How to Restore Your PONTIAC GTO 1964-1974

Don Keefe

CarTech®

CarTech®

CarTech®, Inc.
838 Lake Street South
Forest Lake, MN 55025
Phone: 651-277-1200 or 800-551-4754
Fax: 651-277-1203
www.cartechbooks.com

© 2012 by Don Keefe

All rights reserved. No part of this publication may be reproduced or utilized in any form or by any means, electronic or mechanical, including photocopying, recording, or by any information storage and retrieval system, without prior permission from the Author. All text, photographs, and artwork are the property of the Author unless otherwise noted or credited.

The information in this work is true and complete to the best of our knowledge. However, all information is presented without any guarantee on the part of the Author or Publisher, who also disclaim any liability incurred in connection with the use of the information.

All trademarks, trade names, model names and numbers, and other product designations referred to herein are the property of their respective owners and are used solely for identification purposes. This work is a publication of CarTech, Inc., and has not been licensed, approved, sponsored, or endorsed by any other person or entity.

Edit by Paul Johnson
Layout by Monica Seiberlich

ISBN 978-1-61325-308-3
Item No. SA218P

Library of Congress Cataloging-in-Publication Data

Keefe, Don.
 How to restore your Pontiac GTO : 1964-1974 / by Donald Keefe.
   pages cm
 ISBN 978-1-934709-69-6
 1. GTO automobile--Maintenance and repair--Handbooks, manuals, etc. I. Title.
 TL215.G27K44 2012
 629.28'722--dc23

2012010135

Written, edited, and designed in the U.S.A.
Printed in U.S.A.
10 9 8 7 6 5 4 3 2 1

Title Page:
In the course of 40-plus years, many GTOs have been down a drag strip at one point or another, or they have been driven aggressively on the street. You need to keep an eye out for signs of abuse or racing.

Back Cover Photos

Top Left:
The advantages of a professional spray booth cannot be overstressed because a professional paint booth that's correctly prepared and operated provides the optimal environment for painting. A booth offers temperature and humidity control, keeps contaminants away from the surface to be painted, and controls overspray. (Photo Courtesy Scott Tiemann)

Top Right:
Look down inside the case at the mainshaft gear and the countergear. If there has been a gearbox failure and it's locked up, you can see the damage to the gear sets. Use a 3/16-inch-diameter punch to drive the reverse gear lock pin upward and out of the rear extension (tailshaft). (Photo Courtesy Rocky Rotella)

Middle Left:
Use a rotary cut-off wheel to remove the rusted lower quarter panel. It takes some skill to do this procedure properly. You do not want your car to be the first time you use one of these. Use a MIG welder to butt weld the bottom replacement panel to the top quarter panel. The panel is also welded to the wheel well lip and around to the bumper section.

Middle Right:
At this stage, you have ground the welds flush to the quarter panel. This is the final metal-working stage before you apply thin coats of body filler. You want the surface to be as smooth as possible.

Bottom Left:
We didn't know what lurked inside this Pontiac V-8 until we disassembled it and thoroughly inspected all of the components. A crucial part of inspection is not only identifying obvious and not-so-obvious damage, but it's also to determine what component problems, parts failures, and assembly issues that caused the problems in the first place.

Bottom Right:
The completed seat looks as good as new and is ready for installation.

OVERSEAS DISTRIBUTION BY:

Brooklands Books Ltd.
P.O. Box 146, Cobham, Surrey, KT11 1LG, England
Phone: 01932 865051 • Fax: 01932 868803
www.brooklands-books.com

Renniks Publications, Ltd.
3/37-39 Green Street, Banksmeadow, NSW 2109, Australia
Phone: 2 9695 7055 • Fax: 2 9695 7355

CONTENTS

About the Author 4
Acknowledgments 4
Introduction 5

Chapter 1: Selecting a Project 6
   What Are Your Goals? 7
   Level of Restoration 8
   Rarity, Condition and Originality 9
   NOS, Used or Reproduction Parts 9
   Evaluating a Project Car 9
   Club Benefits 12
   Use the Internet to Your Advantage 13
   Some Friendly Advice 13

Chapter 2: Disassembly 14
   Planning, Tracking and Budgeting 14
   Get Organized 15
   Workspace and Tools 16
   Getting Started 17
   Body Off or On? 18
   Repair or Replace? 20
   How Deep Are You Going? 21
   It's Really a Parts Car—Now What? 21
   Safety 21

Chapter 3: Bodywork 26
   Typical Rust Areas 26
   Paint Removal 27
   Repair Patches 29
   Floorpan and Trunk Floor Replacement 30
   Quarter Panel Replacement 33
   Quarter Patch Panel Preparation 40
   Rust Preventers 55
   Dent Removal 56
   Filler 56
   Body Tags 56
   Collision Damage 56

Chapter 4: Painting 57
   Selecting Paint 59
   DIY or Professional? 59
   Safety 59
   Choosing a Body Shop 60
   What Can You Do Yourself? 60
   Spray Gun and Compressor Setup 62
   Masking the Car 62
   Painting 63
   Prepare Body for Painting 64

Chapter 5: Engine 69
   Time for a Rebuild? 70
   Identifying an Engine 71
   Choosing a Machine Shop 73
   Repair or Replace? 74
   Detailing the Engine 76
   Engine Disassembly and Inspection 79
   Engine Assembly 83

Chapter 6: Transmission 88
   Rebuild or Replace? 90
   Turbo Hydra-Matic 400 90
   Automatic Transmission Upgrades 90
   Super Turbine 300 to Turbo 350 92
   Overdrives 92
   Manual Transmissions 93
   Muncie 4-Speed Disassembly 95
   Muncie 4-Speed Assembly 100

Chapter 7: Suspension 108
   Restore Safety, Functionality and Appearance 109
   Inspection and Evaluation 110
   Paint Finishes 112
   Upgrades 112

Chapter 8: Brakes 121
   Repair or Replace? 123
   Check for Condition 124
   Aftermarket Systems 126
   Master Cylinders, Proportioning Valves and Lines .. 126
   1964 Rear Drum Brakes 126

Chapter 9: Interior 133
   Disassembly and Evaluation of Components 134
   Authentic Reproductions 135
   Mix and Match? 136
   Vapor Barriers 136
   Carpet and Sill Panels 136
   Carpet Installation 137
   Door Panel Installation 140
   Deck Package Installation 143
   Dash Pad Restoration 144
   Pedal Assemblies 145
   Steering Wheels 145
   Seat Belts 146
   Kick Panels 146
   Console 146
   Seat Installation 147

Chapter 10: Body Assembly and Alignment 155
   The Process 156
   Surprises 156
   Door Alignment 157
   Front Fender Fitting and Alignment 160
   Hood Installation 162
   Bumper Installation 164

Chapter 11: Electrical 166
   Inspection of the Wiring 167
   Harness Replacement 169
   Trouble Spots 171
   Upgrades 171

Source Guide 175

DEDICATION

To my son, Rob, the inspiration for everything I do,
To Ann, my one true love,
And to my step-daughter, Katie.
I love you all very much.

ABOUT THE AUTHOR

Don Keefe has been writing about cars professionally since 1988 and in that time, has become one of the leading experts on Pontiacs, as well as American experimental and non-production cars. His byline and photography have appeared in *High Performance Pontiac, Collectible Automobile, Hemmings Classic Cars, The Barrett-Jackson Experience,* and *USA Today*. Additionally, he is the author of *Grand Prix: Pontiac's Luxury Performance Car* and has written promotional material for General Motors, scripts for Speed TV, and has appeared on the History Channel's *Dream Machines*. Don lives in western New York and is currently the editor-in-chief of *Smoke Signals*, the official magazine of the Pontiac-Oakland Club International.

ACKNOWLEDGMENTS

When embarking on a project as large as this one, you really find out quickly who your friends are, and aren't. I am very fortunate in that I have wonderful friends in the hobby who have helped me out with with the completion of this book. I wish to thank my editor Paul Johnson for his help and guidance, my parents, Charlie (who instilled my love of Pontiacs) and Shirley Keefe, and my brother Charles.

A sincere thanks to: Kathleen Adelson from GM Media Archive, Jim, Rodney and David Butler from Butler Performance, Dave Bischopp from SD Performance, Paul Delfeld from Ram Air Restoration Enterprises, Detroit Iron, The Eastwood Company, Edelbrock, Tenney Fairchild, Brian Foster from Ames Performance Engineering, Bill and Jeff Hirsch from Bill Hirsch Auto, Les Iden, Wayne Kennedy, Glen Konkle, Rick Mahoney, Jim Mattison from PHS, Lynn McCarty from McCarty Racing, Original Parts Group, Painless Performance Products, Andy Pooni, Mark Rossetti from Hotchkis Performance, Jason Walton, Garrett Weaver from Pertronix, as well as Marci Stephens and Bryan Ackerman from Year One.

A very special thanks to Imran Chaudary, Luc Corbiel, Sam Ranalli, Scott Tiemann and his staff at Supercar Specialties, Tom DeMauro, Melvin Benzaquen and his staff at Classic Restorations, Tony Golembreski, and Rocky Rotella. Without any of you, this book wouldn't have happened and I am eternally grateful for your help.

My greatest thanks goes to Ann, my one true love, who was incredibly supportive and insightful, and successfully kept me sane throughout this project. I love you with all my heart.

INTRODUCTION

When CarTech contacted me about the idea of writing a GTO restoration book, I was of course, very flattered. I was also impressed that CarTech knew exactly what was needed in the already densely populated GTO book market.

My first question was, "How do you envision this book being different than the others in the marketplace?" My editor's response was that he wanted to make this book a process-oriented restoration guide focusing on GTOs, rather than something that would tell you what was correct for a given year or engine—that had already been capably done by other books in the past, most notably the seminal *Pontiac GTO Restoration Guide 1964–72* by Paul Zazarine and Chuck Roberts, and the spectacular *Collector's Originality Guide: Pontiac GTO 1964–1974* by Thomas A. DeMauro. I look at this book as a spiritual companion to those earlier works because, collectively, they give a comprehensive view of what the Pontiac GTO is all about. Those other books show you what is original and correct, and this book tells how to properly go about the wrenching, welding, grinding, stitching, and painting.

This book does not get deep into the rebuilding of engines and transmissions, for a couple of reasons. First, CarTech already has books that cover those topics. Second, these operations, particularly transmission rebuilding, require specialized tools and machine work. By the time you have invested in everything needed, you will be money and experience ahead by having those operations farmed out—or at least the machining done elsewhere. Third, with a limited number of pages, any coverage in one area would have to come at the expense of another. Since those topics are capably handled elsewhere, I concentrate on territory that hasn't already been covered.

This book is geared to home restorers, people rebuilding a car in their own garage to the best of their abilities using a combination of original factory, reproduction, and used parts. I do my best to show what it takes to restore and re-use what you already have and how to know when parts need to be replaced.

The idea is not necessarily to turn your car into a trailer queen, though I cover the major systems restorations with one of the top Pontiac restorers in the country, namely Scott Tiemann of Supercar Specialties in Portland, Michigan. Scott restores some of the most abused muscle cars and factory race cars into 100-point restorations for many of the top collectors around the world.

It is my intention that this book aids you in the restoration process, as well as provides insight and advice. This book teaches the skills necessary to get you out of the surprises that inevitably turn up, and also helps you avoid the majority of them in the first place. Thanks for purchasing this book; I believe you'll find just about everything you need to successfully restore that aging GTO of yours into the muscle car of your dreams.

CHAPTER 1

SELECTING A PROJECT

When it comes to the restoration of any car, Pontiac GTO or otherwise, the proper selection of a candidate differs for different people, but always boils down to making a realistic evaluation of your intentions and your means of achieving it.

With the selection of the proper project car, you must find your own comfort zone—that individual balance of condition, price, and originality that is unique to you. Keep your own skill level in mind, as well as your restoration facility, tools, and the amount of money needed to properly restore the vehicle. Obviously, everyone's tastes, financial situation, skill set, and intended uses are going to be unique, so the idea here is to find the car that is going to suit your intended purposes without getting in too far over your head.

As a family of vehicles, 1964–1972 Pontiac GTOs are especially good choices for a restoration project. They are fast, good-looking machines with a level of brand identity that has elevated them to legendary status. They remain very popular nearly 50 years after their introduction. There is a tremendous amount

A properly restored Pontiac GTO is a thing of beauty. This one-of-a-kind 1969 Ram Air IV GTO convertible is painted Carousel Red, but it's not a Judge—it's a special-order "factory freak." This particular GTO has been professionally restored, and for good reason—it's one rare Goat. Pontiac only made 549 Ram Air IV GTOs for the 1969 model year, and only 14 automatic convertibles were made. A car with this pedigree and market value demands the best professional restoration possible, and therefore, a novice restorer should not attempt to restore a GTO with similar lineage. A car that has some collector value, such as the 1970 GTO 400, is a reasonable candidate for a first restoration job because you should select a car that's not prohibitively expensive. In other words, an art historian's first job shouldn't be restoring the Mona Lisa, or anything close to it. Select a GTO that doesn't require an extraordinary amount of work and within your budget and skill range.

SELECTING A PROJECT

of aftermarket support for them, and they tend to hold their value better than other vehicles in the collectible muscle car market.

One of the reasons that Pontiacs in general, and GTOs in particular, hold their value so well is the availability of original factory and billing information from PHS, formerly known as Pontiac Historic Services. PHS President Jim Mattison is the owner and holder of Pontiac's original billing information, going back to the 1961 model year. By supplying the vehicle identification number (VIN), PHS can provide a copy of the original shipping manifest, showing the options for that car.

Is your 1970 GTO an original Ram Air IV Judge or is it a 350 LeMans in disguise? PHS is able to prove how it was built. For a fee, PHS provides that information and a reproduction of the original window sticker. It is money well spent, and many enthusiasts have used it to decide whether to purchase a particular car or move on to another one.

Having that level of accountability for the authenticity of a real GTO goes a long way toward stabilizing the values of GTOs and weeding out the clones, so a potential buyer can be sure that the car he is looking at is an original GTO and not a tarted-up Tempest or LeMans.

GTOs from the later two years of production are tougher cars to restore, mostly from the standpoint of parts availability. While there are some reproduction items available for the 1974, they are mostly by way of its cousin, the Chevrolet Nova. In terms of availability, it is nothing like that of the 1964–1972 versions. Floorpans, quarter panels, and other sheet metal are available, as are stripe kits, but when it comes to GTO-specific items such as grilles or turn signal lamps, you need to search for NOS (new old stock) or used parts.

The 1973 GTOs are unique, they were a one-year option package on the 1973–1977 A-Body LeMans platform, they had the fewest number built, and they have virtually nothing reproduced. If parts are needed, it will be an intensive search for NOS or serviceable used parts. Body panels are becoming particularly difficult to find, as these vehicles tended to rust fairly quickly and the supply of usable NOS or rust-free Western metal is dwindling. NOS wheel opening moldings? It's doable, but it's not nearly as cost-effective. I touch upon both of these model years in this book, as the process to restore them is the same as for their older siblings. The main focus, however, is on the earlier models.

What Are Your Goals?

Setting realistic goals for your project is paramount to the success of the project. Will this car be a daily driver, local show competitor, and cruise night participant, or a concours-level trailer queen built to capture national awards?

If you are looking to take the gold at a GTO Association of America (GTOAA) or Pontiac-Oakland Club International (POCI) convention, chances are you won't be using this book to restore your vehicle. You will more likely be hiring the job out to someone with that level of experience and skills, such as Scott Tiemann, of Supercar Specialties, in Portland, Michigan, who has

In the course of 40-plus years, many GTOs have been down a drag strip at one point or another, or have been driven aggressively on the street. Keep an eye out for signs of abuse or racing. If you crawl under the car and examine the frame rails and motor mounts, a heavily abused car shows cracks around these components because the chassis has twisted many times during launches. Other tell-tale signs include doors that don't open and shut easily and "tweaked" roofs because the frame has been bent over time.

CHAPTER 1

When choosing the right GTO to restore, carefully evaluate each possible candidate and use common sense. When a prospective GTO requires extensive work causing the restoration to be too expensive, a novice restorer should find another car. In the case of this very rough 1969 GTO coupe with such an advanced level of rust, you need to walk away. In this case, maybe you should run. A car such as this needs new quarters, floor, fenders, trunk, and more. It also needs the frame rails replaced, and that's the domain of a skilled weldor and fabricator, something most first-time restorers are not. This car is at best a parts car, and maybe not even that. In addition, the original driveline is long gone and more parts are missing than are present.

graciously supplied photos from some of his restoration projects. The processes that these photos illustrate are the state of the art, the "right way" to handle a particular task. Your job as a home restorer is to come as close to that level as you can with your own project.

Level of Restoration

My first words of advice? Restore the car for yourself, not for the "next guy." If you pigeon-hole yourself into restoring a car with an eye toward resale value, chances are you won't enjoy the car as much as if you did it the way you wanted. While there is merit in restoring a vehicle to its as-delivered configuration, if there are things you really don't like about it, you're not as likely to enjoy it.

If the car came from the factory with a green interior and you hate green interiors, there is nothing wrong with changing it to a color that suits your tastes, especially if

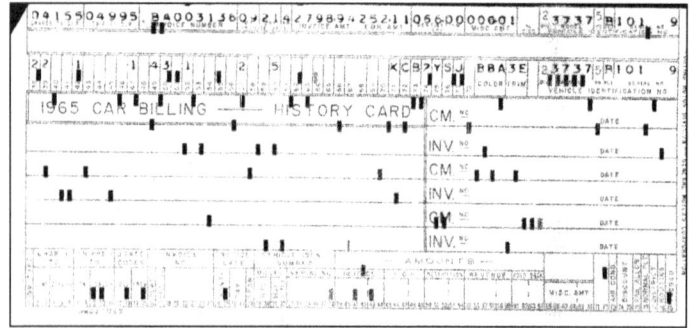

This 1965 GTO history card provides detailed data on the equipment package for a particular car that went through production. The earlier manifest is actually a keypunch card, an early analog form of computer data entry. Although high-tech for the day, it's a time capsule of data management, but the actual information is invaluable. If a seller has this information, it definitely boosts the value of the car because the original equipment package can be authenticated. All Pontiacs since 1961 can have the original Pontiac billing information retrieved and decoded by PHS.

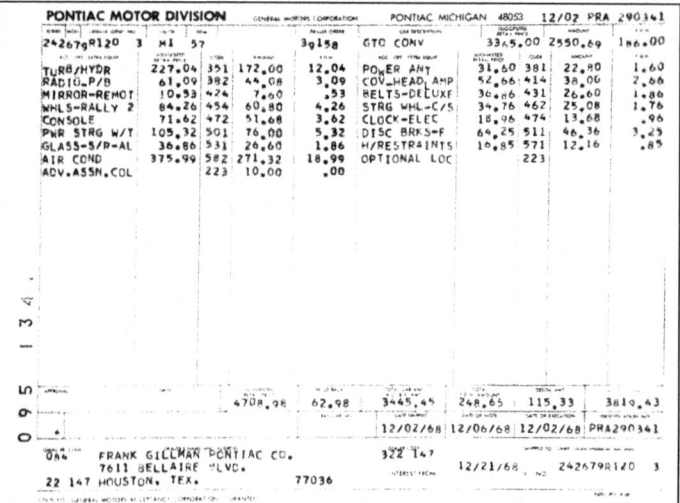

The build sheet for a particular car is another key and valuable piece of documentation. This highly optioned GTO convertible carries power steering and brakes, console, air conditioning, Turbo 400 automatic transmission, disc brakes, Rally II wheels, Soft-Ray tinted glass, power antenna, and many other options.

SELECTING A PROJECT

it needs replacing anyway. If the brown exterior doesn't suit you, why not change it to something you like better? After all, it's your car; restore it as you see fit. But keep in mind, then it won't be a factory-original restoration.

Adding factory options is also a possibility and if you wish to modify the car a bit for better handling, safety, or performance. I recommend that modifications be kept mild enough that they aren't visible or can be easily returned to stock.

Rarity, Condition and Originality

How important is condition? Is rarity more important than condition? For the scope of this book, condition is the most important factor in choosing a car to restore. A relatively clean, complete, unabused, base-engine GTO is a more desirable candidate for restoration than a thrashed, rusted, and stripped Ram Air or HO car. Why? Because the later types of cars are best left to those with the experience and means to bring them back—but when restored, the owners will have too much money invested in them to be practical drivers or weekend cruisers.

Originality is important, but it falls short of condition. While it is important that the GTO you are restoring is actually a GTO, or the Judge you just spent your hard-earned money on is really a Judge, the idea that only a numbers-matching original car is worth saving is a bit silly. How many GTOs had their original engines blown up after a few months and replaced with a service replacement (SR) engine under warranty? A lot of them, especially Ram Air IVs, which the factory ended up building at least one SR block for every one installed in a car. That is why replacement Ram Air IV parts were so plentiful into the early 1980s.

It is likely that at least half of the GTOs for sale have a non-original engine under the hood. Perhaps the 2-speed automatic transmission in that clean 1966 was replaced with a Turbo 350 at some time in its history. Body, frame, and suspension integrity is far more important than the possibility that there's a late 1970s 400 smog engine where that 389 Tri-Power originally sat. You can find correct engine parts a lot easier than you can find rust-free restoration candidates.

NOS, Used or Reproduction Parts

In the quest for replacement parts for your GTO, the question always arises: Is it acceptable to use reproduction parts? Some purists say it is never okay and only NOS parts should be used any time a component needs replacement. I disagree. Reproduction parts are the market's response to the scarcity of original replacements. If enough people are willing to spend 10 or 20 times the original list price for an original item, there exists a market for a reproduction equivalent—period. The market also tends to weed out the substandard replacements, resulting in high-quality, reasonably priced items.

More specifically, the restoration industry is old enough that most of the junk parts have already been weeded out. Several parts suppliers started out as NOS dealers in the late 1970s and early 1980s and had to start developing and offering reproductions in order to keep their inventories at acceptable levels. These businesses have survived because of that evolution.

As with all goods and services, it is true that in the restoration parts market, some pieces are better than others. For the most part, if you are ordering reproduction sheet metal, exterior trim, interior parts, or engine parts for your GTO from one of the established parts suppliers, such as Ames Performance Engineering, Original Parts Group, Year One, and Performance Years, you're going to be fine. In fact, some items have been licensed by GM and some pieces have even been made using original tooling, so technically, they are "continuations." Best of all, if you do have a problem with a particular item, the top parts suppliers will do everything in their power to keep you as a happy customer.

Evaluating a Project Car

Buying a restoration project is generally the same process as buying any other collector car, but with some distinct differences. The main difference is that since it's not a finished project, you must evaluate the candidate based on its current condition and the amount of work you're willing to do. In addition, consider your personal abilities, resources, and of course, finances. It also helps to be able to distinguish a relatively minor flaw from a major one and to see beyond the bad paint, greasy engine bay, and threadbare interior to envision what that particular vehicle could look like as a completed project.

Rust damage is the main enemy of a restoration project. In the case of GM A-Bodies, the main area of corrosion usually starts with rain penetrating the seal of the windshield

CHAPTER 1

These 1972 GTO coupes are in better shape than the 1969 model on page 8, but are still not quite suitable candidates for a first-time project. These cars are mostly complete, but both require extensive body work, and body work is one of the difficult aspects of restoration. While these cars are not as extensively rusted as the 1969 GTO coupe, the restorer must repair or replace most of the body panels. However, these cars are relatively solid undernreath and don't require frame replacement. Though rough, they are feasible to the right person.

This is an ideal car for a first-timer to restore. It's a solid, complete, and running example that is not a complete rust-out. While some surprises are no doubt hidden for the restorer to discover and repair, a beginner will not get in over his or her head with this restoration project. This particular car has the added bonus of being a real 455 HO car, making it rare and hence more valuable than a run-of-the-mill 400. Thus, the restorer should make sure to take the time and invest the money to restore this car correctly. Ultimately, the value of the car reflects the investment in it. While more expensive to get into initially, the total tab and the final results make this one a winner.

and backlight. Water often collects in those areas, causing corrosion. As the breach around the sealed glass becomes larger, water can more easily get into the cowl and trunk areas, causing those areas to corrode. By the time the paint starts to bubble, big problems are already brewing. If the car in question has a vinyl top, the moisture is prevented from evaporating. Soon, the vinyl is covering holes in the roof.

Meanwhile, moisture and salt attack from the bottom and eat away at rocker panels, quarters, floorboards, and most importantly, frame rails. Many times, frame rot can start on the inside and work its way out, so frame rails must be thoroughly examined. Getting the car on a lift often reveals a lot of what is really going on with the entire car.

Find out whether there is more rust than can be effectively repaired. If the damage is limited to bolt-on sheet metal such as fenders, doors, and hood, it is a fairly simple procedure to replace them, and there is enough in the way of replacement panels, both used and reproduction, to meet your needs.

If the corrosion damage extends into welded sheet-metal panels, but does not rise to the level of major structural damage, there is a good chance the vehicle is a viable candidate for restoration. There is a wealth of reproduction sheet metal available to repair most problem areas. For example, if a trunk floor is rusted, but the frame rails are still solid, a reproduction floorpan can be installed, and the overall integrity of the body can be restored.

The idea is to use these panels to repair problems "here and there" and to avoid cars that need every single panel replaced. If the GTO in

SELECTING A PROJECT

Select your restoration candidate carefully because many of the body panels are not offered as reproduction parts. At present, you can buy quarter panel skins and lower quarter patch panels for 1966–1967 GTOs, but you cannot buy reproduction full quarter panels with sail panels, so this adds another level of complexity. If you need to install quarter-panel patches to an existing panel, the required welding and body work may go beyond your current skill level. Therefore, if you find a GTO that requires full quarter-panel replacement or other serious body work, you may be wise to pass on the car.

When you wander the aisles at swap meets looking for parts, you may come across some NOS (new old stock) parts, but you need to determine if the condition or type of part is the best option for your particular restoration project. A reproduction part may fit better and require less prep work than an NOS part. This NOS 1970–1972 right rear quarter panel has quite a bit of "shelf wear." There is a decent amount of surface rust and pitting, as well as some dents and creases, all adding time and cost to the restoration. So this part requires a chemical strip or media blasting to remove the surface rust and then any defects or damage needs to be remedied with body filler. Considering all these aspects, a reproduction quarter is a very viable substitute, and in this case, a preferable alternative.

question needs quarters, rockers, and floorpans from firewall to tail panel, the skill and financial requirements often go beyond what a first-time restoration project can provide. This also applies to cars that need frame repair or replacement. Thus, a first-time restorer should search for a car that doesn't require extensive body work and frame repair because it's beyond what the novice can do. I think we've all known friends or acquaintances who have taken on a project that simply requires too much. These overly ambitious restoration projects typically end in frustration—the car sits in the garage for years and never gets completed.

What to Avoid

Above all else, avoid the urge to restore a rusted-out parts car. A parts car is defined as a car whose condition has deteriorated to such an extent that it cannot realistically be restored and is good only as a donor of parts to other projects.

Unless the car in question has an immense amount of sentimental value—as with a car owned by a beloved family member or one in which you were conceived, born, or brought home from the hospital, or one that you've had since high school—resist the urge. Don't invest money in sweat equity in a car that really doesn't deserve it. If a car has gotten to that point, it's better to move on, or buy it as a parts car.

The majority of parts-car restoration projects end badly. In fact, they hardly ever work out. They are often marriage-wrecking, will-tapping, wallet-drainers, and far too often, the end result is not at all impressive. Restoring a car that should be parted out will have you out of the hobby and collecting Batman comic books faster than you can say, "Holy rusted frame rails!"

Here's an example: If the car you're trying to restore is a stripped, completely rusted-out mess but a genuine factory Ram Air IV Judge that is missing the original drivetrain and everything else that made it special, do yourself and your family a favor and put it on eBay and be done with it. Why? Some people say things like, "Reproduction sheet metal, interiors, paint, and labor cost the same for a base-engine car or a Judge convertible."

This is absolutely true, but it is misleading because being able to find everything needed to put that car back into correct (forget about numbers-matching) condition is what puts you over the top. Have you checked the prices for original Ram Air IV carbs, distributors, or cylinder heads? They are incredibly expensive. Additionally, if you can find it all, you still need to know if the date codes are in the range of your build date.

CHAPTER 1

Unlike many other cars to roll out of Detroit during the 1960s and 1970s, the GM A-Body cars, including the GTO, carried a full perimeter frame. Other cars of the era, such as the Mustang and first-generation Nova, were indeed unibody cars, a collection of stamped-steel panels that supported the front and rear suspensions. The full-perimeter frame provided far greater chassis rigidity than many other cars and therefore the GTOs were an excellent platform for big-inch, high-horsepower engines. If a frame has rusted out, and repair or restoration is impractical or simply not possible, you can buy entire replacement frames. In this case, you're looking at a frame with front and rear suspension for a 1970 GTO. Replacement frames are becoming more common in restoration projects.

In some cases, a frame has rusted beyond repair, but most of the body is in good shape. Thus, you need a replacement frame, and it may be a cost-effective alternative to take the frame from another car. This particular frame is from a 1970 GTO and features rebuilt front and rear suspension systems. It is also a heavy-duty frame, which is boxed and is correct for convertibles, as well as HD frame-equipped coupes. It is a stout frame and a prime candidate for a restoration job, and in particular, it's a good foundation for a high-horsepower build.

It's a vicious cycle and a game successfully played only by the most experienced and wealthiest members of the hobby. These are not cars for a first timer, but if you try one as a first-timer, chances are the project will fail. And out of the frustration, it will be your last project.

Authenticity

The PHS shows it is a real GTO, but can it still be a fake? Yes, it can, though it is unlikely when dealing with unrestored examples. Problems arise when the car has had its VIN and cowl tags removed and installed on another car in better condition. The restoration is performed on that car and the end product is represented as the original car.

Every so often, one of these vehicles comes through an auction. It looks beautiful and correct, but a quick check of the hidden VINs on the body and frame shows it is actually a retagged vehicle—a forgery. While this isn't prevalent, it does happen and continues to do so, and therefore you must be careful to not get stuck with a "clone" car that's worth a fraction of its portrayed value. Very often, the person selling the car is unaware of the switch because it happened two or three owners before and was bought in good faith as an original car. Legal battles quickly arise, lawsuits are filed, and in the end, no one wins.

By the way, taking the VIN tag off one car and putting it on another is a federal crime and the penalties just aren't worth the jail time. Stay away from such temptation.

Club Benefits

Join a club! Though I cannot be considered an impartial observer in this area (I have been editor-in-chief of the Pontiac-Oakland Club International's monthly magazine *Smoke Signals* since 2006), the benefits of joining a car club are worth far more to a restorer than the monthly dues. Even if you are not a "joiner" and don't want to get involved with a local chapter, just having access to the club Web sites, the magazines, and most importantly, the classified ads is a huge benefit when searching for a project car.

One of the other advantages of a club membership is access to the technical advisors. If you have a question about how something is supposed to go together or some detail not covered anywhere else, the chances are very high that the tech advisors are either able to provide the information or point you to someone who can. As a tech advisor for the POCI, I can attest that the amount of time and effort that can be saved is huge. Collectively, the POCI tech advisors have assisted thousands of members over the years and they do it on a volunteer basis.

Whether it is the POCI, GTO Association of America, Antique Automobile Club of America, or a local independent club, join up and reap the benefits of membership.

Use the Internet to Your Advantage

If you are one of those people who "doesn't do computers," do yourself a huge favor—push through your fears and get online. The amount of information, cars, parts, message forums, and experience from other enthusiasts is just too much to ignore. There are some really great online Pontiac forums, and the number of connections you can make for parts, expertise, and general camaraderie make it a no-brainer. If your computer skills are lacking, chances are there is a continuing education class you can take at your local high school or library that will quickly get you up to speed. Or, you can always find a middle- or high-school student to help you.

Some Friendly Advice

The best advice I can give is this: If you're coming into this hobby looking for a first-time project, you'll be far happier finding the car in the best overall condition, with originality and rarity falling behind in importance. After more than 20 years in this hobby, seeing the messes that people have gotten themselves into by choosing the wrong car (and having done so myself as a youngster), I can attest that anything you can do to increase the odds of a successful outcome is a wise choice.

The process of restoring a car is a huge educational experience. You will learn as much about yourself as you do about the car and how it originally went together. You'll learn about the guys who designed and engineered them and wonder about the workers on the line the day it was built. At the completion of a GTO restoration project, you will have learned from what went right as well as what went wrong. There will be things you would do differently in future projects and things you would do exactly the same. You'll also find out who your friends really are.

The question of whether to restore a GTO to factory stock or modified is up to you. While you can build a pro-touring GTO, the purpose of this book is to restore a GTO to its factory-original condition while offering some common-sense modern upgrades to improve performance, drivability, and safety. This 1969 Ram Air III Judge is still with the original owner and features some modifications that were common in the late 1960s and early 1970s, including air shocks, slotted mag wheels, and some bolt-on engine upgrades. Cars of this type are now referred to as "day-two cars," referring to the day after they were brought home and mods began. They feature period-correct aftermarket modifications, yet can be returned to factory original-condition without a lot of work.

CHAPTER 2

DISASSEMBLY

When evaluating your particular car for restoration, be sure you have a realistic expectation of the project, your skill level, and your intended use. This assumes that your car will be restored as a weekend driver/cruise night car and not necessarily for concours competition. Hence, you need to define the level of restoration you're willing to take on. This decision also dictates just how far down you intend to take the car when disassembling.

Planning, Tracking and Budgeting

Use a ledger or spreadsheet to organize, review, and track the progress of your project. Track the parts you need to buy and the procedures you need to perform, and you can have the entire project broken down into stages. Therefore, it helps you complete a component-group restoration and reminds you of all the important steps, but also guides you through the entire process.

For a spreadsheet, assign columns to priority, procedure, parts, projected cost, actual cost, project hours, and projected hours. In the priority column, assign a level of importance to each procedure in the restoration. In many cases, a restorer cannot restore every component or area of a car at once, so assign a level of importance to each task. Therefore, if you cannot afford paint right now, but sometime in the future, you should assign painting a 4.

However, say you want a strong daily driver, but the engine is blowing and leaking oil. You did a compression test and most cylinders are way down on compression. As a result, your engine needs to be rebuilt and that is a top priority, so you assign a number 1 to that project. In the procedure, you need to define what you're restoring on the car, such as

The proper disassembly of your GTO may well be a precursor to your success with the entire project. If you do it the right way from the start, it will save you a lot of time and frustration down the road. Take lots of photos, tag and bag parts, keep a journal, and make short videos to show how things go together. It may take longer to do all of this in the beginning but following these simple rules will help ensure a successful outcome. Fooling yourself into thinking you will remember where every part goes is asking for trouble. (Photo Courtesy Scott Tiemann)

DISASSEMBLY

patch quarter panel, install new seat covers, rebuild rear differential, and so on. Next, define the parts for the part job, such as seat covers, quarter panel, or pinion ring and carrier parts. Once that is accomplished, determine a realistic budget for the parts and the procedures. If you are performing the work yourself, budget in the amount of time it will take and you can choose not to pay yourself. If you have someone else subcontracted to perform a procedure, such as priming and painting, then you need to allocate a realistic budgeted cost. That budgeted cost should come from an estimate provided by the body shop. Finally, fill out the actual cost and hours of a particular procedure once it's been completed.

In reality, you will find out that the planned budget and schedule are often very different than the actual budget and schedule. Therefore, you may have a what you consider as a realistic budget and time schedule for completing the work, but you build in 15 to 20 percent more time and allocated budget. Why? Because even with the best-laid plans, there's unforeseen work and circumstances that arise during a complex project.

Get Organized

When the time comes to disassemble your GTO project car, a few basic things must be taken care of before any wrenches start turning and before any mistakes are made. The idea is to plan ahead and make sure that parts coming off the car are not lost, damaged, or otherwise taken out of service. If they are broken or worn, that is one thing. If they are lost or broken because you didn't properly manage them, that costs you additional time, money, and hassle. The idea of restoring a car should be fun, so make sure that what you are doing is helping that idea along, not hurting it.

I am a very organized person and I know some great techniques for managing a restoration. I learned them all the hard way by not

Supplies to Help You Get Organized

Using a camera can make your restoration project much, much easier. It does not need to be expensive, one of those little point-and-shoot digitals is just fine.

Today, 12-megapixel cameras with a movie-making feature can be had for less than $150. Look for a small, durable camera with a built-in flash to take photos and video. These can be purchased anywhere, from Target to Walmart to Amazon.com. A contractor-grade camera would be a plus, as it can be knocked around more than a regular consumer version. Those are available at Lowe's, Home Depot, and other similar retailers.

An inexpensive yet sturdy tripod is a good investment. They are available anywhere for less than $35.

As parts are removed, they can be photographed. You can also shoot a short video to record how something came apart. This can be helpful if the procedure was difficult or if pieces were missing. That way, you're not spending a lot of time looking for something that wasn't there in the first place.

Other items you should invest in are a notebook (preferably a looseleaf binder with paper), adhesive labels, tags, and Zip-Loc bags, in various sizes.

Parts should be labeled with a code or descriptive phrase, either on the part itself or on the plastic bag, which is then recorded in the notebook. The notebook identifies the part and the related fasteners, as well as how many bags or items there are for that system and any detail you need to remember.

For example, let's say that the left front suspension has been removed. The procedure was photographed and there is a pile of parts now lying on your garage floor. By taking a few minutes to gather all of the main components, tagging the large pieces, bagging the smaller items, coding them with something like "LFS," and recording in the binder when the items were removed and any pertinent details, the chances of problems arising because you lost or forgot something is greatly reduced.

There is no question that using this method of recording and cataloging adds time to the teardown of the car. However, the extra time you invest at the beginning of the restoration saves time and frustration when it is time to put it all back together. Taking a car apart is a lot easier than assembling it.

CHAPTER 2

following common-sense procedures and doing all of the stupid things that people often do. My biggest lesson learned? Never rely solely on your memory! Here are four tips that will keep you out of trouble:

1. Photograph every part as you remove it.
2. Tag or catalog each part.
3. Do not mix components from one system with another.
4. Organize and bag smaller system components and fasteners.

From the list above, you probably get a pretty good idea of the focus of this chapter. The last thing you need is a bunch of mystery bolts or small pieces rolling around on the garage floor getting lost or damaged. The old joke about fixing a car and having extra pieces left over is no joke when it happens to you and you have no idea where those things are supposed to be. The goal of this chapter is to help you prevent these kinds of problems.

Workspace and Tools

The location where your restoration project takes place should be a clean, secure area that does not get high foot traffic or unwanted attention. Ideally, it should be no smaller than a two-car garage. You need one bay for the car itself and the other for space to organize the removed parts and to do the actual work. The work area should have a bench and/or a sturdy worktable that safely holds heavy castings and other parts.

While it is true that people have successfully restored vehicles in smaller spaces and even outdoors, the chances of pieces being lost, damaged, or stolen go up dramatically. It is also beneficial to have a storage area for pieces not being worked on. A remote rented storage area can be helpful for storing larger components, though transportation and cost can become a factor.

The depth and detail of your project dictate tool purchases. Will you be doing your own bodywork and paint? If not, you can skip the body hammers and spray gun and put those resources toward items you will be using.

You do need a quality socket set, screwdrivers, a torque wrench, various hammers and mallets for "massaging" jammed or sticking parts, metal or approved plastic containers for gasoline, oil, anti-freeze and other liquids, and draining pans.

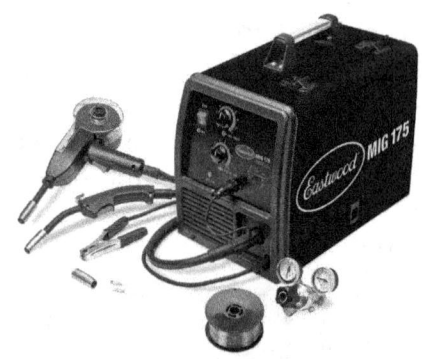

A welder is an essential tool for completing serious bodywork projects. The most popular is a MIG welder because it's easy to use. MIG welding is commonly used for thin-steel body panels because the heat can be effectively controlled to prevent warping the panels. In addition, MIG can weld aluminum and provides high-strength welds for frames, suspension, steering, and other parts. A welder is a handy item to have in your home shop but make sure you have the proper safety equipment and know how to operate it. It is very easy to burn through sheet metal with one. Operating a welder is a science and an art, and not something you proficiently learn in one day. So you may need instruction to learn how to effectively complete projects with it. If you need to learn how to weld, look for continuing education classes in your local school district or at a nearby community college. A perfectly-formed bead is a wonderful thing and is a skill well worth learning.

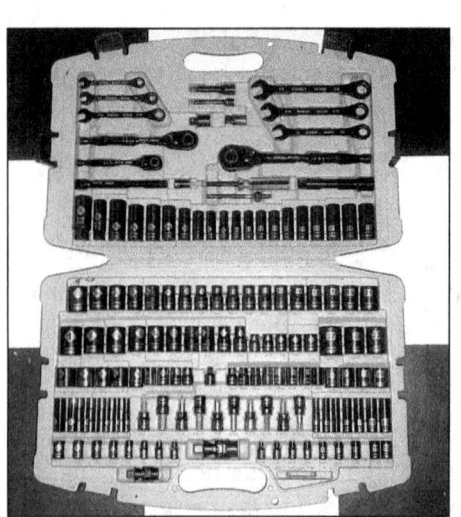

You need a full set of high-quality hand tools, including a full socket set with 1/4-, 3/8-, and 1/2-inch-drive ratchets. You also need a full set of screwdrivers, prybars, hammers, and a variety of specialty tools that can be rented or borrowed. In addition, use Craftsman, Husky, Rigid, or a similar brand that has a lifetime warranty and a reputation for high quality. You don't need professional tools, but if you can afford them, why not? But remember, you're going to be challenged through the entire restoration process, and cheap tools often do not precisely fit the fasteners and round off nuts, strip off bolt head, and make a mess off a job that otherwise could have been accomplished in far less time. A trim removal tool allows you to safely remove windshield moldings without breaking off the delicate retention tabs. A screwdriver used in this operation pretty much guarantees a damaged part.

DISASSEMBLY

For power tools, a compressor is a wonderful and invaluable tool that saves an immense amount of time with most operations. Pneumatic lines, an air-impact wrench, sockets, and grinding wheels ease the burden of disassembly and help speed up assembly procedures. Your shop needs 220-volt electrical service, which may involve some upgrades to your wiring.

Other tools that make life easier include transmission jacks, an engine hoist, an arc welder, and hub pullers of various sizes. These are items that you can purchase, rent, or even borrow (from friends, relatives, or co-workers) as you need them.

Some specialized tools are fairly inexpensive, but greatly assist you in your restoration project. A small assortment of trim-removal tools goes a long way to helping preserve the delicate stainless moldings, as they are often quite fragile and easily break if the clips aren't properly releasing the parts. The fact that they are expensive and usually hard to find makes purchasing the right tool for the job a high priority.

If your project becomes a body-off affair, a rotisserie is a good investment. Having the ability to take a bare body and flip it upside-down for repair and body-panel replacement is a benefit that is well worth the added expense. If you are especially handy and know how to weld, you can build one yourself. There are plans and kits available on the Internet and if you don't want to spend $1,500 or $2,000 for one, this is a very viable alternative. Just put the phrase "auto rotisserie kits and plans" in your favorite search engine and find what is best for your project and budget.

Getting Started

The initial disassembly is likely to be a straightforward affair, though inevitably, there will be some slowdowns. Perhaps some bolts will strip or round out. Maybe some pieces will be rusted together and refuse to separate.

The best way to minimize those troubles is to use the correct tool for the job. That can mean something as simple as using the correct-size screwdriver instead of whatever is close by. In addition, it means using a six-point socket instead of a sloppy, adjustable wrench or a trim tool instead of a screwdriver to remove a delicate windshield molding. Be sure to use a good penetrating oil on rusty bolts (such as exhaust manifold bolts or other engine fasteners), particularly if they have been subjected to heating and cooling cycles. Several good products are available at any auto parts store. Some restorers have their own recipes for penetrating oil, using automatic transmission fluid and kerosene. I have had great success

Some fasteners are torqued with more than 100 ft-lbs and are difficult to remove. A compressor is essential equipment for many of the procedures performed during a restoration. A single-stage air compressor is adequate for many smaller jobs. If, however, you're going to paint, you need a two-stage compressor with a large tank to maintain consistent air pressure for extended periods. It powers air wrenches, grinders, paint sprayers, and countless other items. Take special care when using an air wrench to loosen rusty bolts, as it can easily break off the heads, which is a frustrating and time-consuming operation to correct.

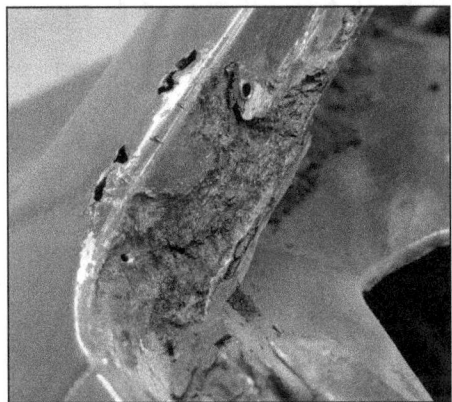

This is a common sight during body disassembly and inspection. Water pooled up around the windshield and backlight and over time it rusted through. Pontiac GTOs are like most other cars of the 1960s in this regard. If you can see rust damage beyond the molding, there absolutely will be more hiding under it. To fix this problem, remove the windshield trim, windshield adhesive, and windshield. Once removed, you can see rust damage from years of invasive moisture. At this stage, you need to thoroughly clean out the area and remove the water, leaves, and whatever else is in there. Then media blast the area to remove all the rust and to get down to the bare metal. In some cases, an entirely new windshield mounting channel needs to be fabricated. (Photo Courtesy Scott Tiemann)

with a product called Blaster. I don't know what the exact formula is, but it has worked better than anything I have used in the past and made easy work of loosening corroded and frozen engine fasteners.

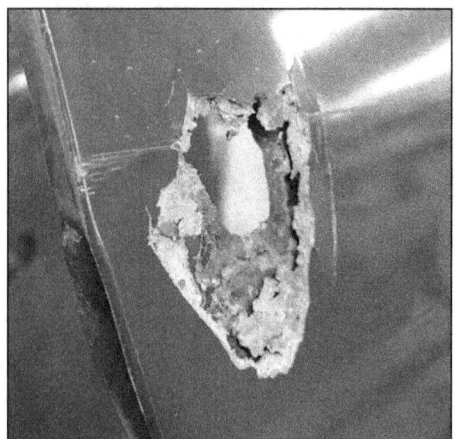

As part of making a specific task list for the restoration process, carefully inspect and evaluate the body. From this list, you can compile a parts list and then develop a cost estimate for completing the restoration project. In the case of this 1964 GTO, body filler was used to repair this rust hole, but it was done incorrectly. This time around it will be done the right way, with the addition of a sheet-metal patch. In this particular restoration, it was important to retain as much of the originality of the car as possible, so the original fender was retained and repaired. (Photo Courtesy Scott Tiemann)

You are sure to find some surprises during the disassembly process. With a car that is 40-plus years old, it is very likely that some areas will be in worse shape than expected. Old collision damage may reveal itself, as well as some substandard repairs. Hidden rust-outs on the inner body structure or frame may be revealed as well. Cracks can also be seen, particularly around engine mounts or suspension mounting points. Also, if your GTO spent time in the rust belt, don't be surprised if your car has a good deal of body filler. Being from Upstate New York, I have seen many cars that appeared to be straight end up having substantial amounts of filler in them. The Northeast is full of skilled Bondo sculptors, so bring a magnet.

If your car came with a vinyl top, expect a significant amount of corrosion damage. It is pretty much inevitable that a vinyl-topped car from that era, GTO or otherwise, will need some rust repair, usually around windshield channels.

Unless you are planning on a correct, as-built restoration, my recommendation is to remove the vinyl top, store the trim pieces in a safe place, and finish the car with a steel top. Alternately, the car could also be finished as a two-tone, using the vinyl-top trim. If you are going to all the trouble of repairing the roof, welding in new window channel, prepping and painting, why set yourself up for another rust problem later on?

Body Off or On?

It's true that body-off restorations are what you typically see in car magazines and at the large collector car auctions. However, your decision to pull the body off the frame and perform a ground-up restoration should be dictated by the condition of the car, your individual situation, and the intended use—not by what everyone else does. Remember, you are the one doing the work (or most of it) and financing the project. You will also be reaping the rewards of your labor, so decide what is best for you and your GTO. If you are restoring the car as a weekend driver, the "necessity" level drops considerably.

If your car happens to be a rust-free example from the Southwest or is not in need of a significant amount of rust repair and/or weld-in panel replacement, skip separating the body from the frame and refurbish them as a single unit. I have seen cars from California, Nevada, Arizona, and New Mexico with completely worn-out interiors, suspensions, and

Successfully finishing a complete GTO restoration is no small task, and when taking on that task, you need to organize and document the entire process. Simply going off memory when disassembling the vehicle and its many components is a recipe for disaster. This book provides detailed instruction and the factory manuals have detailed parts schematics, but you need to document how complex components are disassembled. I strongly recommend that you take extensive notes in a notebook or an Excel file, so that when disassembly commences, the process progresses steadily and smoothly with a minimal amount of hassle. In addition, I also recommend using a digital camera. For a resto job, a small point-and-shoot camera, with both still-photo and video capabilities, is an invaluable aid in the documentation of your restoration. You can even record short movies showing how some of the more complex assemblies go together. These feature-packed little workhorses are in the $150 to $200 range and the quality just keeps getting better.

DISASSEMBLY

drivetrains, but they were in completely rust-free condition.

One car in particular still had the paper tags on the exhaust system after decades of exposure to the elements. Of course, the paint was fried, the drivetrain was worn, and the interior looked like Godzilla's playpen, but every bolt came off without damage and the only rust on the entire car was light oxidation where some paint had worn off.

With cars in this condition, there really isn't any reason to pull the body off. But if you need to replace trunk, floorpans, and quarters, a body-off restoration is the better route, and chances are you will save time with a rotisserie.

Focus your restoration for a particular goal. Not all GTOs are created equal, meaning super-rare high-performance GTOs will always be worth more than the run-of-the mill cars. There are many levels of restoration—from functional non-original transportation to the 100-point concours car that looks the same as the day it rolled off the showroom floor. Most owners restore a GTO somewhere in between these two extremes. These Goat lovers end up with a highly authentic GTO that's restored with some original parts, but also with many reproduction parts. In addition, these cars often have updated disc brakes, modern shocks, digital electronic ignition systems, and other bolt-on parts that don't affect value. Once you develop a goal for your particular restoration, this gives you a clear restoration target to achieve. To arrive at that goal, you define the time, materials, and appropriate parts for restoring your particular GTO. In addition, you are able to develop a realistic budget and invest a wise amount of money in your project and don't overspend.

A rare Ram Air-IV Judge commands prices of $75,000 or more, and therefore, most owners want to restore the car to factory-original condition because it retains its maximum value in that condition. Hence, a car of this pedigree demands professional-caliber body-off restoration if the body needs extensive work. A top professional shop should be enlisted to restore it, especially if it's going to compete in shows. A novice restorer isn't capable of restoring a car to 100-point concours condition.

On the other end of the spectrum, a common 1969 GTO 400 2-barrel automatic car was built in the thousands and does not have the collector cache as the rare Ram Airs, Tri-Powers, or Judges. As such, this

Fasteners, bolts, and nuts that haven't moved in 40 years and have been exposed to road salt, grime, grease, and all types of corrosion don't want to move. In many cases, it's a battle to remove the body parts, suspension, brakes, and so on. During this process, penetrating oil and WD-40 are your friends, and you use a lot of them. Spray the fasteners 24 hours before you plan to start disassembly. Treat the fasteners just before you start. In cases where heat can be applied, use a propane torch so the threads break their bond and can be removed. A good penetrating oil goes a long way to freeing rusty fasteners and speeding up disassembly. I have had very good luck with Blaster brand penetrating oil, which comes in an aerosol can and can be purchased at most auto parts stores.

Many first-time restorers do not attempt a frame-off restoration, and for good reason. A full frame-up restoration is at a level of complexity beyond most first timers. However, the most thorough and highest quality restorations are rotisserie restorations. The body is essentially mounted on a jig, where you media blast, cut out the bad metal, install the good metal, and do all the finishing work necessary. A rotisserie goes a long way to speeding panel replacement. The ability to spin the body shell upside-down speeds replacement of the rockers, quarters, and floorpan. (Photo Courtesy Scott Tiemann)

CHAPTER 2

vehicle is the perfect candidate for a first-time restorer because it doesn't need the highest degree of originality, and the restoration shouldn't come at enormous expense. Critical mistakes with a pedigree car can cost tens of thousands of dollars. With the time, patience, research, and the ability to develop and enhance mechanical and bodywork skills, restoring a high-performance and reliable GTO is well within your reach.

Your level of restoration also determines the parts you will use for that restoration. If you're restoring a rare Goat to compete on the show car circuit, you must carefully select and use parts that are accepted by the particular organization judging the car. In these cases, many restorers use NOS parts. Finding and buying these parts adds a level of expense and complexity to your restoration. These NOS parts may be three or more times expensive than reproduction parts. If you're building a daily driver, high-buck NOS parts are simply unnecessary, and therefore high-quality reproduction parts are the wiser choice. But keep in mind that GTOs are different than Mustangs and Camaros. Many reproduction parts including body, interior, suspension, steering, and other parts, are readily available for the GTO. But some common parts, such as full quarter panels, are currently not offered as reproduction parts. So if your rare pedigree or pedestrian GTO needs full rear quarter panels, you may have to fabricate two panels into one. Once again, that is professional metal-work skill that few budding or beginner restorers possess.

Repair or Replace?

As parts come off your car, make notes about their condition. Can they be cleaned, repaired, painted, and reused or will you have to locate and purchase replacements? Sometimes the decision to repair or replace is not always obvious. If the crankshaft comes out in two pieces, your decision has already been made for you, but it usually isn't that easy. Try to work with what you have whenever you can, even if it means using some creative methods to save the items.

For example, is it better to patch repair the lower section of a front fender or replace it altogether? The answer depends on the severity of the rust damage, the overall viability of the original panel, and the cost to repair versus replacing with a rust-free used piece or a reproduction. If you are handy with a welder, chances are you can save a few bucks by repairing what you have, though the quality of the repair needs to be high enough to ensure the proper appearance and/or function. You may also save some time with body panel alignment by keeping your repaired original fender versus buying a reproduction, though the quality of the repair also plays a role in that operation.

Another area where the decision may not be very easy is with trim pieces. As long as you don't actually break the pieces as you remove them, they can likely be repaired. This is one area where reproduction pieces aren't going to fit quite as well as originals. While reproduction parts are an option when pieces are missing and unobtainable through used parts channels, they should be used only after all attempts to fix the originals have failed.

The damage to this lower windshield molding is not enough to warrant replacement. Once the windshield has been removed from the car, the dent can be removed with some delicate hammer work on the back side of the trim piece. It can then be polished back to its original luster, even removing the steel-wool marks. (Photo Courtesy Scott Tiemann)

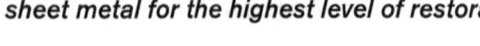

A body-off restoration is the most complete and thorough restoration for a GTO. When separating the body from the frame, you have full access to the frame rails, chassis, and body. The body can be mounted to a rotisserie for media blasting and painting. But most importantly, when the body is separated from the frame, you can cut out all the rusted panels, and replace them with fresh sheet metal for the highest level of restoration. (Photo Courtesy Scott Tiemann)

On the bright side, a professional trim repair shop can effectively repair stainless steel, pot metal, and aluminum trim pieces—even those that most restorers might think are beyond saving. Get on one of the Pontiac-oriented message boards and look for advice on finding a reputable company that provides good results for the money.

How Deep Are You Going?

The truth is, plans change, and sometimes for the better. As you are disassembling your car, you are learning a lot. You may well be learning things you don't want to know, and the scope of the restoration may end up changing. What may have started out as a repaint and interior freshening may end up as a body-off project if a substantial number of surprises pop up.

It is okay if your initial plan for the restoration needs some modifications or even a complete rethink. While it may take some extra time to change course or line up some additional specialists to get the job done, the idea here is to take it in stride. Don't get upset about the initial easy plan that becomes a major job. Most importantly, don't become discouraged, even if you feel you were misled about the condition of the car when you purchased it. With the availability of reproduction sheet metal and the power of the Internet to find just about any used part, most problems can be worked through. Keep your composure and your eye on the prize: a successful outcome.

It's Really a Parts Car– Now What?

If you find the worst-case scenario has happened and your restoration project is not a viable candidate, but rather is a parts car, you still have several options. Above all else, don't fall in love with it. Falling in love with a parts car is like falling in love with a really bad girl. Both will leave you disillusioned, heartbroken, and of course, financially drained. Fall in love with the idea of owning a GTO, not necessarily this particular parts car. If you need to break up with this GTO, consider thes options:

- Sell this GTO as a parts car. This works best if the car hasn't been significantly dismantled.

The restoration is well underway in this photo. The front clip has been removed and the cowl is exposed. You need to determine the level of restoration to your GTO. If you're restoring a car to be judged, then a full body-off restoration is warranted. If your car is this clean and doesn't require much body work (and more importantly if it will be a daily driver), you don't need to disassemble it down to the frame. Therefore, if you believe that you will save time in the long run without compromising the quality of your driver restoration, leave them together. (Photo Courtesy Scott Tiemann)

- Buy another GTO and use your current car for parts. This can actually be your best plan, particularly if the second car is in need of pieces that are still good on your donor car.
- Part it out and use the proceeds to purchase another GTO. This is a good option if the GTO is no longer a complete car but a huge pile of parts. Chances are you can make some money to find a better car and aid others in their projects by going in this direction.

Trying to restore a parts car is almost a rite of passage. Resisting the urge to restore a parts car is a sign of wisdom.

Safety

One area that I cannot stress enough is the use of quality jackstands and related equipment. This is an area where cutting corners can literally kill you. Spend the money to get quality equipment because there is nothing worse than a tragic outcome.

Also, proper ventilation is a must. While many cars are sprayed in a paint booth for professional results, some restorers paint their cars in their own shop. If you are going to be painting in your shop, be sure to have the proper masks and filtration. Some paints are ridiculously toxic, and even welding galvanized metal creates very dangerous fumes. Be sure to check with your paint manufacturer for guidelines to the proper use of their products. Different types of paint require different precautions and procedures.

Make sure you are doing everything the right way; nothing slows down a restoration like hospitalization and lengthy recovery times.

CHAPTER 2

Electrolysis: The Greatest Rust Removal Idea Ever

As we all know, there are a variety of processes to remove rust from metal. Some of the more common are sanding or sandblasting, wire brushing, acid dipping, and chemical stripping processes. While these methods are effective, they can be expensive, messy, and some run the risk of damaging the metal, either by wearing through it or making it brittle and difficult to work with. Concentrate the stream coming out of a sandblaster on one spot of a fender for a few seconds and you're going to put a large hole right through it.

Also, what can be done to free an old engine that has been locked up due to the piston rings rusting to the cylinder? You can fill the cylinders with automatic transmission fluid or drop the short block in a barrel of oil for a few months. Maybe it frees up and maybe it doesn't. What if you don't have a few months to wait—is there an alternative?

A possible answer to the problem in these instances is electrolytic rust removal. Electrolysis is nothing new. Actually, it is a very old concept and has been successfully used by antique tool and tractor restorers for decades. For some reason, it is not as well known in the automotive field, but has incredible potential to help engine builders and auto restorers inexpensively get rust off their parts and out of their lives.

The process is ridiculously simple: Electrical current is run between the part to be restored and an electrode. The part is submerged in a liquid solution (electrolyte) that conducts electricity. Electricity frees electrons from the electrolyte and adds them to the metal part, returning it to the original iron or steel. Where other rust-removal methods take away rust and possibly even good metal, electrolytic rust removal takes nothing from the metal. Unrusted metal is untouched, as is plating in good condition and most kinds of undamaged paint.

While this process does not restore the lower 6 inches missing from your rust-eaten fender or remove the pitting from your exhaust manifold, it does completely remove the rust still present. Best of all, it is a very simple process to set up and you probably have most of the equipment you need already. If you don't, everything is easily obtainable and dirt-cheap.

Electrolysis is one of the most effective ways to remove rust, and it allows the part to shed its rust while retaining solid metal. Hence, you're not stripping away good, useable metal in the process of reconditioning the parts, and sandblasting can remove good metal as well as corroded metal. Performing this procedure is also fairly simple; all you need is a plastic wash tub, a box of Arm & Hammer Super Washing Soda, and a battery charger (I use a 4-amp 12-volt trickle charger). This tub is the perfect size for a exhaust manifold. Rubber gloves are also a good idea, especially if you are prone to skin irritation or prefer not to be mildly shocked. You should also conduct this rust-stripping process in a well-ventilated area because it gives off fumes.

Equipment

- Plastic container large enough to completely submerge the piece to be de-rusted. Plastic construction is necessary to prevent shorts, which could produce a fire or shock hazard. The plastic container can be as small as a household bucket for small items or as large as a kiddie pool for engine blocks, rear ends or other large components. If your item is too large for the container or sticks out of the solution, one side can be treated and then flipped over to finish the entire piece.
- Ordinary 12-volt car battery charger. This unit provides the electrical current necessary for the process.
- Box of Arm & Hammer washing soda. Add one tablespoon of washing soda per gallon of water used.

Adding more won't really help with conductivity. Fill the container with water, mixing up the solution to dissolve as much washing soda as possible. Washing soda helps the water conduct electricity and as a side benefit, provides a mild degreasing effect. You can also add some laundry detergent to further degrease your parts. Others have used lye or baking soda to achieve similar effect, though lye is more hazardous to work with, is a skin and eye irritant, and attacks aluminum. Baking soda is not as effective. Washing soda does the best job without being caustic.

- Scrap piece of iron. The electrode delivers current needed for electrolysis. Avoid stainless steel or galvanized steel; toxic fumes can result. The ideal electrode is a length of metal that can be bent around the submerged object and be tall enough to clear the waterline. If that isn't readily obtainable, it's no big deal. In my own experiments, I have used small pieces of steel tubing and even a discarded iron brake drum.
- Rubber gloves to keep hands clean and provide a little electrical insulation, as you can give yourself a small jolt if you touch the electrode or the item to be cleaned while positioning things in the water. It's low enough voltage so it's not going to injure you, but you'll know you were zapped.

For demonstration purposes here, I used an old brake drum from a Chevy Lumina as the sacrificial anode. The part I am removing rust from is a vintage Pontiac V-8 exhaust manifold. Always make sure the positive lead on the battery charger is connected to the electrode and the negative lead is connected to the part to be cleaned. If the connections are reversed, the part is quickly eaten up by the process. The negative lead can be submerged with the part, though the positive lead must remain above the waterline or it is eaten up by the electrolytic process.

Getting Started

Follow these four steps for a problem-free procedure.

Step 1

Be sure to perform this procedure outdoors or with adequate ventilation, as small amounts of hydrogen will be released. Fill the plastic container enough to completely submerge the item. Mix one tablespoon of Arm & Hammer washing soda per gallon of water.

Fill your washing tank and mix the proper amount of washing soda to create the required amount of wash solution. Measure out the number of gallons or use a Sharpie to mark a certain level on the container. Add one tablespoon of washing soda per gallon of water used. Adding more washing soda doesn't really help with conductivity.

Fill the container with water. Use a large serving spoon or other utensil to stir and thoroughly mix the washing soda with the water. The washing soda should dissolve in the water to make the washing solution. Completely submerge the part in the tank.

Once properly set up, the process starts and stops automatically. It is best to be at 4 amps or above. If you're having trouble getting to that level, try moving the electrode closer to the part, clean any corrosion off the electrode, or change to a stainless-steel electrode. In my own experiments, I was able to pull more than 7 amps with a stainless electrode, which dramatically reduced the cleaning time and sent a strong and steady stream of bubbles to the surface.

The rusty foam on the top of the water is a by-product of the process, as is a small amount of hydrogen gas.

Note that the positive terminal is above the waterline, while the negative terminal is below it.

CHAPTER 2

Electrolysis CONTINUED

Be sure to have adequate ventilation or perform the operation outdoors.

Step 2

Connect the battery charger's positive lead to the electrode. Be sure that the positive lead connection is above the waterline, or it too becomes consumed by the electrolytic process.

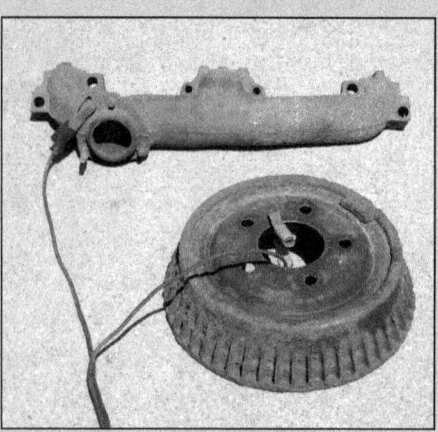

For the purposes of demonstration, I used an old brake drum as the sacrificial anode. I am stripping the rust from a vintage Pontiac V-8 exhaust manifold in this electrolysis process. Always make sure the positive lead on the battery charger is connected to the anode or sacrificial part and the negative lead to the part to be cleaned. If the electrical leads are reversed, the process essentially disintegrates your part in the solution. The negative lead can be submerged with the part, but the positive lead connected to the anode has to remain above the waterline or the electrolytic process eats it. Take my word for it, I found out the hard way!

Step 3

Connect the battery charger's negative lead to the item to be cleaned. If necessary, the negative lead can be submerged, as it is not damaged by the process. Remember, polarity is very important. If you put your rusty part on the positive lead, it is eaten up in short order. The electrode always gets the positive lead, and the part to be de-rusted always gets the negative lead.

Make sure the part and the electrode are close together for maximum effect, but not touching, as that will short it out and possibly damage the charger if it doesn't have internal circuit breakers.

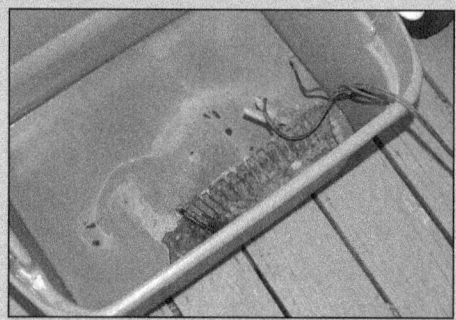

Attach the negative lead to the exhaust manifold and place the positive lead on the drum brake. Place the manifold and the negative lead in the solution; connect the positive lead to the drum and keep it above the waterline. The electrolysis process quickly starts a stream of bubbles. It is best to be at 4 amps or more. If you're having trouble getting to that level, try moving the electrode closer to the part, clean any corrosion off the electrode, or change to a stainless-steel electrode. Warning: Do not, under any circumstances, use stainless steel as a sacrificial anode, as it generates some very toxic fumes. The rusty foam on the top of the water is a by-product of the process, and a small amount of hydrogen gas is released. Note that the positive terminal is above the waterline, while the negative terminal is below. Be sure to have adequate ventilation or perform the operation outdoors.

Step 4

The process begins when the charger is turned on. A fine stream of bubbles begins rising to the surface, indicating the rust is being converted. Getting good contact is a necessity for this process to work. Depending on how good the contact is, the system draws up to 4 to 7 amps, and complete rust removal is achieved from a few hours to a few days, though an overnight session is most likely adequate for most purposes, especially if the system is pulling more than 4 amps.

When the rust is completely gone, the process stops automatically. Electrolytic rust removal is self-limiting and does not "overclean." The formerly rusted areas are black in color, though pits and other surface imperfections may be present. The part is very susceptible to rusting again, so be sure to completely dry off the part off with an electric hairdryer or heat gun and immediately prime and paint or spray with oil or silicone spray.

DISASSEMBLY

The OEM manifold for the Pontiac V-8 has a lot of surface rust because the high-heat paint has burned off and moisture allowed the rust to form on the surface. Since there are no cracks or major flaws with the cast-iron manifold, it is worth restoring and electrolysis returns it to like-new condition.

The electrolysis process removed the rust from the surface of the manifold. Essentially, the process plates the part with iron, reversing the oxidation process. Now those broken studs will come out out easily.

Though the electrolyte becomes very cruddy with dirt and rust, it never loses its effectiveness. Evaporation and the electrolytic process lower the water level so you probably need to top off the container periodically. Add only water; additional washing soda is not needed. If the solution becomes too disgusting to deal with, it can be discarded without negative environmental impact. You may wish to strain out the rust particles so it doesn't clog your drain, though. Be sure to contact your local municipality for disposal compliance information.

The electrolytic process is the gentlest way to remove rust. With a little care and even less money, you can return your vintage GTO parts to their former splendor or get that seized-up engine apart with a minimum of hassle.

After removing the rust from the cast-iron exhaust manifold, the sacrificial anode part (in this case the brake drum) looks like this. The half of the brake drum that was submerged gave up electrons and quickly oxidized.

Shop Manuals on Disc

The computer has really made life easy for those looking for information. If you haven't found a copy of an original Pontiac shop manual for your GTO, there is a very attractive alternative that saves time and money.

Detroit Iron Information Services now offers officially licensed copies of Pontiac shop manuals that cover all years of GTO production through 1973. They are reproduced, page for page, on CD in an Adobe PDF format, which most computers can read.

These manuals are especially handy for a number of reasons. First, you don't have to search and scrounge for an original, which have become collector items and carry a premium price. Second, they take up virtually no space. Finally, you can just print out the pages you need for a particular job and if they get lost, ripped, or covered with grease, you can just print out another one.

CHAPTER 3

BODYWORK

Good bodywork is the foundation of a quality paint job. You can't have one without the other. How many times have you looked at a shiny, new paint job at a distance only to inspect it up close and find a visual nightmare of poor panel alignment, waves, and sanding scratches? This is the result of a lack of preparation for the paint. The finer points of painting and body alignment are covered in Chapter 4; this chapter lays down that foundation with proper bodywork.

Looks can be deceiving. This 1970 Judge convertible seemed to have a solid body not requiring extensive body work. However, it was hiding some significant problems. In addition to both rear quarters needing to be replaced, it needed new floorpan panels, as well as new portions of the trunk floor. The interior was removed to reveal that the floorpans were rusted in certain areas and needed to be replaced. Inspecting the trunk also revealed a certain amount of rot that necessitated patches. While both quarter panels seemed to be solid from the outside, a lot of rust was lurking around the wheel wells and these needed to be replaced. (Photo Courtesy Scott Tiemann)

Typical Rust Areas

From 1964 to 1972, Pontiac GTOs were built on the same GM A-Body that was shared with the Chevelle, Skylark, Cutlass, and of course, the Pontiac Tempest and LeMans. As you expect from cars sharing the same basic platform, they all suffered from the same problem areas where water and road salt collect and corrode sheet metal.

The windshield and backlight areas are prone to window gasket failure, which lets water collect in those areas. As the corrosion progresses, the moisture moves downward and the corrosion follows. In the front, the windshield base is compromised, as are the cowl and firewall areas. Out back, water can collect in the trunk floor, the seams of the trunk wells, the rear quarters, and wheel wells. At the same time, road salt and water are working on the mating seams of the rear quarters and outer wheel wells, as well as the rocker panels.

Fortunately, all unrestored GTOs don't end up as rusted-out parts cars. While it is tough to find a solid GTO in the Northeast or Midwest, the elements are far kinder to Southern and Southwestern examples. Regardless of what corrosion damage you might find, if the overall structural integrity of the car is still sound, often the car is a good candidate for restoration.

Paint Removal

A proper foundation for paint means removing old paint. Many body shops scuff up and paint over an existing finish to save time and money. While this might be fine for repairing a fender-bender or freshening the look of a used car for resale, it is necessary to remove the paint down to the metal so you have the best paint adhesion and of course the best results. Not doing so is putting way too much faith in old materials and labor you really aren't familiar with. Taking the time to do it right will give the results that you want— no one wants to see a substandard finished product every time you open the garage.

There are several methods for paint removal and if done correctly, each does a very good job. Each has certain benefits and drawbacks. When each method is done incorrectly, the results can be disastrous.

Sanding

It's tedious, time-consuming, and messy, but it is the time-honored method of paint and rust removal. There is a balance here that has to be maintained—the balance between saving time and being too aggressive with the paper grit. If you are using a right-angle grinder/sander, be very careful, as it can generate enough heat to warp sheet metal. It also removes more metal than necessary and leaves very deep scratches, which can add time to repair. A dual-action (DA) orbital sander is not as aggressive—it is easier on the metal but takes longer to accomplish the same job.

My suggestion is to start with a less-aggressive grit and use a DA orbital sander. As you become more familiar with how they perform, you can get more aggressive with the paper grit, maybe even switch over to a right-angle grinder and work from there.

Chemical Stripping

Chemical stripping falls into two categories of application—industrial and brush-on. In the industrial application, the entire body is dipped in huge vats filled with an acid or alkaline solution that takes off all paint and rust, leaving only the bare metal. Brushing on a chemical stripper softens paint and filler, making it easy to scrape off, revealing clean, bare metal. I have worked with both and no matter how you do it…it ends up a gooey mess.

The brush-on application is a practical way for the at-home restorer to strip the paint from the body. In addition, it is a good way to get paint and filler off large panels, such as roofs, hoods, decklids, and doors.

I have had good luck using stripper on the main area of a hood, while leaving the edges for a sander later. That way, I took advantage of the time-saving chemical strippers offered while still preventing damage to new paint in the future.

Whatever brand of stripper you use, make sure you have plenty of ventilation as the fumes can be strong. Gloves are mandatory as well, as chemical strippers can cause severe drying of the skin and/or chemical burns.

If you have the option to take the body shell and panels to a commercial company to do the stripping for you, it is a big time-saver, albeit a fairly expensive one.

Acid Dipping: Acid dipping is also known as chemical milling. In addition to removing all paint, primer, and filler, it also removes a certain amount of the metal, depending on the amount of time the part is immersed. Race car builders have used the process for decades to remove weight from a car body while still maintaining the original material and appearance. The downside to acid dipping is that it is corrosive to

Chemical strippers work well but are messy and disposal can sometimes be a problem. They are applied with a brush, and due to their viscosity, they stick to vertical surfaces without dripping off. The stripper doesn't need a thick coat to be effective, but it does need some time for the paint to start bubbling and lifting. The directions say to let it sit for 30 minutes to three hours but I suggest letting it sit for at least three hours. After the paint is lifted, scraping with a putty knife is necessary. You may have to apply a second coat or wire brush off the primer coat to get it off. (Photo Courtesy Eastwood Products)

metal. It also tends to work-harden it. There is also the possibility that if not properly rinsed, acid can remain in seams and other areas, destroying paint and causing further corrosion.

Alkaline Dipping: Alkaline dipping uses liquid on the other end of the pH scale from acid. The advantage is that while it is very effective at getting rid of rust and bondo, it leaves the "good," or non-corroded, metal alone. This process is costly and the alkaline must be removed from the seams to prevent potential paint damage. Given the choice of the two, the alkaline process is better for restorations. The RediStrip process is offered at franchises around the United States and is especially good for restoration work.

As with acid dipping, be careful about getting the stripper in body seams and other places where it can be trapped and cause paint damage later.

Media Blasting

For many years, sandblasting was the only available form of media blasting. While it is very effective at removing rust, paint, and old filler, it is a process that can easily destroy sheet metal, both from the abrasive action and from the frictional heat it develops. Plus, if you aren't careful, you could blast a hole right through a fender. Sandblasting sheet metal requires an even technique and inexperienced restorers destroyed many parts learning this lesson.

Today, new processes are just as effective without the detrimental effects of sand, most notably soda blasting. While soda blasting might sound like spraying a Coke or Pepsi firehose at the body, it actually refers to baking soda (sodium bicarbonate). If you look at it under a microscope, you see that it is not really a powder but is actually crystalline. When the media is accelerated to high speed, millions of tiny explosions occur and the paint is stripped away.

Baking soda is fine enough as a very gentle paint remover. In fact, it is so gentle that you can remove one paint layer at a time. Best of all, you can save time by not having to mask everything off, as the soda does not hurt chrome, rubber, or glass. Obviously, this is not the most effective means of rust removal, but it takes off light to moderate surface rust on sheet metal. In addition, unlike sandblasting, you won't risk warping or blowing a hole in the sheet metal. For paint removal, it's a very good choice. The media leaves a rust-inhibiting coat on the bare metal, which needs to be cleaned off before priming or painting.

Equipment can be rented or purchased, and certain companies will do the job for you. Eastwood and Harbor Freight, among others, have a wide variety of reasonably priced kits and soda media for home use. Eastwood also sells a combination of baking soda and aluminum oxide, which is formulated to work with its blaster and more effectively remove rust, though it does harm trim and glass.

Of course, there are other types of abrasive media such as plastic, pulverized walnut shells, even dry ice. For the home restorer, the soda blaster represents the best overall media-blasting system available, from the standpoints of cost, ease of use, safety to delicate trim, and ease of disposal. Baking soda is eco-friendly and you are not trying to get rid of non-biodegradable refuse, as with the acrylic medias used in plastic media blasting. The equipment is not terribly expensive, it is ridiculously simple, and for all intents and purposes, it's idiot-proof. Where you can quickly and easily cause sandblast damage, the soda blaster is much more forgiving without having to sacrifice results. When you add that up and see how quickly it does the job, combined with the ease of disposal, the choice really is a no-brainer.

Media blasters come in many different types and sizes. Sandblasters have been around for quite a long time and effectively strip the paint and rust off the body panels of your A-Body car. For the home restorer, soda blasters, which use baking soda as the medium, are a great choice, as they are fairly inexpensive, safe to glass and trim, strip paint very quickly, and are environmentally friendly. They also leave a rust-inhibiting coating, which needs to be removed before priming and painting. The blaster works just like a sandblaster, using an air compressor, a hopper for the baking soda, and a hose and nozzle. Work the area carefully to avoid stripping any area you want to preserve, and be sure to wear proper clothing, eye protection and a respirator. (Photo Courtesy Eastwood Products)

BODYWORK

This 1964 GTO body was stripped using the soda blaster and the end result is a thing of beauty. All of the paint was removed, leaving a beautiful foundation for a show-winning paint job. (Photo Courtesy Scott Tiemann)

Repair Patches

Metal patches made to original body panels go a long way to saving money and retaining a measure of originality. The 1964 GTO shown here was the original *Car and Driver* magazine test car that appeared in the now-legendary "GTO vs. GTO" article in the March 1964 issue. As such, this particular GTO has an immense amount of history behind it, and it was deemed important by both the owner, Tenney Fairchild, and the restorer, Scott Tiemann of Supercar Specialties, to integrate as much of the original sheet metal as possible into the restoration.

Fortunately, this GTO was in remarkably good condition for a rust-belt car, having spent nearly 20 years in storage. While it displayed corrosion in most of the typical spots seen in cars of this age, it had not advanced very far, so it was feasible to repair much of the damage with simple, hand-fabricated patch panels cut from sheet metal.

The process was fairly simple. One fender was stripped down to the bare metal inside and out. Scott carefully cut out the rusted section using a reciprocating saw, and then cut a patch out of 18-gauge sheet metal, closely matching the shape of the hole. He then tacked-welded it in place, placing the welds about 1 inch apart.

After inspecting the repair for fit, the patch was completely welded in. The welds were then ground flush with the original sheet metal and the front side of the repair was completed.

There was also some rust damage to the fender support brace just behind the original rust damage. That area was also treated to the same preparation, a patch was cut, welded in, and the welds ground flush. This process returned the fender to its original appearance and structural integrity without replacing the factory-installed panel. A small amount of filler may be needed to completely smooth the area prior to painting, but at this point, the repair is complete.

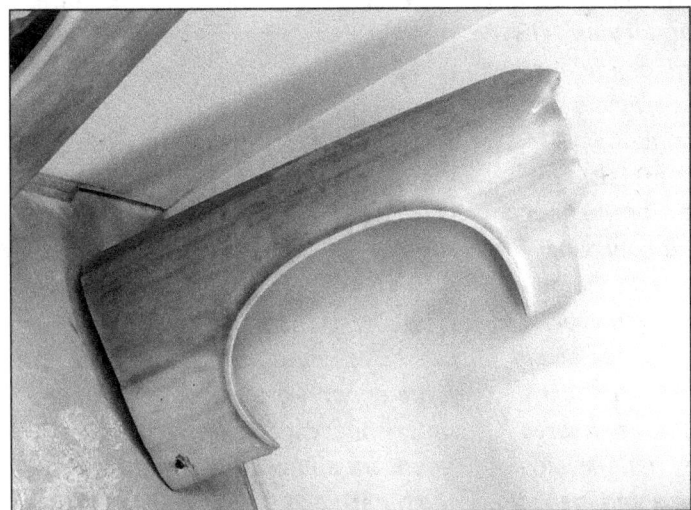

Once the paint and rust are removed from this 1964 GTO fender by way of a soda blaster, the repair can begin. (Photo Courtesy Scott Tiemann)

This close-up shows that the rust-through damage is fairly localized and doesn't extend to the edges. This fender is a good candidate for a repair patch. (Photo Courtesy Scott Tiemann)

CHAPTER 3

Floorpan and Trunk Floor Replacement

Floor and trunk pans are areas that are frequently rusted out from continued exposure to moisture and salt. Depending on where your car is from, the damage could be as minor as pinholes in a foot well to entire sections no longer being present. Fortunately, the solutions are as large or small as the damaged areas.

Before reproduction floorpans became available, repair methods ran the gamut from using NOS sheet metal obtained from dealers to cutting floors out of rust-free Western cars to welding in fabricated patch panels. Other more creative methods, such as using expanded sheet metal covered with fiberglass cloth has been used, as was riveting on a piece of sheet metal or even just laying a piece of sheet metal over the hole and letting the carpeting hold it in place.

For some reason, where I come from in Upstate New York, it was all the rage in the 1970s and 1980s to steal stop signs and cut them up to make floorboards. I'm not sure what the reasoning was, as the metal used was much thicker than production car floorboards and was not even steel—they're silk-screened aluminum. I suppose it was more the thrill of obtaining the stop sign than its suitability as a replacement panel.

In any event, the aftermarket came to the rescue, saving these would-be scofflaws from months of possible jail time and community service, as well as helping law-abiding restorers regain the structural integrity they lost to the elements.

Replacement floorpans and trunk floors are engineered to fit right and restore integrity to the body. Like the originals that they replace, the reproduction floor panels are stamped from the correct-gauge sheet metal and feature the same ribs and contours as the originals to make their installation as trouble-free as possible. Companies that manufacture and sell these panels include Year One, Ames Performance Engineering, Original Parts Group, Performance Years, National Parts Depot, and Dynacorn.

Further aiding the restorer are the sizes of replacement pans available. In some cases, the rust damage is limited to one area, such as below the accelerator, brake, and clutch pedals.

The factory carpeting has a vinyl mat area that can trap moisture from wet footwear, leaving the area prone to rust-through. For jobs such as this, quarter sections are available for front and rear on both sides.

Replacement floorpans also come in left and right halves, front to rear, as well as full-floorpan stampings.

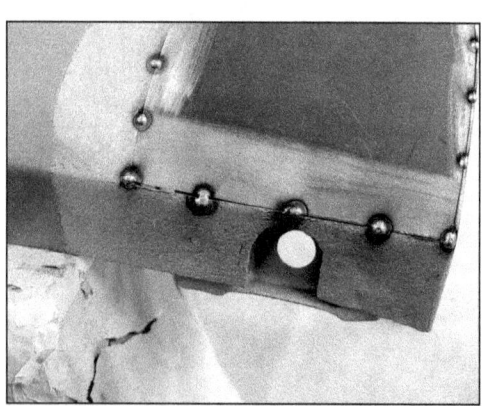

MIG-welding body panels—whether it's fenders, quarter panels, or floorpans—is an art. If you have not used a welder before, it's wise to take a class and develop the necessary skills. If you're a quick learner you can practice in your garage. Body panels are typically 14- or 16-gauge sheet-metal steel, and if your MIG welder is set too high or you apply too much heat to a particular area, you can easily burn through the sheet metal and ruin the component.

Therefore, set the welder at a lower voltage for welding thin metals. I recommend at least practicing the tack and stitch welding required for the floor installation on some scrap metal before attempting to install the floorpans. The patch panel and the existing sheet metal should overlap slightly and the gap should be minimal so fill welding is not required later. Apply the weld every 4 to 5 inches, quench the area with water or air, and then apply the next tack weld. If you don't allow the welded area to properly cool before applying the next tack weld in the same area, the panel warps. If it warps, corrective measures must be taken using a hammer and dolly to straighten the body panel, which is time consuming and frustrating. Tack weld the patch into place and inspect the repair for fit. When it is deemed satisfactory, completely weld in the panel, making sure that the heat is not so hot that it warps the metal. Then grind the weld flush and prime it. (Photo Courtesy Scott Tiemann)

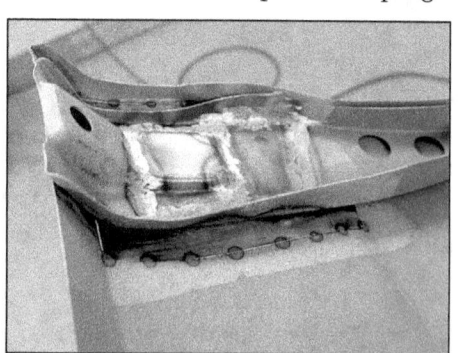

If the support brace just behind the outer sheet metal is also rust damaged, cut and weld in a patch as on the outer-section repair. Grind the repair smooth so the fender regains its original appearance and integrity. (Photo Courtesy Scott Tiemann)

BODYWORK

Once the floorpans are rusted and weakened, they need to be replaced. Several tools can be used to cut out the rusted-out floors of a GTO. Most use a plasma cutter. If you use a plasma cutter, use it with care and precision. You can inadvertently cut through the frame rail, floor support, and other components much faster than you'd think. So be deliberate and careful because you don't want to patch and repair those from inadvertently cutting them with a torch. To remove the floors, use a rotary cutoff tool, which takes some time and is hard work. Use a 3-inch disc in 1/32- or 1/16-inch thickness, and do yourself a favor by buying a high-quality disc, such as one from 3M. Use the cutoff wheel to precisely cut out the rusted and weakened factory floorpans. Use the replacement pans as templates for cutting. Take precautions to ensure the original floor bracing is not harmed in the process. Though these look bad, they are actually in great shape. Most of the rust seen on them is from pieces falling from the floor panels, not from the braces. (Photo Courtesy Scott Tiemann)

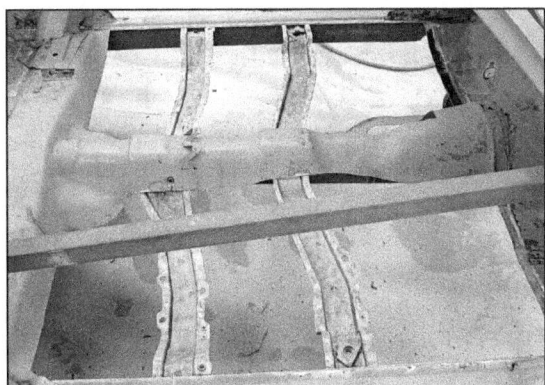

The floorpans are a major structural component of the body, and therefore when cutting out the floors, the body can move out of alignment. You don't want to install the floorpans when the body isn't square. Hence, you need to install these brace bars and take the proper measurements to ensure that the body is square. This is not really necessary for a floorpan replacement, but if your car is also getting quarter panels it needs the support. These floor braces have been soda blasted and primed. Once the floor braces are stripped, the pans are ready for installation. (Photo Courtesy Scott Tiemann)

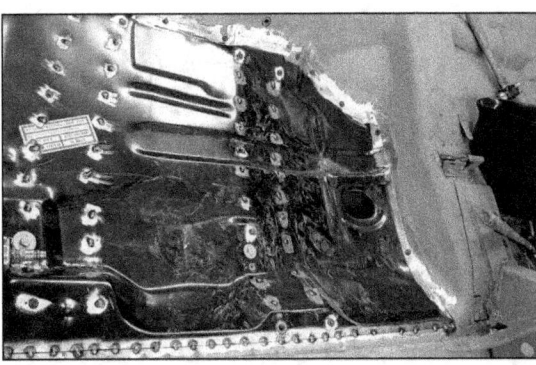

While some purists may use a clean floor from a donor car, you can install a reproduction floor on your GTO. Mark the alignment for the new floorpans, then measure and cut for a butt weld to the existing sheet metal. To maintain accurate alignment throughout this tack welding stage, drill holes around the perimeter of the replacement sheet-metal floor to hold it in place. This is done to locate them and keep them in the proper position during the welding process. Also drill holes in the areas just above the floorpan supports, so they can be easily welded to it. Then, using a MIG welder, place tack welds every 3 or 4 inches along the floor braces. Be careful when applying these welds because you don't want to burn through the thin sheet metal or apply too much heat, causing the floors to warp. (Photo Courtesy Scott Tiemann)

These replace the entire floor from the rockers to the firewall to the wheel wells and trunk. They can even include support braces and rocker panels, if you wish—essentially the entire bottom of the body. This is an attractive alternative in cases where the rust is severe, though some restorers prefer to weld the smaller pieces together, as they are easier to handle than one large piece and save money on shipping costs.

Keep the condition of the passenger compartment floor and the trunk floor in mind when evaluating the car. Make sure that you are poking and prodding the entire area with a rubber mallet and a screwdriver. In addition to rust holes, look for weakening of those areas with heavy surface rust.

If you find that you can get the floorpans to deflect even a little with your hands, it is a clear indicator that their strength has been compromised by corrosion. They should be replaced, even if there aren't any visible holes because the structural integrity of the body is compromised, and ultimately it's a safety issue. You don't want to have seats falling through the floors six months after the car is finished. Take the time

CHAPTER 3

Professionally installed floorpans look similar to this when viewed from underneath the car. The seams, panel stamping, and alignment with the floor braces make it appear as the original one-piece unit. Grind down the tack welds and prime and paint the floor. Once the area is properly finished, the repair is nearly invisible and restores the integrity of the body. A floor replacement, such as this, adds value to the restored car. On the other hand, if the stamping and panel alignment is off, a potential buyer or show judge will recognize this issue and the car will be worth less and points deducted. Replacing floors for the first time takes care, attention to detail, and diligence. (Photo Courtesy Scott Tiemann)

to carefully evaluate what you have while the car is all apart, because it will never be easier to weld in new floorpans than it is at this stage.

The procedure for welding in new floorpans involves careful measuring and cutting away of the original floor. The idea is to remove only as much metal as necessary to properly install the panel to solid, original metal. Be careful to avoid cutting the support braces; they may be reusable. If you are finding that you are cutting into more and more rusted metal, keep cutting until you find solid metal, even if it means having to purchase additional panels. What good is it to weld in fresh reproduction sheet metal to thin, corroded, compromised sheet metal? Again, safety and structural integrity is what you are going for.

Once the corroded metal has been removed, the area should be prepared with a grinder or reciprocating saw to smooth the edges. As with the patch panel described earlier, the new pan should be tack welded every 1 inch or so and checked for warpage and fit. Once

A thorough inspection of this 1970 GTO Judge convertible revealed major rust damage in several areas. In particular, the quarter panels suffered major rust damage, and these parts required replacement in some cases and major repair in other cases. Water spray from passing cars often leads to more rust on the driver's side of the car, and in this case, the driver's side is far worse than the passenger's side.

Although the driver's side was worse than the passenger's side, the passenger-side quarter panel still needs to be replaced. Use an air-powered rotary cut off tool to cut out the rusted outer skin below the beltline. Use the replacement panel to guide the cut off tool across the rusted skin and achieve a straight cut. Drill out the factory quarter-panel spot welds, so the panel can be removed. Use a special spot weld drill bit, which drills a 1/8-inch hole in the center and then cuts away the top metal in the spot weld until it is freed from the bottom half of the weld. Note that this rocker panel is still in very good condition and the outer wheel well only has minor rust-through along the edges. (Photo Courtesy Scott Tiemann)

BODYWORK

that is achieved and the job is satisfactory, finish welding in the pans and then grind down the welds for a correct appearance.

Quarter Panel Replacement

On areas where there is enough corrosion to negate the use of simple patches and warrant the replacement of entire exterior quarter panels, reproduction units should be obtained, as well as the support pieces behind them. This operation is quite involved and requires a great deal of preparation and planning.

Once you have made the decision that replacement is necessary, it is time to order parts. It is advisable to wait until they arrive before cutting anything, as it is too easy to cut more away than is necessary, which complicates the process and slows things down. This is especially significant when using lower-half quarters instead of the full units that extend into the C-pillar.

Once you have the new panels, carefully clamp them to the car so you can scribe lines to determine where to cut. If you are going for a full quarter replacement, use the factory seams as a guide for cutting. If you are performing a full quarter replacement on a coupe or hardtop body style, the seam that mates to the roof panel has lead as a filler. Use a propane torch to remove the lead, but make sure that you are not heating the roof panel enough to warp it. Just use as much heat as needed to remove the lead.

Be sure to wear a mask when performing this task and use caution. Lead is a poisonous substance, and you don't want to risk your health. Be careful and use plastic filler when finishing the area.

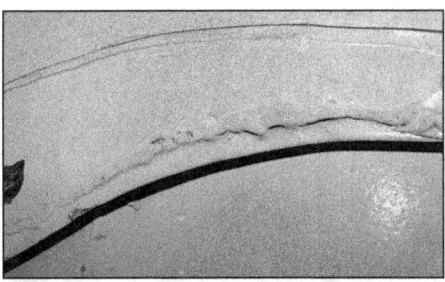

The inner wheelhouse on the passenger side had some rust-through damage, so a repair was necessary before the new lower quarter was installed. (Photo Courtesy Scott Tiemann)

Measure, measure, measure. When positioning the new quarter panel into place, take note of how the new panel aligns with other adjoining panels and their contours, the outer wheelhouse, bumper, and other critical points. It is not difficult to install a quarter panel a little too high or low and throw off everything in the process.

Quarter Panel Replacement

Cut Out Rust

1 *Use a small rotary cutoff tool to cut out the rusted portion of the inner wheelhouse. Carefully cut above the frame rail and between the trunk support rail as well as 4 to 5 inches of the rust-affected area. Cut out the rusted metal, leaving a void for the patch to cover. Cut a patch by hand with shears to replicate the edge of the cut as well as the lower edge of the wheelhouse (Photo Courtesy Scott Tiemann)*

Tack Weld to Wheelhouse

2 *Tack weld a 4- to 5-inch-wide by 24-inch-long piece of .040-inch-thick sheet metal to the solid metal wheelhouse. Measure the thickness of the original metal and use the same thickness in all repairs. Once the tack welds are placed, use a rotary grinding tool to smooth down the tack-weld heads. Place a bead along the entire seam and then smooth it down. Make and install a patch that loops around and meets the replacement outer wheelhouse. (Photo Courtesy Scott Tiemann)*

CHAPTER 3

Weld Seam

Smooth Out Seam

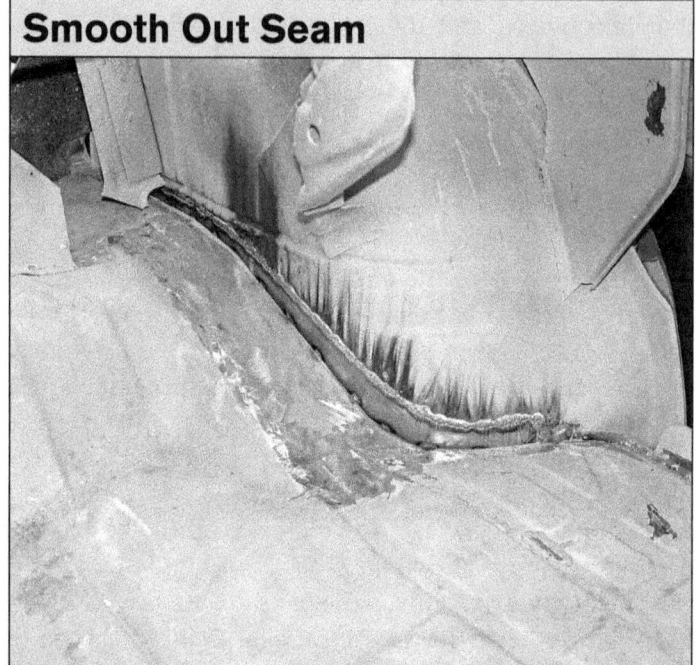

3 Use a MIG welder to place a bead of weld down the entire seam. When performing this work, ensure that the welder is correctly set, so you do not burn through the small patch you're installing. The corner of the patch meets the inner wheelhouse, and the quality of this work is exceptional. You should strive to achieve the quality of work pictured here. As well as the quality of the welds, care must be taken with the grinding down of the welds. It is important to grind the weld and not any of the surrounding metal, as it needlessly weakens the metal and causes an uneven contour. (Photo Courtesy Scott Tiemann)

4 The wheel-well housing repair has been completed and so has the area of the trunk adjacent to the wheel well. The rust in that area also necessitated that a corresponding patch in the trunk floor be installed. Once the tack welds and then the full seam welds are placed, use a rotary tool to smooth out the seam so it looks factory new. Remember to work on the welds and not the metal itself. (Photo Courtesy Scott Tiemann)

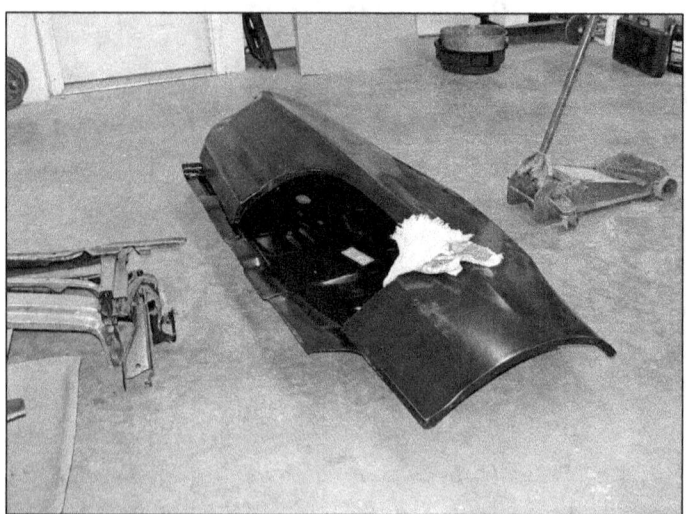

Shown here is a full replacement quarter panel for the passenger's side. Although the replacement panel includes a full rear quarter, only the lower half is used for this particular repair. In addition, there is a dent above the beltline on the panel, but with some coaxing and body filler the dent will be repaired. (Photo Courtesy Scott Tiemann)

This assortment of body parts also includes replacement inner wheel-well panels. In this particular case, the pieces came from Ames Performance Engineering. (Photo Courtesy Scott Tiemann)

34 HOW TO RESTORE YOUR PONTIAC GTO 1964–1974

BODYWORK

Weld on Wheelhouse

5 Use a MIG welder to weld the reproduction outer wheelhouse onto the inner section and to the inner section of the trunk sump area. Smooth the welds with a rotary tool to achieve a clean look. (Photo Courtesy Scott Tiemann)

Align Panel

6 To install the panel, it must align with the adjoining body panels and be anchored in position. While the doors and fenders can be moved around once installed, the quarter panel is not removable and therefore it's imperative to get the alignment correct. At this stage, look at all the adjoining body panels and ensure that they are correctly lined up. Look at the quarter panel and door gap; the same goes for the quarter panel and trunk lid gap. All these components need to be in alignment.

Drill through the adjacent sheet metal and bolt the panel into position. As with the rest of the panels used for this restoration, the quarter panel must be temporarily fastened and located with bolts, allowing for shift-free positioning while it is tack and finish welded. Butt weld the lower quarter-panel section to the top half. Place body panel clamps and locking pliers on the bottom of the quarter panel and the inner wheel-well housing. From inside the trunk, weld the quarter panel to the trunk floor panel and the wheel well. (Photo Courtesy Scott Tiemann)

Weld Quarter Panels Together

7 Weld the upper quarter panel to the lower quarter panel using a butt-weld joint. Use a MIG welder to place a thin stitch weld along the entire seam of the quarter panel. This is extremely delicate work that requires correct welder settings and attention to detail. If the welding is too hot, you run the risk of warping the panel and ruining all your hard work. Once the stitch welds have been completed, use a rotary tool with a 36-grit, 5-inch, flexible 3M wheel disc to grind the beads smooth on the quarter in preparation for final finishing. As mentioned before, carefully grind down the weld and not the surrounding sheet metal. (Photo Courtesy Scott Tiemann)

Align Panel with Bumper

8 With the bumper installed, properly align the upper and lower quarter panel with the bumper. This level of body fit and alignment is needed for a concours-level restoration and will be rewarded with gold awards. (Photo Courtesy Scott Tiemann)

Remove Paint

9 Strip the entire body of paint in preparation for dent repair, paint, and alignment. Soda blasters are great for home restorers due to the low cost and the fact that the media is gentler than sand beads. However, you can use a two-step process, which begins with plastic media blasting and ends with a careful sandblasting of whatever rust remains. (Photo Courtesy Scott Tiemann)

Align Remaining Panels

10 As mentioned earlier, the driver's side of this Judge was worse off than the passenger's side, requiring an extensive teardown and rebuilding with reproduction sheet metal. In this case, the extent of the rust damage was far beyond a quarter-panel patch, and therefore the entire quarter panel needed to be replaced.

Before you cut off the rear quarter panel, align the panels that will still remain on the car. That way, you can properly align the replacement quarter panel when you're installing it. (You don't want to find out after you installed the quarter that the trunk lid and door were not properly aligned and have unsightly gaps between your new quarter panel and adjoining parts.) Start with the front fender and make sure the gap and alignment are even with the front seam of the door, and also make sure the trailing edge of the door properly aligns with the existing quarter panel. Once that has been accomplished, you can move onto cutting out the quarter panel. The process was started with a cut along the factory seam. (Photo Courtesy Scott Tiemann)

Drill Out Factory Spot Welds

11 Rust has ravaged the driver's side of this Judge. Corrosion has destroyed the entire quarter panel, and the inner wheel well has extensive rust damage. Essentially, this entire area of the body must be reconstructed. Having such a valuable car cut up like this may look intimidating, but that's what it takes to build a show winner out of a rusty car. When rust damage is this extensive, the repairs are substantial, but you need to take a planned, methodical, and patient approach to install each body part. The inner wheelhouse, the trunk floor, outer wheelhouse, and then the full quarter panel will be replaced and/or repaired—in that order.

If you have this level of metal deterioration, drill out the factory spot welds to free up the quarter panel. Use a cutoff wheel to cut through the original spot welds on the edge of the panel. Cut off the quarter panel at the trunk lid frame, the deck panel, and interior-side bulkhead panel. In addition, cut off a portion of the trunk adjoining the wheel well. Fabricate a patch for this area of the trunk. The tools you use to make the cuts are dictated by the amount of space available and could be a small or large cutoff wheel, plasma cutter, air chisel, or spot-weld drill bit. (Photo Courtesy Scott Tiemann)

BODYWORK

Inspect Wheel-Well Housing

12 A close inspection revealed that the outer wheel-well housing was damaged, wrinkled, and rusted to the point that it needed to be replaced. However, the inner half could be saved with a patch similar to that on the other side. This side of the trunk floor must also be replaced with reproduction sheet metal. (Photo Courtesy Scott Tiemann)

Sandblast Support Bracing

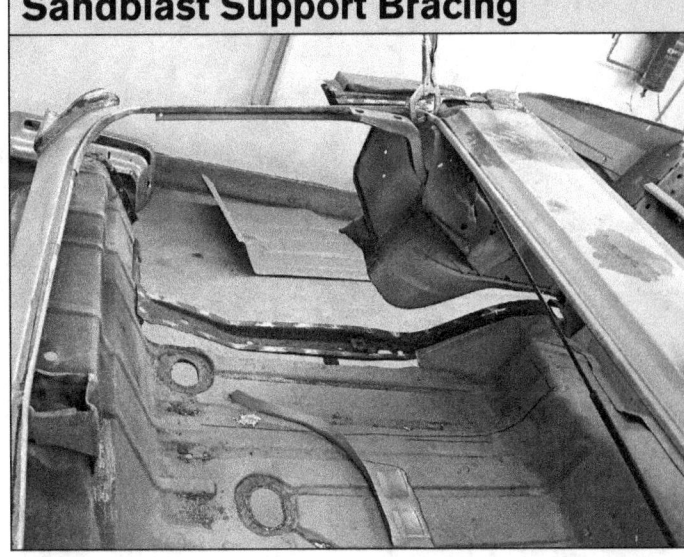

13 If your trunk support bracing is structurally solid, carefully sandblast and prepare it for reassembly. If the bracing underneath is in good shape, retain it and weld the new trunk floor section to it. (Photo Courtesy Scott Tiemann)

Remove Rust Behind Quarter Skin

14 Carefully use a sandblaster to remove the rust from the panels behind the quarter skin. This provides for a good foundation for the rust-inhibiting primer and paint. Here, the trunk and rear bulkhead body structure are solid and free of corrosion. But if your particular GTO has more rust in this area, all of it must be removed from the panels and body. If the rust isn't completely removed, it will start coming through the sheet metal, and eventually, the body work must be re-done. (Photo Courtesy Scott Tiemann)

Weld In New Trunk Floor

15 Weld the new trunk floor section into the good metal. Spend the time to make sure the trunk floor section is in proper alignment with the adjoining panels and the seams properly line up with rest of the trunk floor. The outside edge of the trunk patch has a lip stamped into the reproduction trunk panel. Weld the trunk patch to the existing trunk section using a butt joint. Use a set of welding clamps to keep the pieces in alignment and promote good spot welding. Once again, drill the panel and use tack welds to attach the patch to the trunk support members. Place spot welds every 3 or 4 inches to secure the panel to the trunk brace. (Photo Courtesy Scott Tiemann)

CHAPTER 3

Install Inner Wheel-Well Patch

16 Using high-quality reproduction parts, you can cut the patch from an inner wheelhouse. That way the contours match perfectly to the inner wheel-well sheet metal. It's far easier to cut reproduction body parts down to size than to fabricate a patch piece out of raw sheet metal. First, measure the patch for the butt weld. Then spot weld the patch to the inner and outer wheel well. Grind the spot welds flush to the sheet metal. The inner wheelhouse pictured here had a patch welded in as on the other side. (Photo Courtesy Scott Tiemann)

17 Cut two pieces for the outer wheelhouse repair from reproduction parts. The first piece is a long 4- to 5-inch-wide lip of the outer wheelhouse that was cut with a small cutting wheel. The piece runs from the rocker panel all the way around the wheel-well opening. Fit the first piece and MIG tack weld into place.

18 Keep as much original sheet metal as possible. Tack weld the wheelhouse piece into place and then finish with a MIG welder. Then smooth it with a sanding disc so it looks like a fully integrated piece. (Photo Courtesy Scott Tiemann)

Hang Quarter Panel

19 At this stage, the inner wheelhouse has been repaired, the outer wheelhouse has been replaced, and an adjoining section of the trunk has been replaced. Hence, all the body work for the wheelhouse and adjoining parts have been completed. Now it is time to hang the quarter panel itself. Drill the quarter panel front to rear with 1/8-inch holes every 6 inches or so to secure it to the upper quarter. Locate the full quarter panel with bolts, tack weld, and then finish welding it in. As with the previous sheet-metal installations, the results lined up perfectly in this example. (Photo Courtesy Scott Tiemann)

BODYWORK

Locate Data Tag

20 The Judge's original data tag was removed to prevent damage while the bodywork was performed and also to prep the area under it for paint. New, correct rivets to re-attach it are available from TrimTags.com. While it is legal to remove the data tag for the purposes of restoration, removing a VIN tag riveted to the body, as in the early GTOs, is a federal crime. Don't do it. (Photo Courtesy Scott Tiemann)

Avoid Painting Over VIN

21 The VIN of the car is stamped into some body panels, and it is often hidden to thwart theft. It is important when painting these areas to not have the paint obscure these numbers. (Photo Courtesy Scott Tiemann)

Select Paint

22 Rust-inhibiting paints, like Hirsch Miracle Paint, act as a barrier to moisture, completely encapsulating the metal. Some of these paints are affected by UV rays, so a topcoat is needed in some cases. (Photo Courtesy Hirsch Automotive)

Pull Dents

23 Years ago the only option for pulling out a dent in a body panel was to drill holes in the panel so a slide hammer could be attached. Once the dent was pulled out with the slide hammer, the holes needed to be filled in with lead or body filler. And that was a hassle. Today, this handy stud welder is a great way to fasten a stud to a damaged panel, making slide-hammer attachment a snap.

Place a stud into the welder, touch the bare metal within the dent, and pull the trigger. The stud is instantly welded onto the panel. Best of all, there isn't enough heat generated to warp the panel and once completed, the stud can be ground off and the surface primed. (Photo Courtesy of Eastwood Company)

CHAPTER 3

Quarter Panel Patch Preparation

Time and corrosion have taken their toll on this driver-side quarter panel, and as result, replacement is the most viable option. The recipient of the quarter-panel patch installation is this 1967 GTO hardtop, which is owned by Tom DeMauro, editor of High Performance Pontiac magazine. Tom purchased the Goat back in 1987, and it is a typical rust-belt machine. Years of exposure to salt and corrosion requires a quarter-panel replacement. While this GTO doesn't have a particular pedigree, Tom has a great amount of affection for it, so he invested the money to have the quarter panel repaired. The car has many high-performance upgrades, so it runs, handles, and stops better than a stocker. However, it obviously needs some help in the body and paint departments. Tony Golembreski at Melvin Benzaquen's Classic Restorations in Sloatsburg, New York, replaced the rotted-out rear quarter.

A thorough and careful inspection of the rear quarter panel from underneath the car, the trunk, and from the wheel well shows the extent of rust damage. This outer wheelhouse is rusted through and cracked. You can also see that the lower quarter-panel skin is rusted through right above the trim panel. Once the trim panel was removed, more rust was found beneath it. The trim panel trapped moisture in the quarter panel and rusted out the metal as it always does. But the rust didn't stop there—it extended back and around the car and underneath the taillights. These rust patterns are very typical of an East Coast or Middle Atlantic GTO. Quite a bit of body filler had been added to this quarter as well, as a previous owner tried to repair it, and the repair job was marginal at best.

Cut Off Quarter Panel

1 To cut off the quarter panel that extends underneath the rear bumper, the bumper itself needs to be removed. Remove the four bolts holding the bumper to the bumper bracket. Remove the bumper to access the rear of the quarter panel. If the bolts are rusted solid, the heads can be ground off with a rotary grinder.

BODYWORK

Remove Bumper

2 Once the bolt heads are ground off, the bumper comes off easily. If your bumper is still very straight and the fit is excellent, it can be re-chromed and reused.

The replacement sheet metal includes this stamped lower rear quarter-panel patch, trunk extensions, and outer wheelhouse. The pieces are available from Original Parts Group (OPG). While the parts are all stamped from correct-gauge sheet metal, the quarter-panel patch and trunk extension need some modification to fit properly.

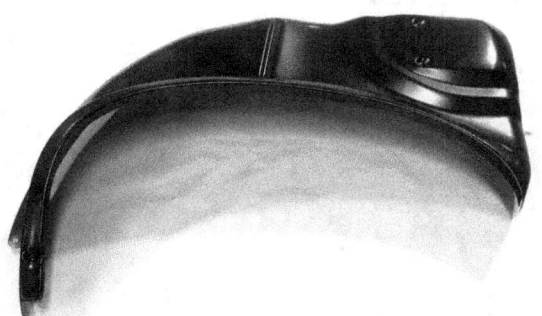

The inner wheelhouse is also from OPG, and like the others, it is close to the factory original, but not the same exact part. These reproduction parts just need some time and fit work to be properly installed in position.

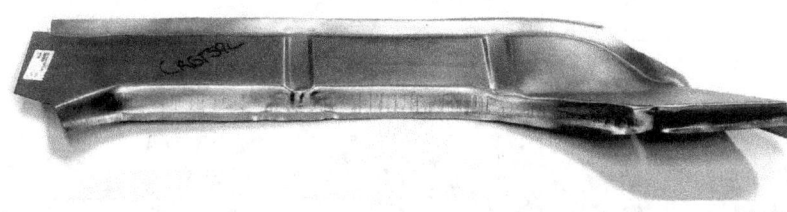

This lower quarter panel was not stamped from factory dies, and therefore, it is not an exact replacement. Consequently, a piece such as this often requires some trimming and fitting to be installed on the car because it's marginally different than the original.

Remove Lower Quarter Molding

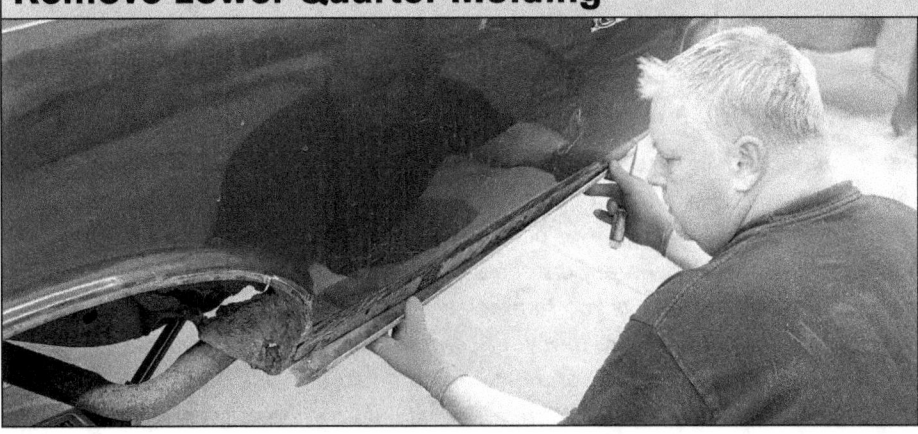

3 Remove the factory lower quarter molding. If very little of the quarter molding actually holds the piece on, it can be pulled away. Commonly, the clips must be released with a trim tool, but it simply wasn't necessary here, as the molding was barely attached to the quarter panel.

Remove Trim Piece

4 Pry off the trim piece to the quarter panel. Moisture may be trapped behind the trim piece, with the expected corrosion eating up the lower portion of the quarter, trunk extension, and outer wheelhouse. If rust has come through along the entire length of the quarter panel, there is too much corrosion damage to do a simple body-filler patch. The rust-affected quarter panel and wheelhouse must be cut out and replaced.

Align Quarter Panels

5 Test-fit the panel. Use a wide-jaw locking pliers to keep the body panel in place. Use a scratch shawl or a Sharpie pen to mark the original piece along its entire length. Reproduction panels and even NOS panels often don't fit the same exact way as the factory-original panel.

Align the top quarter panel with the lower quarter panel and be sure it aligns with the wheel-well opening and the seam at the bumper. Gaps along the edges are common. If the panel is too short in any area, use a piece of metal from the old quarter panel or cut a piece of sheet metal from the same-gauge sheet metal and tack weld it in place. With diligence and practice you should be able to fit most panels. If you get stuck in a particular area, take some digital photos of it and take them to a respected body man or enthusiast; he can often help you find the best solution.

Place Tape for Quarter Panel Cut-Off

6 Once you verify the size of the quarter panel, scribe a line along the factory quarter panel, using the upper edge of the quarter-panel patch as a guide. Place a piece of tape to run the entire length of that line. When the sparks start flying from the cutoff wheel, it's hard to see the scratched or marked line. The tape gives an easy-to-see reference point for cutting off the bottom of the quarter panel.

Use Rotary Tool to Cut Off Quarter Panel Skin

7 Take your time and use both hands to get a straight, clean cut along the axis of the quarter panel. Be sure you use the proper safety equipment when performing this procedure. Use a grinding wheel to cut the section of the quarter panel to be replaced by the patch panel. A 3M general purpose 3-inch cutoff wheel, or similar wheel, allows you to precisely cut through the sheet-metal skin. Be sure that your compressor can sustain 90 psi for the duration of the cut. Also be sure to use proper hand and eye protection, as metal cuts can be very serious.

BODYWORK

Remove Rusted Lower Quarter Panel

8 Use a rotary cutoff wheel to remove the rusted lower quarter panel. It takes some skill to do this procedure properly. Practicing on scrap metal is a good idea, or you can have someone with experience show you how. With a clean and straight cut, the rest of the panel can now be removed by drilling out the rest of the tack welds. Use a MIG welder to butt weld the bottom replacement panel to the top quarter panel. The panel is welded to the wheel-well lip and around to the bumper section.

Patch Panel Installation

Cut Around Quarter Panel Lip

1 Carefully use the cutoff wheel to cut around the quarter panel lip. Once that is done, you can pull down the quarter panel. Over the years, a lot of moisture and debris has collected inside this quarter panel. On the bottom of the quarter panel, drill through the tack welds and remove the quarter panel, along with all of the debris collected in the sump formed by the trunk extension.

Fit Trunk Pan

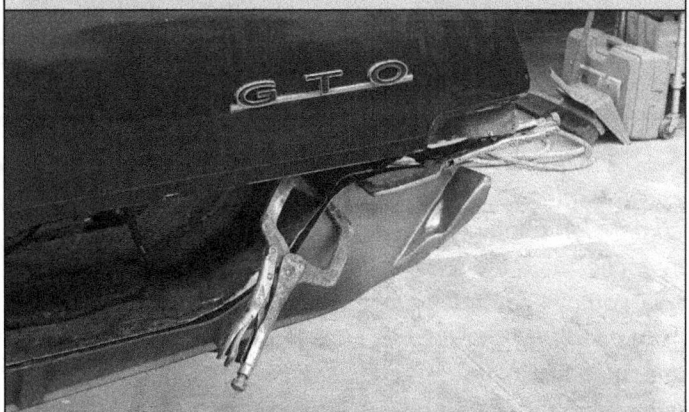

2 With the quarter panel removed, you have access to the trunk and can test-fit the trunk pan extension. This piece ended up needing a fair amount of work in the rear to line up correctly.

Punch Holes in Patch Panel

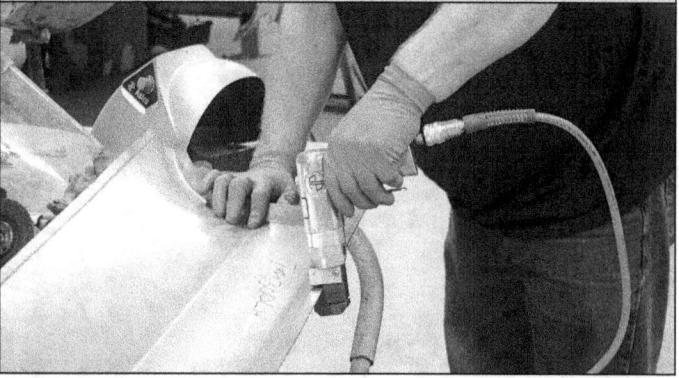

3 An air punch is a commonly used body shop tool and makes 1/2-inch holes every 4 or 5 inches along the outer perimeter of the patch panel. If you cannot afford to rent this tool, hand drill these to make the panel fit, so it can be securely fastened to the remaining quarter panel.

HOW TO RESTORE YOUR PONTIAC GTO 1964–1974

CHAPTER 3

Use Grinding Pad to Remove Material

4 Use a 3M (or similar) grinding pad to remove paint, old body filler, and rust. While this takes some time and patience, it's relatively easy work, so apply even pressure and move the disc around the panel. Avoid generating too much heat in any one area because this could warp the panel. Once the panel is down to the bare metal, this helps ensure the weld will successfully join the two pieces of metal.

Fit Patch Panel

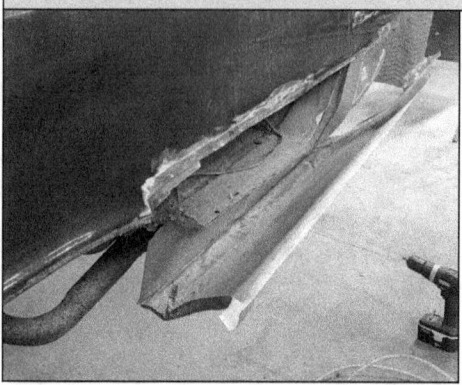

5 Clamp the panel to the car and align it in its proper position. Install the sheet-metal screws through the bottom of the quarter panel and into the quarter-panel extension. Once secured to the quarter-panel extension, the patch can hang there until the next step is completed. Install the 14 screws on the top portion, including two behind the rear bumper area, as well as five on the lower section that meets the trunk extension.

Fabricate Flange on Patch Panel

6 Use an air-powered flange-making tool to fabricate a flange that provides a better mating surface because an overlap joint is created rather than a butt joint. The tool slightly stretches the metal so there is a slight joint overlap for added strength. At-home restorers may be able to rent a flange tool if buying it does not make sense. If you cannot access this tool, a hammer, dolly, and anvil can be used to create the same flange, but it takes more time and some skill to develop the flange by hand.

A MIG welder can create a lot of heat during the butt-weld process, and as a result, can warp the body panels, which is a very bad thing. Therefore, make sure the welder is set on a low-voltage setting for welding thin sheet metal and give each spot weld a chance to cool before placing another spot weld.

Fit Patch Panel

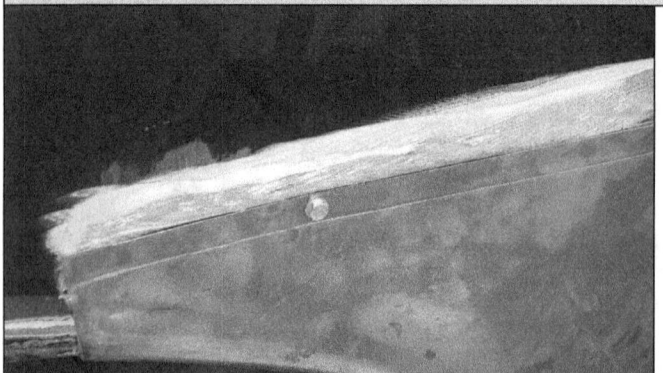

7 Place the lip of the quarter-panel patch over the flange on the top panel. Drive sheet-metal screws through the patch panel into the factory quarter. After the patch panel has been anchored to the top panel, check it for fit. If you look closely, you can see this patch panel has a stamped flange. It was not used for two reasons. First, it is too shallow to be useful. Second, and more important, it could potentially allow moisture to collect around the welds, as the bottom edge of the factory quarter goes over the patch panel, leaving the back side exposed for water to accumulate. Position the patch, tack the panel in place, and completely cover the edge with a bead of weld. The stamped-in flange is shallow enough to be completely covered with a light coating of filler. Then unscrew the quarter-panel patch and set aside.

BODYWORK

Shape Patch Panel

8 Use a hammer and dolly to shape the contour of the patch panel so it follows the contour of the factory quarter. If you haven't spent much time working metal, firmly hold the dolly behind the metal and patiently work the metal into the desired shape. Smaller, focused blows are needed to shape the metal, rather than large, heavy blows. Remember, metal working is an acquired skill and you may need to spend some time developing these skills before attempting to shape a patch panel. You can hone these skills by working scrap metal on a bench, taking a course in metal working, and/or refer to Matt Joseph's books *Automotive Body Work and Rust Repair* and *Automotive Sheet Metal Forming and Fabrication*.

Inspect Passenger Quarter Panel

9 The factory passenger's side does not match the patch on the driver's side, so you must correct the difference and get both sides into similar configuration.

Adjust Driver-Side Quarter Panel

10 Make a vertical cut about 2 inches long on the top edge of the trunk floor extension, then fold the trailing edge forward and fabricate a small patch to fill the void between the extension and the rear end body panel.

Align and Clamp Inner Wheelhouse

11 Align the inner wheelhouse to the rear trunk extension panel and clamp once the desired position is determined. In order to align the inner wheelhouse to the rear trunk extension, cut the leading edge of the wheelhouse and bend it upward to meet the trunk extension. Once bent and raised into position, clamp it.

Fit Patch Panel to Trunk

12 Cut a small patch from sheet metal and then clamp it to the trunk patch with body-work pliers. Tackweld the extension into place. It was made to join the trunk floor extension to the rear end body panel.

CHAPTER 3

Measure and Fit Outer Wheelhouse

13 *If the outer wheelhouse is rusted through and cracked, you want to keep as much of the original sheet metal as possible. Measure the section that needs to be replaced. Apply those measurements to the reproduction wheelhouse, and then use a cutoff wheel to cut it off. Allow for no less than 1/2 inch of overlap.*

Install Wheelhouse Patch

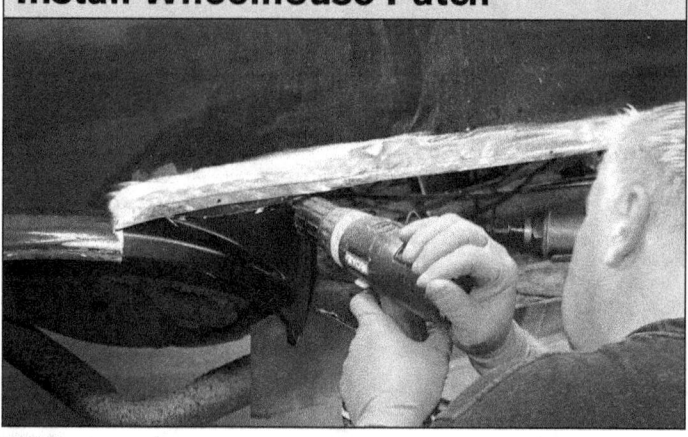

14 *Once measured, use metal shears to cut a precise edge. Then place the wheelhouse patch into position and verify the fit. When in the proper position, drill a hole in the top right-hand corner and then screw the patch into the trunk patch or the inner wheelhouse.*

Anchor Outer Wheelhouse to Trunk Patch Panel

15 *Drive a sheet-metal screw through the outer wheelhouse and into the trunk patch panel, so it is held into position for welding.*

Weld Quarter-Panel Body Parts Together

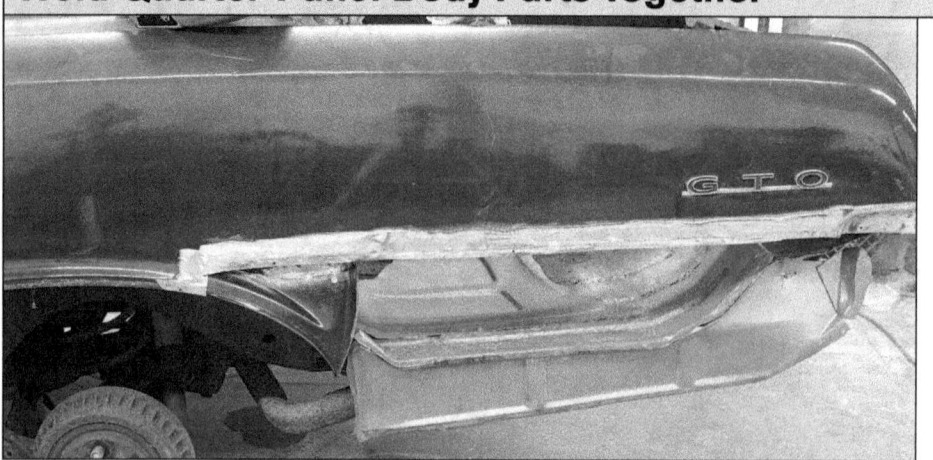

16 *All the adjoining parts are now fitted up, screwed together, and ready for welding. Here you can see the outer wheelhouse trunk patch and the inner quarter panel. All of these components have now been properly fitted so the quarter panel skin can be reinstalled for welding.*

Test Fit Quarter Panel Patch

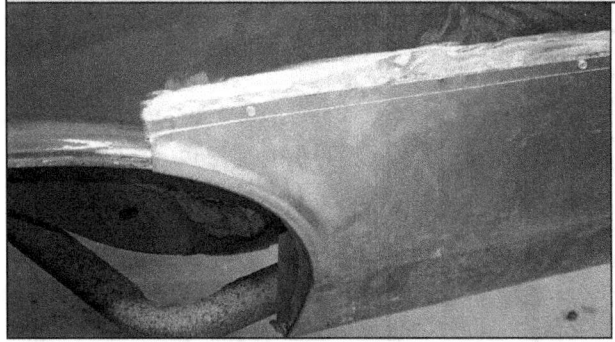

17 Use three sheet-metal screws to re-fasten the lower quarter panel to the top quarter panel and over the wheelhouse patch and trunk extension under it for another test fitting. Make sure the panels properly align, so all the pieces of the jigsaw puzzle now fit into place. Now that the test fit has been successful, remove the quarter-panel skin again, so the outer wheelhouse and other parts can be welded. Depending on the model year of your GTO, you could temporarily reinstall some of the trim pieces to further verify the alignment of the panels prior to welding.

Weld Quarter Panel Pieces

18 Use a MIG welder to place a bead of weld on the outer-fender housing and the adjoining inner-fender housing. When stitch welding the outer-fender housing, manage the application of heat when placing the bead weld on the seams. The selection of the welder settings is paramount. You want enough amperage and heat to have the weld properly take hold but not blow holes in the metal. Conversely, you don't want it too cold to have the welds fall off. Show me three 1967 GTOs and I'll show you three different settings for both plug welds and stitch welds. Using the rusted quarter-panel section that was removed as a test for the proper amperage settings is the best way to determine what the best settings are for a particular car.

Weld Wheelhouse to Trunk Extension

19 Weld the trunk extension to the inner wheelhouse. Apply a bead of weld along the seam, a few inches at a time, and allow it cool, then switch to the opposite side of the seam to spread out the heat. Welding thin sheet metal is a delicate art so the proper welder settings are important. Be careful not to burn through or warp the panels. Then weld the cut to solidify the new contour of the trunk extension.

20 Weld the small patch joining the trunk extension to the rear-end body. Place a full bead on the patch and the inner quarter panel to secure it in position.

Weld Trunk Extension to Trunk Floor

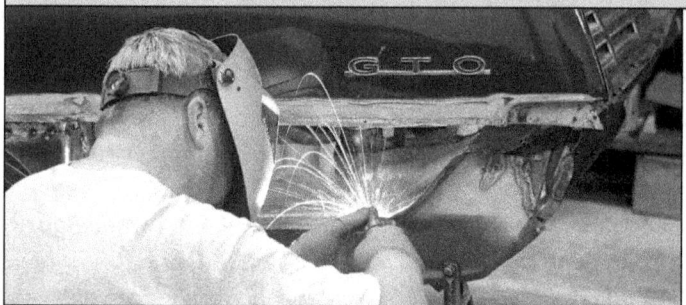

21 Stitch weld the top edge of the trunk extension to the trunk floor. The panel provides the necessary support to the trunk floor.

22 Weld the trunk floor to the inner quarter-panel support, providing additional strength and improved structural integrity. Your newly welded panels should be straight because they didn't warp or bend from the over-application of heat. Stitch welding is very forgiving in this area and practicing on scrap metal beforehand gives some insight into the proper settings for each phase of the operation.

Place Stitch Welds on Inner Quarter Panel

23 These stitch welds are at the back of the inner quarter panel. Be careful not to apply too much heat and warp the panels.

Grind Down Welds on Seam

24 A rotary air grinding tool grinds down the welds to develop the smoothest surface possible. You want to shape the body panel and leave behind the smoothest and most correct profile possible. This is done in preparation for applying all-metal body filler. Grind the welds, not the surrounding metal.

Apply Body Filler to Inner Quarter Panel

25 Body filler should not come in contact with your skin so put on a pair of nitrile gloves. When preparing body filler for application, be sure that the filler and hardener are thoroughly and properly mixed. If the filler doesn't have enough hardener, it does not dry properly. If it does not dry correctly, many problems may result. The filler doesn't have a strong bond with the metal, and therefore the primer and paint don't adhere to filler properly. The filler could absorb moisture and rust later on.

Many filler products need to be mixed, while other products are premixed. Once mixed, use the filler to cover the welds as well as to smooth and seal the area. There are number of products that are suitable for this type of body work. You can use all-metal filler, which contains aluminum, and as a result is stronger than regular body filler. All-metal filler is ideal for metal leveling and it can be used on aluminum as well as sheet metal. When applying body filler, apply the thinnest coat to cover the area. With most body work, the body filler should not be thicker than 1/8 inch.

BODYWORK

Prepare Quarter Panel Patch for Installation

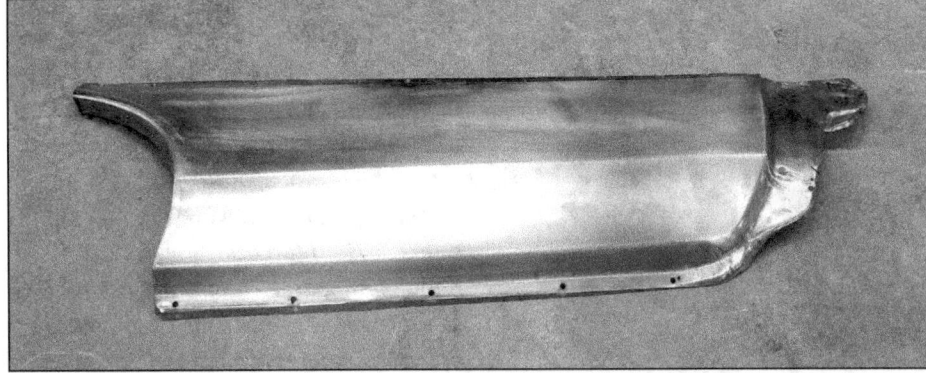

26 Use a wire brush to clean the quarter-panel patch. A vertical dent was discovered on this particular panel. It appears to have been made during the stamping process. If you look at the right side of the patch below the seam, you can see the dent. To true-up the panel, a hammer, dolly, and some blunt force trauma were used to bring it back into shape.

Shape Quarter Panel Patch

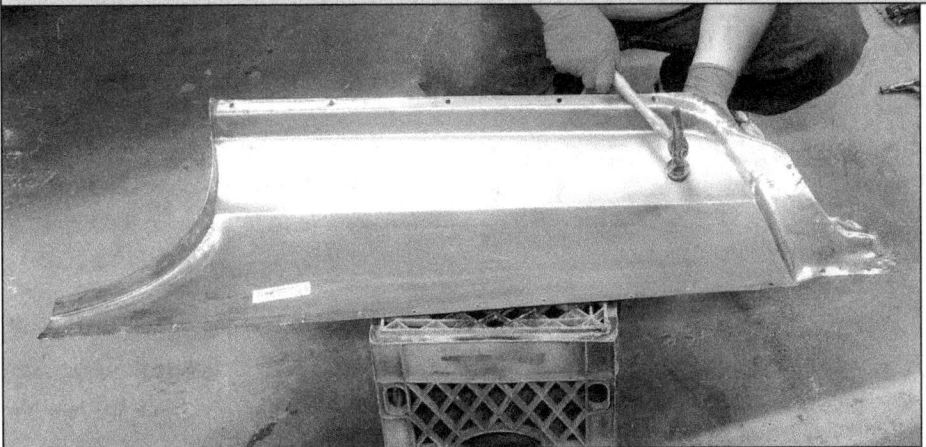

27 Remember, metal working is an art. To get the quarter-panel patch back into shape, use a medium metal-finishing hammer and a medium dolly loaf on the backside. The loaf needs to follow the profile of the quarter-panel patch and the hammer has a convex face for working the metal. Use small, firm taps rather than heavy blows to slowly bring the area back into shape. Rushing it can do more damage. This kind of straightforward and easy repair job can be performed on a milk crate placed on the floor. But it is easier and more comfortable to manipulate the hammer and dolly on top of a bench.

Align Quarter Panel Patch

28 The quarter-panel patch has been test fitted to the car several times, so it should align with the welded inner quarter panel, trunk patch, and wheelhouse patch. Properly align the panel as you did before, and then drive sheet-metal screws through it to hold it in place. Here, four screws fasten it at the trailing edge of the panel.

HOW TO RESTORE YOUR PONTIAC GTO 1964–1974

Shape Quarter Panel Patch

29 Even though quite a bit of panel fitting has been performed, the quarter patch may not line up perfectly. Use the pick end of a finish hammer to move the metal around, so the patch-panel edge lines up with the factory quarter. Hold the dolly in your right hand from inside the trunk and lightly tap the sheet metal until both seams come into alignment. Once again, be patient and take the time to do it right. One small move at a time shapes the metal and eventually you achieves the finished shape.

Tack Weld Quarter Panel Patch

30 Weld the patch panel to the vehicle in two major steps: tack weld and then stitch weld. First, place tack welds all along the seam of the quarter-panel patch to firmly anchor it in position. Place a tack weld every 3 inches and quench the weld with air to cool the area and prevent warping. MIG welders can apply too much heat and warp the panels if you're not careful. Grind off the heads of the tack welds; they don't need to be flush.

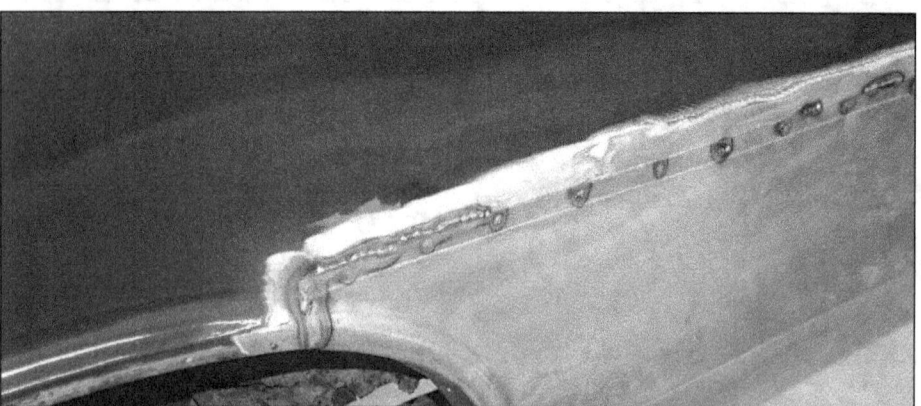 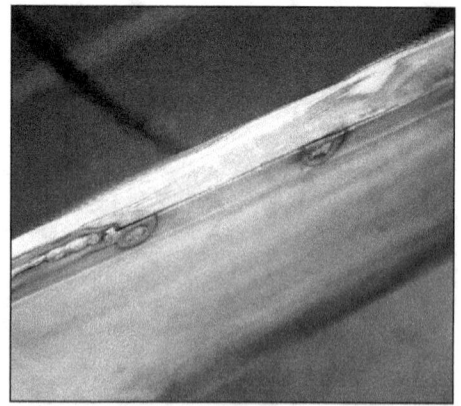

31 Once the tack welds have firmly anchored the patch panel into position, enlarge them so they are nearly together. This once again manages the heat application during welding and helps prevent warpage. Once the second round of tack welds is placed, go ahead and connect all the welds with a stitch weld to fully close the gap between the two pieces of metal.

32 The stitch welds connect the tack welds and a full bead is starting to form. Together, they locate, secure, and seal the panels, becoming one piece.

BODYWORK

Patch Inner and Outer Wheelhouses

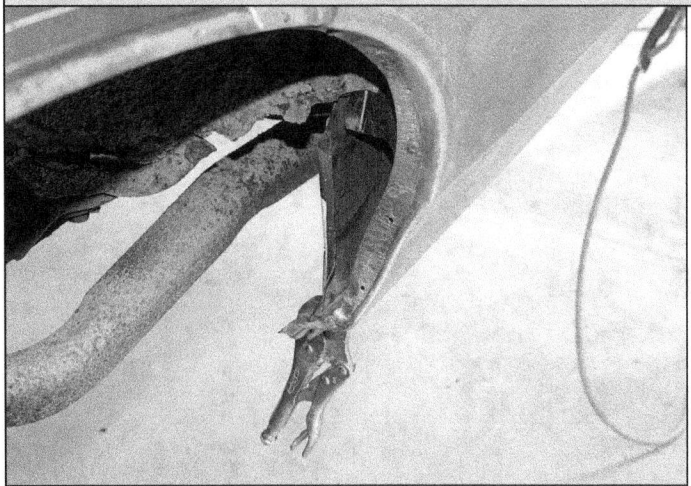

33 A majority of the work has been completed the quarter-panel patch, but a patch panel is also needed for the rusted areas of the inner and outer wheelhouses.

Cut Patch Piece for Inner Wheelhouse

34 This is probably the most complex and difficult step of the quarter panel patch job. After you cut the desired piece out of 16-gauge sheet metal, it needs to be formed to the profile of the wheelhouse. Use an English wheel to stretch and form the sheet metal piece to the profile of the outer wheelhouse. (For more details on this process, refer to Automotive Sheet Metal Forming and Fabrication by Matt Joseph). Once the piece has been test fitted and the fit verified, the rusted sections need to be cut out using a cutoff wheel. The new metal can then be clamped into place.

Tack Weld Wheelhouse

35 The wheelhouse patch needs to be welded into position. To do that, drill three 1/16-inch holes through the patch panel into the trunk extension and lower inner quarter panel. Place three plug welds to connect the outer wheel patch to the trunk extension. During the plug weld process place the welds in the panel and quickly quench with air to prevent warping.

36 This close-up shows the tack welds that join the wheelhouse patch to both the trunk extension and the quarter-panel patch.

HOW TO RESTORE YOUR PONTIAC GTO 1964–1974

Tack Weld Lower Quarter Panel

37 At this point, the entire rear quarter-panel section is coming together. These integrated parts provide body integrity and clean lines. Once the work is completed, it will look as it did when it came from the factory. Drill holes through the lower quarter-panel patch and into the trunk extension. Then place plug welds through the quarter-panel patch every 3 inches.

Grind Down Tack Welds

38 Use the rotary air tool with a 60-grit sanding pad to grind down the tack welds, preparing it for final finishing. Then grid the welds smooth for the entire quarter-patch panel. Be careful not to spend too much time grinding in one area and move the grinding tool down the seams. This way excessive heat is not produced and the panels do not warp.

Smooth Panel Seams

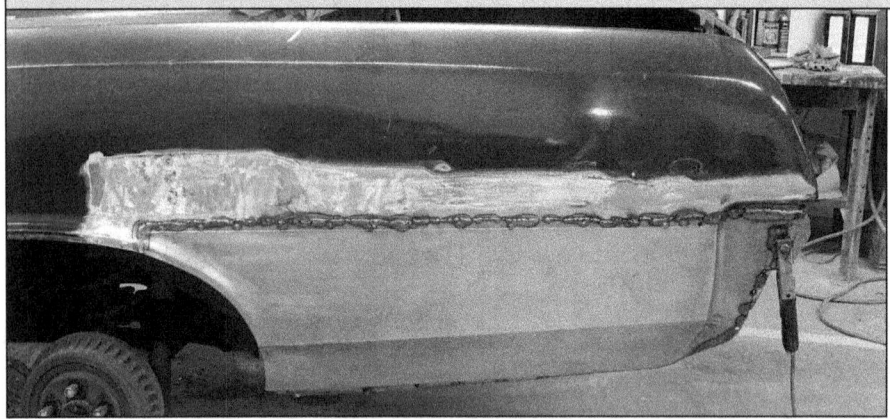

39 At this stage, welds have been ground flush to the quarter panel. This is the final metal-working stage before you apply thin coats of body filler. You want the surface to be as smooth as possible. If the welding and grinding has been correctly completed, you just need a thin coat of body filler. Often, novice body workers haven't properly installed the panel, completed good welds, or smoothed out the welds. In turn, an excessive amount of body filler is used to correct these mistakes. Eventually the whole job comes undone because a thick coat of body filler often shrinks, cracks, and then rust forms. You need to ensure that all steps have been correctly completed because the outer appearance of your car (i.e., the paint) is only as good as the body work underneath it.

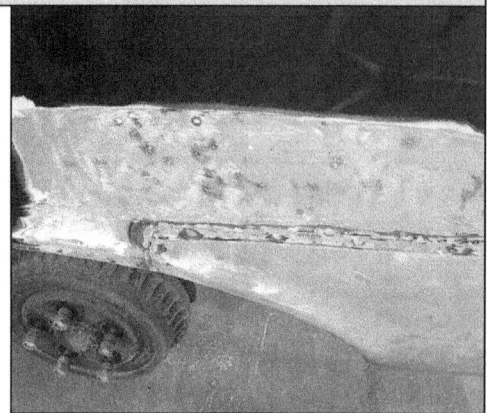

40 The quarter-panel patch has been fully prepared for body filler. The seam has been tack and stitch welded and then the seam has been smoothed over. Notice how well the upper quarter panel and the patch align with each other. With a patch like this, only a small amount of body filler needs to be applied, and therefore you need not be concerned with shrinking or cracking of the body filler.

BODYWORK

Apply Body Filler Base Coat

41 *A variety of body fillers are suitable for this type of work. Just be sure the filler and hardener are properly mixed before application. Use the straightedge applicator to apply two thin coats of filler. Here, Real Metal body filler is applied for the base coat. Try to apply as thin a coat as possible. Your body filler should be no more 1/8-inch thick or you may run into shrinking and cracking problems. Applying it too thick ends up with a lot more sanding later.*

Apply Body Filler Final Coat

42 *Use a lighter, smoother filler for the top coat. You can clearly see the ridges of the filler, but blocking removes these ridges and produces a smooth profiled final finish. Block sand the base coat with 120-grit sand paper. As a rule, the coarser-grit sandpaper shapes the body filler, while the finer-grit sandpaper smooths the body filler. Often, using a dual-action (DA) sander is an alternative to sanding blocks and other tools. The DA can be used in a rotary or orbital motion.*

Block Sand Body Filler

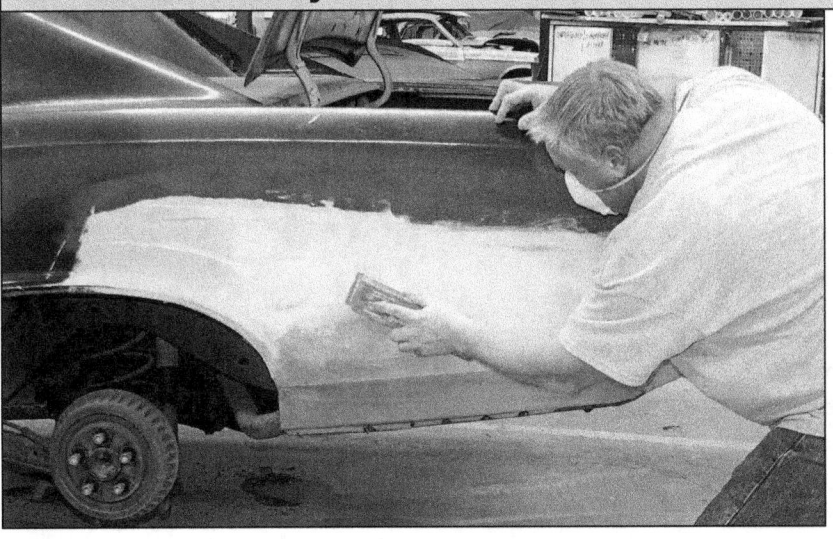

43 *Block sanding thins the filler to provide a smooth, uniform surface and a suitable foundation for primer and, ultimately, the final top coat. While every stage of the repair is important, this stage is critical and many body techs spend a lot of time smoothing and shaping the surface. Primer can fill small imperfections in the filler, but the filler surfaces need to be as smooth as possible. For the top coat, use 240-grit sandpaper for a smooth flat surface area and then use 320-grit paper to eliminate any small surface imperfections. It is easier to shape and smooth the body filler before it's completely dry.*

Cross Sand Body Filler

44 Cross sand the body filler until it feathers into the bare sheet metal and looks like one smoothly flowing surface. Use a 14-inch sanding block with 120-grit, then switch to 240-grit, and finally 320-grit to provide a fine surface finish.

Spread Top Coat of Body Filler

45 Mix body filler and spread it across the upper quarter and lower quarter patch panels. Apply the top coat as thin as possible, and apply a spot coat. Use the same 14-inch sanding block. Start with 120-grit, switch to 240-grit, and end with 320-grit for a smooth surface finish.

Apply Body Filler to Trunk

46 Also apply a coat of protective spot coat to the trunk. In addition to protecting the back side of the weld, the spot coat goes a long way toward hiding the repair. Sanding should also be done on the back side but it but does not need to be as perfect as on the outside.

Apply Body Filler to Bumper Area

47 Apply the filler with a straightedge in a smooth and linear fashion, a clean sweeping motion that covers the entire area to be filled in one carefully-placed application.

Mix Primer

48 The primer used as a guide coat is regular old spray-bomb sandable primer. Why is it okay to use such a cheap primer out of a can? Because it is used not as a base for any paint but rather as a way to visually inspect the panel for high and low spots and other imperfections. It also dries very quickly, so sanding can begin without much waiting time. Completely sand off this primer, re-apply, and sand off again multiple times in the block sanding process. In a home restoration project, it doesn't make a lot of sense to invest in high-end primer at this stage of the process. When the block sanding is completed and the panel is free of imperfections, consult your body shop manager to select a primer that works with your chosen paint system. Follow the manufacturer's instructions for mixing the primer. Use the proper measuring cups to achieve the optimal ratio. This is something you cannot guess at. After measuring the correct primer and element, thoroughly mix it so it's properly blended.

Apply Primer Guide Coat

49 Spray a primer guide coat so the high and low spots of the paint can be identified. If major flaws or imperfections are revealed, you may have to use spot body filler to fill in the low areas and then sand it out and prime it again. Spot putty is essentially the same as most primers but has a thicker paste-like consistency. Use it to fill chips, low spots, sanding scratches, and other imperfections in the primer. Apply it in much the same way as filler, using a small flexible squeegee; the coat is much thinner. Block sand to match the contour of the surrounding primer surface and then cover again with primer.

Rust Preventers

Before you replace the quarter panel (and anytime that you run into areas hidden by outer sheet metal or interior pieces), it is a great opportunity to prep the metal with a rust preventer that seals the metal from the elements.

There are three brands that are quite similar in formulation and in application, POR-15, KBS Coatings, and Hirsch's Miracle Paint. While all can be thinned enough to run through a paint gun, this is one time that brushing is acceptable, as these products dry smooth without brush marks. Once dried, they offer an incredibly tough coating that gets stronger if exposed to moisture. Some are sensitive to UV light and may need a top coat if exposed to light. Check with the manufacturer for specifics.

Dent Removal

With many books on bodywork and dent removal, I am not going into too much detail here. I recommend picking up a copy of CarTech's *How to Paint Your Car on a Budget*, by Pat Ganahl, as it covers that topic in much more depth than space allows here.

That being said, simple dent removal requires appropriate tools. There are almost as many types of body hammers as there are dents to repair. Eastwood has a full line of body hammers that make it easy to remove dents in areas where you can get behind them and pull or tap them out.

In the past when you couldn't get behind the dent, holes were drilled in the panel and a slide hammer was inserted to pull the dent out. The idea was that it was easier to repair a couple of small holes than it was to take apart a car far enough to expose the back side of a dent.

That mindset still holds true today, but there is a really great little tool that makes the job easier and it is a lot easier to fix the damage. The tool is a portable stud welder, marketed by Eastwood, H&S Auto Shot, Harbor Freight, and others. With a stud inserted and the trigger pulled, it instantly spot welds a stud onto a dented panel, provided the paint and any surface contaminants are removed. From there, a slide hammer is connected to the stud and the dent can be pulled out in the normal fashion. Once the operation is completed, the stud can be ground off the panel with little or no warpage.

Filler

In the old days, lead was the preferred material for body filler. Experienced body men found it was easy to work with. It flowed nicely and was fairly hard when cooled. It took primer and paint like the rest of the body and when done correctly, lasted for the life of the car. Unfortunately, lead is poisonous, heavy, expensive, and did I mention poisonous?

Today, plastic fillers offer the same positive qualities of lead without the weight, high cost, and health risks. They can give varying amounts of shaping and hardening times and are clearly the preferred choice.

When using fillers to level off dent repairs or grinding marks in sheet metal, the rule is, less is more. If you need more than 3/16 inch of filler, it would be wise to go back and keep working on the dent or repair in order to bring it closer to level. This way, the filler is less prone to crack, craze, or separate from the parent metal (see Chapter 4 for more details on body filler).

Body Tags

This subject really makes me uncomfortable because there are legal ramifications involved with the removal of tags from a body. While it is legal to take off a data tag to prepare the area under it for paint or to repair rust, it is not legal to take a VIN tag off a car. It is actually a federal crime to do so.

If the area around your data tag is not rusted or damaged, it would be a wise move to leave it where it is and very carefully soda blast the area. If it needs to come off, photograph it first. With a pliers, carefully pinch the rivets to decrease their diameter, allowing them to be pushed through the hole so you can remove the data tag. Once the tag is off, put it somewhere safe, like a safe deposit box. The last thing you want is for it to get lost, as your car's heritage will be in question for eternity if it is.

When it is time to reinstall it, use the correct rivets and a rivet gun from TrimTags.com and apply some adhesive seam sealer in the center of the rivets to replicate the factory preparation.

Collision Damage

If your GTO has a significant amount of collision damage, enough to require a frame straightener or hydraulic rams to bring it back into shape, take it to a collision shop for repair. These shops have the frame-straightening jigs and a variety of tools to professionally repair collision damage, and this is industrial equipment the at-home restorer cannot afford. Of course, there are people who have successfully pulled out crumpled tail panels and quarters at home, but in my opinion, these are repairs that are completely out of the scope of a home restoration. Doing it wrong will at best worsen the damage and at worst make the vehicle unsafe.

If your GTO has been rear-ended, T-boned, or has taken a front-end hit hard enough to bend the frame rails, you owe it to yourself and anyone who rides in your car to make sure it has been accurately straightened. With the latest generation of laser-guided frame-straightening equipment, there is no excuse for a car that crab-walks down the highway or one that the body panels cannot be properly aligned because the frame is not square and true. The money you spend to have it done right by trained professionals is money well spent.

CHAPTER 4

PAINTING

When considering options for painting, you may end up with even more questions. If you had been undecided about the level of your restoration, perhaps waffling between an upper-end, driver-quality car and a true concours-level effort, choosing the paint and exterior finishing will likely help sort that out. As with just about everything else, it depends on your plans for the car and how much you can budget for that portion of the restoration.

There is a huge difference between a driver-level paint job and a points-judged effort. That is not to say that the paint for a driver is necessarily inferior from a materials or durability standpoint, but there is a much higher level of preparation when going for gold awards. This ultimately drives up the cost to where the final finishing ends up being the largest part of the restoration budget—even more than the drivetrain rebuild, or the suspension preparations, or the interior refurbishing.

It's been said before, but it needs to be said again, painting a car is an art and a science. It takes the right materials, correct techniques, and some experience to achieve professional results. It also requires a commercial paint booth and an assortment of professional equipment. A commercial paint booth can cost $10,000 or more and is the size of a typical garage stall or larger. So this isn't equipment an at-home restorer is typically going to buy. In addition, in some states, it's illegal to paint a car at home. For most paint types (enamel, lacquer, polyurethane), the materials are hazardous and expensive. A gallon of urethane paint (the most commonly used today) often retails for $130 to $200, so this is a significant

The end product of expert body work, paint, and trim preparation can be seen in a concours-level restoration like that of the Car and Driver test car. This 1964 Royal Bobcat GTO was the actual car tested in the infamous "GTO vs. GTO" article that appeared in the March 1964 issue. Now owned by Tenney Fairchild, Scott Tiemann and his staff at Supercar Specialties restored this historic machine. It has won gold awards at both Pontiac-Oakland Club International (POCI) and GTO Association of America (GTOAA) national conventions. (Photo Courtesy Scott Tiemann)

CHAPTER 4

investment. Keep in mind you need to invest in primer, base coat, and clear for most multi-stage paint systems. In addition, a large amount of preparation work is required for a quality outcome, but it also takes the mastery of several different operations, all of which are essential to a high-quality result. A quality outcome also revolves around where this operation is going to be performed. Will it be a high-tech paint booth with state-of-the-art temperature and humidity control, filters for dust and overspray or a damp, dusty, cement-floor garage?

As mentioned, the main difference is in the preparation. The concours-level paint, the type that earns the gold awards will have the benefit of perfectly straight, wave-free bodywork under multiple, expertly laid coats of primer, block-sanded to perfection. On top of that are several coats of color, each laboriously hand-sanded, and then the clear coats, again each hand-sanded. The top coat is sanded, buffed, and waxed to a point that the finish looks as if it is 6 feet deep. This level of preparation is what it takes to get the top honors.

On the flip side, having a finish this perfect will most likely render the car a trailer queen or it is likely that the owner is a nervous wreck every time the car goes out into traffic. The type of car that you see at a cruise night, does not have particular use for a finish like this, and it is not necessarily desirable to have paint this perfect. The cost differential is also enough to keep most restorers from putting that much money into a street-driven vehicle. If you cannot relax enough with your car to drive it around, it's not really a driver anymore and the fun factor goes out the window—if being able to drive it is your primary objective.

A driver-quality paint job is something closer to what you have with a new car. From 10 feet away, it is virtually indistinguishable from a full-tilt show car and looks fantastic on the road or at a cruise night. It has plenty of shine and is very durable. The Woodward Dream Cruise is full of cars that fit this category. The truth is, a good, driver-quality paint job is 90 percent or more of what a show-car finish is and will likely be enough to get you first-place trophies in local shows but will not quite be enough to impress concours judges.

In order to save time and money, you can cut some corners with a driver-quality paint job. Not every coat of primer is going to be hand-sanded to perfection. Additionally,

The advantages of a professional spray booth cannot be overstressed because if it is correctly prepared and operated it provides the optimal environment for painting. A booth offers temperature and humidity control, keeps contaminants away from the surface to be painted, and controls overspray. While you can build a temporary paint booth to paint your car at home, the process takes a lot of time, preparation, and work. Even a temporary paint booth doesn't control contaminants as well as a professional one. If dust is present, it will show up in the paint and produce flaws that must be fixed. The dust factor alone should be enough to send your car to a professional body shop.

Body work and painting are often the most expensive portion of a restoration project. To paint a GTO or any classic car the right way is expensive, but the top-quality results are worth the investment. So you should strongly consider having a shop paint your car. Along with the superior painting area, a successful body shop employs highly-skilled technicians able to give your car the best possible outcome. You may pay more up front, but the savings in time and quality is significant. Plus, if you end up with less-than-acceptable results, how much of a savings is that? (Photo Courtesy Scott Tiemann)

you may be able to get acceptable results with a single-color stage, rather than multiple coats. If the color is non-metallic, you may even be able to skip the clear coat altogether, if the paint is formulated for that. There are a lot of options here, and your body shop should have very attractive alternatives if you're on a tight budget. Every car and budget are different, and some consulting on that topic with your shop manager will help you find the right paint and prep level for your situation.

Selecting Paint

There are many very good-quality paint systems. I use the term "paint system" because manufacturers of modern paints produce and market their paint lines to coincide with every step of the painting process, including primers, color coats, top coats, even thinners, flex agents, and catalysts. It actually makes sense to work with one line of paint products from one brand. The reason is that they are engineered to work together and provide the best overall performance, in terms of application, durability, and appearance. You might be able to get by with a primer from one, color coat from another, and clear from a third, but why? There is risk to that approach with no real benefit.

Before you get to the primer stage, consult with your body shop to choose a paint system that is right for you and your GTO. Most body shops have a brand that they work with. This brand often has certain qualities that are the best fit for their facility and their technicians. Maybe it is nothing more than there is a good sales rep for that brand in the area. The truth is, all manufacturers make high-quality paint systems, and most of them market low-cost "used car lot" lines as well. Researching the options Online and consulting with your body shop manager will help you narrow your choices.

Right now, the current trend is to work with catalyzed base-coat/clear-coat systems. They offer a great combination of ease of application, coverage, shine, and durability with minimal maintenance. Though they are enamels, they can be color sanded, as the catalyst hardens the entire thickness of the paint, not just the surface as with conventional enamels of the past.

Additionally, this new generation of paint systems is far superior to the original "magic mirror" lacquer finishes applied to GTOs from the factory. Manufacturers such as DuPont, PPG, Sikkens, Sherwin-Williams, House of Kolor, and countless others market these systems with excellent results. Again, consult with your body shop for the best selection of the paint for your application and price range.

DIY or Professional?

I am going to be upfront with you on this subject. Unless you have access to a shop with a modern paint booth, compressor, spray guns, proper respirators, and full-body overalls, and you have a good deal of experience with this equipment, you should have a professional do the work. It is as simple as that. There are many factors to take into account, including your experience level (or lack thereof), the type of facility you will be using, local zoning regulations, and most important, safety.

Personally, I wouldn't even consider painting a car myself. I realize that it's far out of my skill set and I don't have the time or inclination to learn the proper procedures. While I can handle a spray bomb, that doesn't qualify me for the job. I know enough about painting, and myself, to hand that part of the restoration over to someone more skilled and experienced.

There is also another factor to consider. Here in New York State, where I live, the huge level of zoning regulation has really precluded the home builder from painting their own vehicles. This trend is spreading across the country. Safety is the main reason for this sort of regulation, though it is certainly not the only reason. How many times has neighboring property been damaged because of unskilled painters allowing overspray to travel even blocks away? How many times has someone become sick from fumes? The answer is enough times for people to demand regulation.

Safety

The truth is: Painting a car is one of the many areas where an unskilled or underskilled painter can cause real health hazards, both for you, as well as your family and neighbors. The hydrocarbons, solvents, solids, and other chemicals contained in paint can cause damage not only to your lungs but to all organs and long-term exposure is not always necessary. The Occupational Safety and Health Administration (OSHA) recommends the following procedures to limit exposure:

- Wear a full-face respirator. Supplied air (outside air) respirators are preferred.
- Wear full-body overalls.
- Use a downdraft-type paint booth.

I am not trying to make it look like some sort of nightmare scenario will inevitably happen if you try painting yourself, but it's likely that unanticipated problems will arise once you get started—and by that time, it is often too late. Also, time is money, and nowhere will it be more evident than if you try to paint your car at home, mess it up, and then take it to a professional shop to fix it. The fix often involves a strip down to the bare metal, negating all of the time and money you spent on your do-it-yourself attempt.

In this scenario, the cost is significantly higher than having just sent them the car in the first place. If you aren't experienced and 100 percent sure you can do this, save yourself the mental trauma and a good deal of cash and let a pro do it.

Choosing a Body Shop

When it comes time to select the proper people to paint your car, cost is not the most important factor but it is fairly high on the list—after all, you are footing the bill. You obviously want the best work available for the amount of money you have budgeted. In addition to cost, you should look for quality of work, positive word of mouth, and repeat customers.

You can start by logging onto the many Pontiac and GTO message boards, such as the Performance Years Tech Forums, the POCI Message Board, and other such meeting areas for Pontiac GTO fans. Starting a topic thread such as, "Looking for a reliable body shop in Toledo," or wherever you live, will no doubt get a variety of opinions. You may have to sift through some obviously unqualified opinions, but it will help point you in the right direction and give you a few leads you didn't have before.

This is an area where belonging to a club, such as POCI, Antique Automobile Club of America (AACA), or GTOAA, benefits you. By joining a national club and its local chapter, you put yourself in front of fellow GTO fans in your area whose prior experience greatly aids you in the proper selection of a body shop to paint your car. This is a benefit that will pay huge benefits, much more than the cost of the membership fees. You can learn who the members have used in the past, who they have avoided, and who have earned their repeat business. Best of all, you can actually look at your fellow members' cars and see who got the best result for their money.

What Can You Do Yourself?

With all of those cautions, it doesn't mean there is nothing for you to do in the area of paint preparation. If you're planning to restore only one car, investing in paint guns, blocks, sanding materials, and other equipment is probably not worth it. Let's face it prepping, painting, and blocking a car is an art. While savvy and skilled novices can perform a commendable job, your first paint job will not be as good as the work of a qualified professional.

On the other hand, if this project is the first in many restoration projects, it makes sense to invest in the equipment and develop the skill to paint a car. A temporary paint booth can be created in your garage and you can obtain good results, but it takes time, dedication, and patience. If you choose to have someone spray your car, you can perform a lot of the prep work yourself.

Best of all, because the prep work is typically the most expensive portion of the labor costs involved with a paint job, you can actually do the majority of it yourself and if done correctly, you can save a bundle of money. Ideally, if you are able to do the majority of surface prepping, you should be able to afford a higher-quality paint job than if you sent the car without any prepping. This is also more in the spirit of the do-it-yourself mindset of most hobbyists.

Fillers

Once the bodywork is near completion, the focus shifts from welding and panel replacement to making the surface as perfect as possible. This is long and tedious work, but it pays dividends, both in the quality of the finished product and the reduced labor costs to you.

Contrary to popular belief, at least in my neck of the woods, quality body repairs are not made solely out of body filler. Quarter panels are not to be replicated out of Bondo. As a result, body fillers have a somewhat shady reputation in some parts of the country, but the truth is that they are necessary for a high-quality paint surface. In fact, filler is even used at the factory. In the old days, roof-to-quarter-panel seams were filled with lead and other imperfections were similarly treated. When the paint is stripped off your GTO (if it hasn't been subjected to major bodywork in the past), you will most likely find some lead filler from the factory. Even during the GTO's initial assembly, it was not usually possible to get the high-quality body seams without some sort of filler. It is still true today with new cars.

PAINTING

Unlike the Bondo abusers of the Northeast, filler should be applied to panels so it is not more than 3/16 inch thick when completely sanded. If you have spots more than 3/16-inch lower or higher than the rest of the surface, more bodywork is necessary, which may require grinding, hammering, or welding. Once those are made as close to the surrounding bodywork as possible, filling is then an appropriate solution, not before.

These days, the quality of plastic fillers has progressed to a point where the use of old-style lead fillers is completely obsolete. There is no longer any justification for the use of lead, as it is toxic, expensive, and requires special ladles and panel-distorting heat to use. It also takes quite a lot of experience to apply and work with it correctly. Lead filler has gone the way of the buggy whip and Betamax VCR. Avoid the temptation.

In the quarter-panel patch replacement procedure outlined in Chapter 3, I actually used two different types of plastic body filler—a standard "lightweight" version used for the top surface under the primer and all-metal, a stronger version that contained powdered aluminum. For the patch, I used the real metal filler to seal and waterproof the welded areas. The reason it wasn't used as the top surface for the primer to adhere to was because it does not sand out as smoothly as the lightweight filler.

The proper use and handling of plastic filler is fairly simple, but it can be a harsh irritant if it or the chemical catalyst comes into contact with your skin. Wear rubber or plastic gloves and avoid breathing the fumes. Also make sure that the area to be filled is completely free of paint, oil, grease, or other contaminants, as they do not allow the filler to properly adhere to the parent metal. If the area is relatively small, make sure there is a border of bare metal at least 1 inch all around the area being worked on. This helps to properly shape the fill and avoids contamination. Whatever the size of the area to be filled, the metal should be prepped with 40-grit sandpaper to ensure that the metal is rough enough for filler to adhere to it.

After familiarizing yourself with the proper ratios of filler and catalyst (as outlined in the manufacturer directions) use a plastic putty spreader to mix the two to achieve a completely homogenous color. (The catalyst is dyed so you know when the two are uniformly mixed.) The more catalyst you use, the faster it sets up, so make sure you give yourself enough time to properly apply it to the body surface to be filled.

Use a flexible plastic putty spreader to apply the filler, using enough pressure to push the filler into crevices around welds, low spots, etc. The pressure also helps reduce the chance of excessive filler being applied that has to be sanded off anyway. Use smooth, broad strokes and use the spreader to wipe away excess filler before it sets up. Depending on the brand of filler you use and the amount of catalyst folded into the mix, you have about 20 minutes to perform the job.

Block Sanding

Once the filler has hardened and covered the desired area in roughly the correct contour, block sanding can begin. This procedure is pretty simple, but rather tedious. After finding a sanding block specifically designed for the purpose and the right size for the job, start with a fairly rough grade of paper—40- to 60-grit sandpaper knocks down high spots in the filler and gets the general contour into shape. A long, rigid sanding block works well for doors, and a flexible unit is appropriate for contoured areas. The more pronounced the contour, the smaller the block should be.

The block-sanding procedure can be sped up significantly with the use of an orbital sander, particularly in the early stages when knocking down excess filler is needed and the final contour is still a few steps away. Keep in mind, however, the speed in which an orbital sander operates could cause too much filler to be removed, necessitating a redo. Use a mask to avoid inhaling the plastic filler dust.

Periodically check on your progress, especially with the rough sandpaper—you don't want to go too far with it. Using a spray can of dark primer as a spot coat or a primer specifically made for the job, spray the area with a light coat and allow it to dry. From there, closely inspect the panel for high and low spots as well as the correct contour.

Once you have gone as far as you can with the rough-grit paper, you can then proceed with 180-grit sandpaper. The idea at this stage is to make the surface as perfect as possible, save for the inevitable sanding scratches. Mark high and low spots and use spot putty to fill the low spots, if they are less than approximately 1/16 inch deep. Spot putty is the consistency of toothpaste and is essentially the same chemical compound as found in primer paint, but it is quite a bit thicker. It fills sanding scratches and other minor imperfections. Anything deeper than that should have conventional filler applied.

CHAPTER 4

Once the panel has been inspected and any problems corrected, you can move on to 320-grit sandpaper. It is helpful to use wet/dry sandpaper. Use a spray bottle with water to help keep the sandpaper from getting clogged up with filler. Keep sanding and spot coating until all imperfections are gone, right down to the sanding scratches. Since the paint needs something to adhere to, don't go smoother than 320-grit.

The enemy of any paint job is contamination. Dust, dirt, or any debris is often the culprit of a ruined or poor paint job. In turn, the cleaner the painting environment, the cleaner the paint job will be. If you're going to paint at home, you must construct a temporary paint booth and keep it as clean as possible—close to "operating room clean" is ideal. Once body filler has been applied, shaped, and sanded you need to prep the entire area to be painted. Therefore, you need to wash the area with a silicone-free solvent so the parts are clean. Clean the panel all the way out to edges and the borders of the masking tape. You can use a wool pad or Scotchbrite pad to clean and rough up the surface for excellent paint bonding.

The actual procedure is not complicated, yet takes many hours to perform. It certainly isn't easy work, but some real effort here can pay big dividends in the quality of the finished product. You will also save money by doing this yourself.

I know of one show-winning Pontiac where the owner spent six weeks block-sanding just the rear quarter panels. The car was black and it was intended to be a points-judged gold show car. The results were stunning. While that level of effort may be more than you need, keep in mind that a quality paint job needs as perfect a surface as possible. Any imperfections will show through the paint. Lighter colors may hide minor imperfections at a casual glance; darker colors hide nothing—black demands perfection.

Spray Gun and Compressor Setup

To paint at home does require some serious equipment. First you're are going to need a powerful air compressor with a large tank. A small 2-hp single stage compressor with a 10-gallon tank will not provide the required 25 to 50 psi over a long enough period of time to paint a car body. Therefore, you need a large twin-stage 3 hp or larger compressor with a 50 to 60 gallon tank. These typically retail for $700 on up.

Now you're going to need the requisite air hoses and a regulator to ensure you are maintaining consistent air pressure. A couple decent air hoses will cost you about $100, and you will have to buy a spray gun.

Pros often use one gun for primer and another gun for paint. While you can use the one gun for both, you need to always thoroughly clean the gun. Inexpensive guns that provide an adequate paint spread retail for $100. However, the high-quality paint guns DeVilbiss, Sata, and others retail for $300 to $600. While we can't cover every single aspect of spraying your car, we will provide some of the basics.

The paint manufacturer provides specific air pressure levels for the certain amount of paint, so follow those instructions to obtain the best results. You need to set your air compressor to deliver 25 to 50 psi when the spray gun is activated. Most regulators are set at about 30 psi, and this translates into about 25 psi at the gun. You need to practice against paper before you start spraying any primer or paint. On the spray gun itself, you will find a knob to adjust the paint spread or pattern, and another knob adjusts the thickness or the amount of paint traveling through the gun. The gun should deposit most of the paint in the middle of the application area and less towards the edges. Point the gun at a piece of masking paper, and pull the trigger a bit further to allow fluid.

Masking the Car

To mask off the sensitive parts on the car takes the right materials and attention to detail. A thorough and complete masking job of an entire car often takes a full 8 hours. Masking paper is available in several widths, but many body workers opt to use 3-foot-wide rolls, which are ideal for covering glass, trim, and other parts. These rolls come in 1,000-foot lengths.

The tape needs to follow the curves of the trim and glass, and you must make sure that the tape extends to the edge of the trim. You can use an X-acto or razor blade to make precise cuts of the masking paper to precisely fit the particular part being masked. If the paper or the tape extends to metal body work, you have to repaint that particular area. On the other hand, if paint bleeds through a gap in the tape, you have to remove the paint from glass or trim, which is far easier.

Remember, the chassis, suspension, and all other parts are exposed to overspray. Mask in paper that extends from the chassis to the floor, so no overspray gets under the car and ruins the finish of any component.

Painting

Some classic muscle cars demand original paint to maintain authenticity and acceptance within the community. The GTO community and popular GTO shows accept a wide variety of paint finishes on owner cars. There are a number of paints available today. Acrylic lacquer, acrylic enamel, urethane, and now water-based paints are options. Each type has definite benefits and drawbacks. Lacquer is the easiest to apply and touch up, but it is also the least durable. Few GTO owners select laquer because the new urethane paints provide far better durability. Acrylic enamel is very durable but it is more difficult to apply than lacquer. Urethane paint is one of the most durable and for all intents and purposes has replaced the acrylic paints. But like acrylic enamel, it is difficult to spray when compared to lacquer.

Applying Primer Coats

Once you and your painter are satisfied with the filler and sanding portions of the job, it is time to apply the primer. The final primer coats should be applied at a body shop in a paint booth and block sanded between each coat. How much sanding varies, but the price and the amount of prep between coats is a topic for you and the shop manager to work out.

It is likely that the shop has a set schedule of procedures and costs. You may be able to work something out with the manager where you can do the block sanding between coats to save some money—it never hurts to ask if you are so inclined.

Applying Top Coats

With the surface preparation completed and the primer coats sanded, it is time to actually start laying down the paint. Since every car is different and every body shop approaches this portion of the restoration in a unique fashion, I do not get into too much detail here. The idea is to make sure that you and your body shop manager are on the same page, with a clearly defined set of goals and objectives.

Your list should include:

- Type of paint system.
- Level of preparation and division of labor (block sanding of primer, etc.), if any.
- Inspection of paint between coats (make sure that the problems are solved before moving to the next coat).
- Sanding and buffing procedure.

In this era of spectrometer color sampling and computer-aided mixing, the chances for variations in color have been greatly reduced. However, common sense still applies and mixing up a suitable amount of paint for the job is still a priority. Today, fortunately, it is easier to match colors between two different batches, should something go wrong.

Color Sanding and Applying Clear Coats

Depending on the paint system, you may have the option to color sand your paint job between coats. If you can, this is a great opportunity to fix any imperfections, which end up showing through and reducing the quality of the restoration. Dust, runs, sags, orange peel, and other problems can be corrected at this point. One of the great qualities of catalyzed enamels is that once they are dry, they are very hard, very durable, and their hardness goes through its entire thickness. This allows for color sanding, which accomplishes two things. Number one, it provides a suitable surface for the next coat to adhere to. Number two, it allows the painter to remove the aforementioned imperfections.

So, if the painter gets a little heavy-handed with the paint gun and the paint runs a little or a bug inadvertently gets into the spray booth, lands on a fender, and gets stuck, all is not lost. With some careful wet sanding and subsequent cleaning of the surface, you are ready for another color coat. (Eventually, your clear coat will be applied, if that is part of the paint system you choose.)

When the top coat is sprayed, whether a clear or color coat, it also undergoes the same sort of prep as the color coats except that there are more steps in the sanding procedure. The top-coat sanding starts with a 1,500-grit paper, moving up to 2,000-grit. To the naked eye, sandpaper this fine doesn't look much different, but it polishes the paint to a point where it can then be buffed and waxed.

If you are planning to have painted pinstripes, add them after the top color coat but before the first clear coat. If you aren't using clear, add them after color sanding but before polishing.

If you have a GTO Judge or any GTO with tape stripes, graphics, or decals, add them after all polishing has been done but before final waxing. Be sure to remove all polishes and compounds from the areas where the decals are applied. Fortunately, reproduction stripes and decals are available for just about any combination of GTO made and the quality is very good.

Using NOS stripes, if you could even find them, would probably not be a great idea. With 40-plus years since they were made, they are most likely discolored and the glue has lost its adhesion qualities. Reproductions are available from a variety of sources, such as Phoenix Graphix and Stencils and Stripes Unlimited, as well as larger restoration parts houses.

If you've done your homework, the finished product, whether driver-quality or concours-ready, will be an exhilarating thing to behold!

Prepare Body for Painting

Prep Body Panel

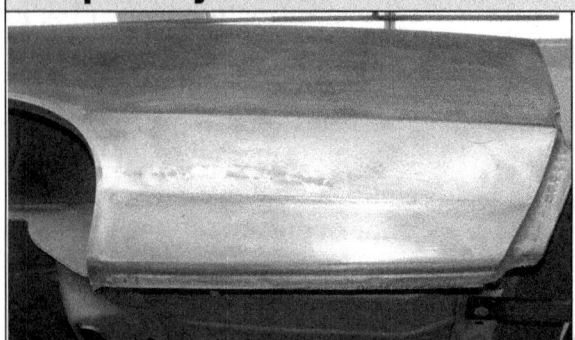

1 The rear quarter panel of this 1965 GTO has been sanded to the bare metal and is ready for a primer coat. When applied, a primer provides both mechanical and chemical adhesion to the body part. A typical primer grabs onto or adheres to the small sanding scuffs or scratches in the surface. Etching primer delivers a mechanical adhesion and chemical adhesion by chemically bonding to the painted surface. When it comes time to prime the surface, be sure the surface is clean and properly prepared for the type of primer you're using. The primer coat must have strong adhesion for the paint to be long-lasting, durable, and of course eye appealing. If the surface is not, properly prepared you risk a lot of money by having to paint the car again. (Photo Courtesy Scott Tiemann)

Remove Dents

2 After the primer was applied, some small dents just below the crown and just above the accent line became apparent, so additional body work was necessary to achieve a completely smooth surface. Depending on the depth and location of the dents, you can use the appropriate hammer and dolly to work the dents out of the body and apply a light coat of filler to smooth over the imperfections. (Photo Courtesy Scott Tiemann)

Smooth Body Filler

3 For completely flat surfaces, like the door skin on the 1964 Royal Bobcat GTO, a rigid 24-inch or longer sanding block is ideal for shaping the filler into its final form. Use long, even sanding strokes. It quickly knocks down high spots in the filler and covers a large surface with every stroke. A variety of automotive sanding blocks are available today: rubber, plastic, wood, and special foam constructions. Eastwood offers a seven-piece Dura-Block set made of molded, closed-cell EVA for $65. The Dura-Block set contains cylindrical and square blocks, which are required for most automotive body work. For curved or sculpted surfaces, an 11-inch or similar cylindrical block is required, and this is helpful for a wheel-well opening.

When starting on this door, the technician used 60- to 80-grit to shape the filler, then 120-grit, and finally 320-grit for smoothing the final surface. With finer grits of sandpaper, such as 320, use wet/dry paper and a spray bottle to keep the sandpaper from clogging with sanding dust. (Photo Courtesy Scott Tiemann)

Apply Primer

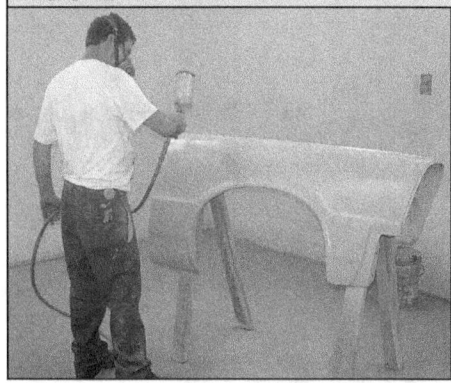

4 Spraying primer is similar in procedure to shooting a top coat. Bolt-on body panels can be painted separately. This is advantageous because with the panel off, as with this 1965 GTO front fender, both sides of the fender can be primed, which gives better corrosion protection and more control over the finish. If there is a lot of paint overspray floating around, prime the fender in a paint booth and wear a proper breathing mask. If you are going to attempt this operation at home, please take into account all of the necessary safety precautions and make sure your town or city allows the use of a paint sprayer outside a professional body shop. Many municipalities have outlawed painting in a residential area, so make sure you are in compliance. (Photo Courtesy Scott Tiemann)

5 Many restorers use PPG DP-40 primer for bare sheet-metal panels. Load the spray gun with a properly mixed ratio of primer and spray the primer on a freshly-stripped panel, such as this, to seal the metal. This helps prevent moisture from penetrating the sealer and rust from forming. In addition, it provides an ideal base for body filler. Use a plastic straightedge to apply body filler over the DP-40 and block sand. After the block sanding of the filler has been completed, lay down a second coat of primer. Using this procedure, the filler is sandwiched between two layers of primer.

You can shoot parts installed on the car, but if you hang the parts, and shoot them in a booth you have access to the entire surface of the panel, and this is the ideal way to spray the panel. Make sure the paint spread and the amount of paint going through the gun are properly adjusted. Before you start shooting a part, make a test spray on some paper to make sure the gun is properly adjusted. This bolt-on sheet metal is painted separately from the main body in order to obtain full access to the entire piece. Otherwise, the door-mounting points do not get the same application of primer and paint. (Photo Courtesy Scott Tiemann)

Apply Spot Coat of Primer

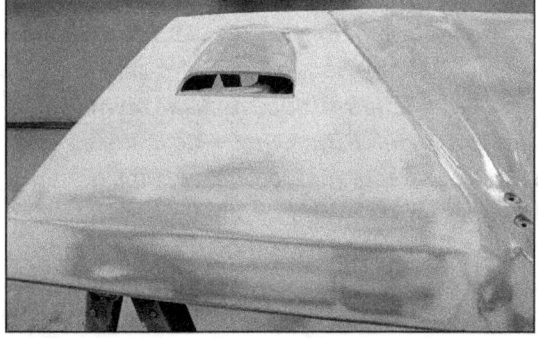

6 Keeping tabs on how your work is coming along is as simple as using a spot coat of primer. Spraying a quick spot coat reveals the inconsistencies in the panel surface. On this 1964 GTO hood, you can see that the surface on the passenger's side is perfectly smooth and is ready for either the next round of finer sandpaper or the first coat of primer. (Photo Courtesy Scott Tiemann)

Apply High-Build Primer

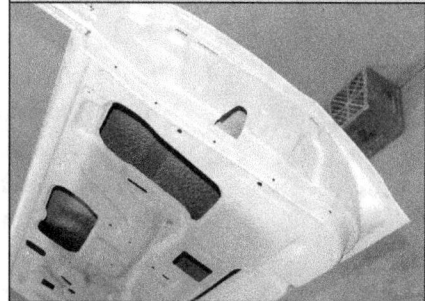

7 Surfaces that are too contoured to block sand can benefit from "high build" primers. These primers are generally thicker than regular types and do a better job of filling low spots, sanding scratches, and other surface imperfections. They are usually sandable and are great for covering small blemishes.

Also, the factory-applied sound deadener is inside the door shell. This coating can be found on many interior body panels, as it also acts as a rust inhibitor. It is lost in a chemical-stripping process, especially if it has been in a full-immersion tank. If the door has been re-skinned in the course of a restoration, the deadener also needs to be replaced. While not commonly seen in a restoration, it is acceptable to use spray-can rustproofer/undercoating/sound deadener, but make sure you get a product that dries completely. It actually goes a long way to reducing road noise that reaches the interior. (Photo Courtesy Scott Tiemann)

CHAPTER 4

Sand Primer Surface

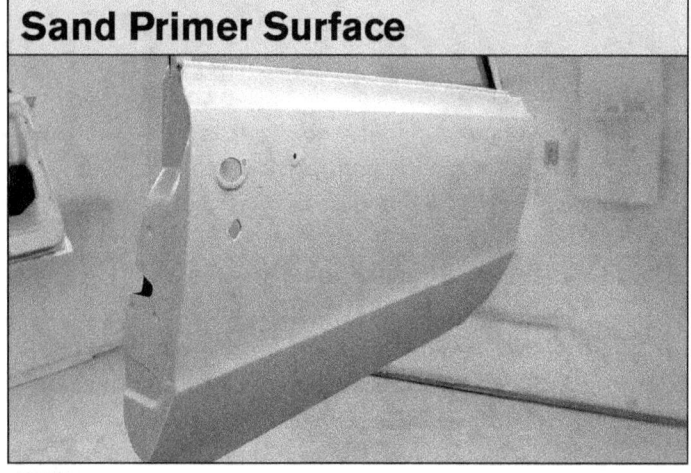

8 At this stage, the first coat of PPG Primer has been sprayed on. Now, sand the surface using 180-grit sandpaper and then wet-sand with 220-grit sandpaper. Work the imperfections out of the primer coat so you have a perfect surface ready for the base coat. The better the primer coat, the better the final paint job will be. If you identify any low spots, apply spot primer and then sand the area flat. Due to recent regulations, lacquer paint is rarely used anymore and catalyzed urethane enamels have replaced the original-style finishes. The primer coat must remain as clean as possible in preparation for applying the paint. (Photo Courtesy Scott Tiemann)

Paint Hood

9 The underside of this GTO's hood was painted at the same time as the exterior surface. Since it does not undergo the same level of color sanding and polishing, and will probably not receive as many coats as the top side, the color appears different. This is not really a concern, as this difference could also be found in new GTOs as they came from the factory. (Photo Courtesy Scott Tiemann)

Mask Body Surfaces

10 Use a high-quality tape, such as 3M High Performance masking tape and use the appropriate masking paper. Masking paper is available in a number of colors and widths to match your needs. Masking the windows, trim, and any other non-body-colored painted surface requires some diligence and attention to detail. Use an X-acto knife or razor blade to precisely cut the paper for the window, trim, or other item. Apply the tape around the window openings so it precisely follows the compound curves. Make sure the tape does not overhang or extend to the body or you will have to touch up this area. If some paint leaks onto the glass or trim, you can clean this up later.

If the body has been separated from the frame, painting requires much less masking. However, if the body is on the frame, you need to create a protective skirt around the perimeter of the car, so the suspension, axles, exhaust, and all the other parts are not exposed to overspray.

In this photo, the 1964 GTO has been heavily masked to protect the interior from overspray, so the doorjambs can receive the proper color coat along with the rest of the exterior. These areas are not typically block sanded, as they have a lot of compound curves and are not as readily visible as the rest of the interior. A variety of adhesive tapes can be used for different parts of this procedure. Foam tape does a good job of keeping paint out while gripping and sealing the paper and metal surfaces alike. It also seals the gaps where you don't want paint. (Photo Courtesy Scott Tiemann)

PAINTING

Tape Door Trim

11 Install the door glass along with the lift mechanism and hang the rest of the door hardware and the semi-finished door assembly on the body. Place these protective tape strips on any exposed chrome trim. (Photo Courtesy Scott Tiemann)

Apply Base Coat

12 Use a chemical cleaner, protective gloves, and a lint-free cloth to thoroughly wipe down all primed surfaces. This ensures the door or panel surface is as clean as possible. Then, apply a base coat of paint. In this particular instance, catalyzed urethane enamel has been applied to this 1965 GTO. You can plainly see the prep work that went into this concours-level car was extensive. The panels are absolutely wave-free, which is a testament to the expert bodywork and countless hours of block sanding. Also, a blemish cannot be seen even before color sanding and polishing, so the finish simply glows. (Photo Courtesy Scott Tiemann)

Apply Base Coat and Clear Coat

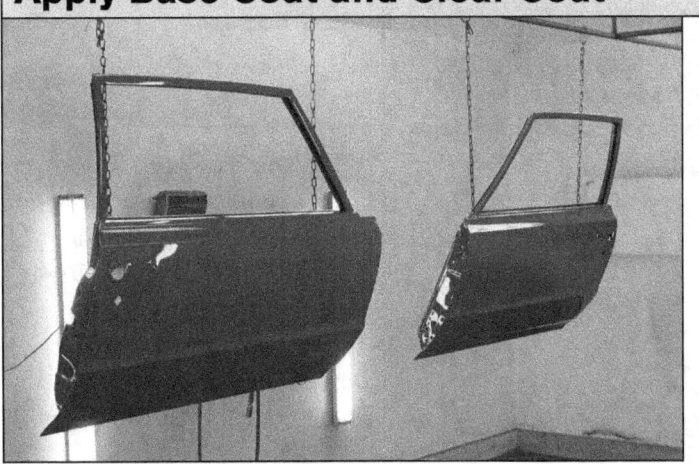

13 As with the priming phase of the operation, spray base coats and the clear coats on the bolt-on sheet metal, which is separated from the main body, ensuring superior results. You can use PPG Deltron for the base coat and DCU 2002 for the clear. Though it looks beautiful and shiny, there's quite a bit of sanding and polishing yet to do. Apply the clear coat and then start color-sanding. It is recommended not to sand between color coats because it can hurt the luster of metallic finishes. Non-metallics can be sanded, but only if there is an imperfection that needs to be repaired. Color sanding is often only done on the clear coat.

Color-Sand Door After Clear Coat

14 You can dry- or wet-sand; the choice is up to you. With wet sanding, water removes the paint from the paper or sanding media so you're able to get more mileage out of the sanding paper. Color sanding removes the imperfections in the clear coat, but you need to be careful not to apply too much pressure and sand the clear coat off and get into the base coat. If you do, the part will have to be repainted. It's a good idea to use a chemical cleaner to pick up the paint residue before color sanding. When color sanding, start with 600-grit sandpaper and work your way up to 2,500-grit. Be sure to color sand the surface evenly so it has the same appearance from edge to edge. Starting with 600-grit, progress to 800 then 1,000, on to 1,200, 1,500, and 2,000, finally finishing up with 2,500-grit. The properly sanded panel will have a consistent dull appearance over the entire surface. If any part of it is shiny, it needs to be sanded to match the panel. From there, the finish is buffed to its final luster. (Photo Courtesy Scott Tiemann)

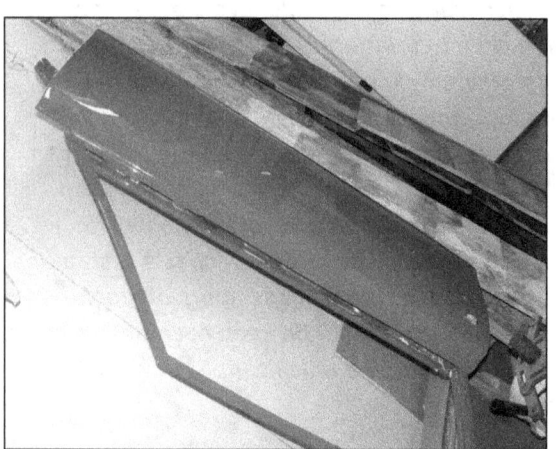

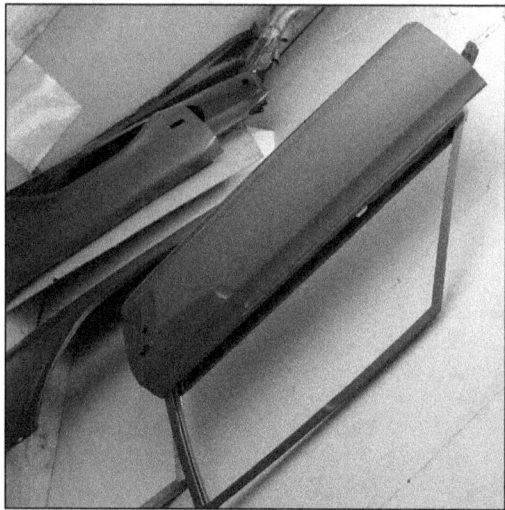

15 At this point, the color sanding has been completed, time for installation and final polishing. Select a buffing pad that's suited for the particular charateristics of the surface. If your paint has very mild scratches, you need a less aggressive buffing pad. Set the buffer speed at low so you don't damage the paint surface. Use light pressure and place the buffer pad flatly on the surface. Work the pad across the surface and buff the entire surface in equal proportions. A fine abrasive paste is used to bring out the final shine, and you should use a high-quality buffing compound, such as 3M Perfect It 3000 Buffing Compound or Meguiars. The formulation of the abrasive will vary according to the paint manufacturer's recommendations. (Photo Courtesy Scott Tiemann)

16 During the color-sanding process, start out with 600 and as you evenly apply pressure to the sanding block you need to create a uniform dull finish. The matte finish first seen at the 600- and 800- grit levels begins to become glossier once the grit moves past 1000. Sanding over the clear coat and reducing the uneven surfaces creates a white residue and that can be wiped off. Take time to create a uniform finish before using 1500-, 2000-, and finally 2500-grit sandpaper. Often, the blocking and buffing determine how good the paint is. (Photo Courtesy Scott Tiemann)

Protect Door Handle

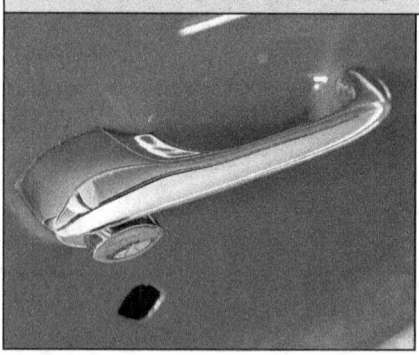

17 The door handle is installed on the door after the color sanding but before the final buffing takes place. The lock is installed as the final exterior component of the completed door assembly. (Photo Courtesy Scott Tiemann)

CHAPTER 5

ENGINE

All 1964–1974 Pontiac GTOs used some version of what we now refer to as the "traditional" Pontiac V-8. It was produced from 1955 through 1979 and a modified version continued for another two years. By the time the GTO rolled around, the Pontiac V-8 had a decade of improvements under its belt and a special version of the venerable 389 was developed for use specifically in the GTO. It featured cylinder heads from the 421 HO and a special camshaft designed to provide additional top-end power. Both 4-barrel and Tri-Power versions were offered with horsepower ratings of 325 and 348, respectively.

As the years passed, displacements and horsepower ratings increased—the base 389 grew to 400 ci, with new, freer-flowing cylinder heads. Optional round-port heads debuted in the 1968 Ram Air II. A 370-hp Ram Air IV was introduced for the 1969 and 1970 model years. An optional 455-ci engine also entered the line-up in 1970. A low-compression 455 HO replaced the Ram Air IV in 1971 and both the 400 and 455 remained in various versions until 1974 when they were replaced with a new 4-barrel version of the 350, which was used for just one year. It was rated at 200 net horsepower.

Achieving a factory-correct engine restoration with all stock equipment and finishes is no small feat, but it's something you can certainly accomplish. Unless your GTO is 100-percent complete and original, it may take some time to get all the required parts. With some research, patience, and skill, you can get it all "correct."

In the case of this 1969 GTO convertible, no expense has been spared to correctly restore this engine and the engine compartment; it's as close to perfection as any. The engine paint, valve covers, air cleaner, accessories, hose clamps, and other equipment are all correct. But the restorer didn't stop there; the date codes on the hoses, belts, and plug wires are correct for the build date of the car.

An engine restoration for a pedigree Tri-Power, Ram Air IV, Judge, or other rare GTO is well deserved. You may not want to make this investment in a pedestrian 1969 GTO 400 2-barrel automatic because you won't recoup the investment from selling the car. In addition, the level of engine restoration should be determined by your personal taste, its intended use, whether your car is numbers-matching and of course, your budget. A daily-driver engine can be restored to the region of 75-percent correct and appear similar to stock. After all, it doesn't take a lot of money to make an attractive engine compartment, but making it 100-percent correct does. (Photo Courtesy Scott Tiemann)

Time for a Rebuild?

The engine currently in your GTO may or may not be the original engine that was installed at the factory. Perhaps your car came without an engine altogether. Whatever your situation, this is a great time to build a Pontiac engine. Why? Because you can benefit from a level of aftermarket support for the Pontiac V-8 engine that is truly remarkable. My intention is to outline some ideas for rebuilding your engine to take advantage of this support while still maintaining the spirit of the original.

As street performance engines, Pontiac V-8s were among the best available. They boasted a generous displacement, fantastic low- and mid-range torque, and a responsiveness that left many race-inspired mills at the starting line. For the street racing movement of the 1960s and 1970s, most "competition" was stoplight to stoplight, so a big, torquey V-8 like a 400 or 455 Pontiac with a lot of low-end grunt was the usual winner in a short distance over a more high-strung engine like a Boss 429 or a 426 Hemi. Give either of those engines another block to rev up, and it was a different story.

The Pontiac engines are street-oriented performance engines, while the Boss 429 and 426 Hemi are race-oriented engines used on the street. General Motors left sanctioned racing in 1963, so only street performance could be offered. For that purpose, the Pontiac V-8 fit the bill admirably.

Today, those same characteristics of responsive street performance can be easily integrated into your GTO and substantially upgraded, whether it is for a restoration-style build or something a little hotter. Better bottom-end componentry, freer-breathing heads, computer-designed camshaft profiles, and more efficient exhaust systems can greatly increase power and reliability without disrupting the external appearance of your engine.

Aftermarket Resurgence

Over the past 20 years or so, the popularity of the muscle car movement generated a lot of interest in Pontiac engines. After all, they powered the GTO, the original muscle car. The aftermarket responded, first with intake manifolds, then cylinder heads, then a Pontiac-based race block, then forged-steel stroker kits—all amazing developments, considering they are currently supporting an engine family that has been out of OEM production for three decades. In fact, it is now possible to build an entire Pontiac V-8 engine in displacements of 600-or-more cubic inches without using a single original part. This is further proof that while there aren't any new Pontiacs being made anymore, there is a very strong and loyal fan base, which helps keep interest and values up.

If you are considering an engine rebuild, I assume you are not looking to build a mega-dollar race engine for your Goat. Instead, you probably already have an engine that will be pressed into service for this project, and you are looking for something reliable, powerful, and not straying too far from what the Pontiac engineers envisioned.

What if I told you that your 389 could become a 453, your 400 a 468, or your 455 a 474, all while still looking 100-percent stock and not costing significantly more than a stock rebuild? It is all possible from the magic of a stroker kit. By retaining

This 389 Tri-Power from a 1965 GTO is ready to be disassembled and rebuilt. Visually examine the block and look for any cracks or damage in the casting. Look for any carbon deposits between the block and the head because that could indicate a head gasket failure. That could mean there's serious internal engine damage, such as scored pistons and cylinder walls. In addition, look at the intake and exhaust manifolds for any cracks, breaks, or other obvious damage.

As part of any inspection process, you should Magnaflux the block, heads, intake, and exhaust manifolds to ensure they're free of damage. The process identifies cracks and other deformations that are not obvious to the naked eye. Before turning any wrenches, generously apply penetrating oil on all bolts, so you're able to remove them without stripping them. Here, the casting number-77 cylinder head stamping is clearly visible on the number-2 (front) exhaust port. Most years have the head casting number on the center exhaust ports. (Photo Courtesy Scott Tiemann)

the standard production Pontiac engine block with nothing more than a standard prep and clean-up overbore, the addition of a new balanced rotating assembly with forged pistons and rods and your choice of a cast or forged 4.25-inch stroke crankshaft, you can reap the benefits of up to a 1/2-inch stroke increase with much more durability than the stock cast pieces.

If you add a set of freer-flowing heads and a more aggressive camshaft, you could easily put out 525 or more completely streetable horsepower and have an engine that really lives up to the legendary status of the GTO. Several reputable companies can help you find the right combination for your specific block, including Butler Performance and SD Performance.

Throw Out the Stock Pistons and Rods

Even if you aren't planning on a big jump in displacement, there is no longer any reason to reuse the stock cast connecting rods (PN 541000) in your Pontiac V-8. While they are fine for driving to the grocery store, they should not be considered high-performance items, even though they were installed in all factory GTO engines. Why build in a weak link? By the time you rebuild them and add new bolts, you could buy brand-new forged-steel connecting rods that are light years ahead of the production pieces in terms of strength and overall durability. Yes, you can purchase new forged-steel connecting rods for under $300, so why use the stockers?

The same goes with pistons. There are so many good forged pistons now that a stock-style cast piston is not worth bothering with. Prices have dropped over the past several years, while quality and selection have improved.

The truth is, most engines being rebuilt for stock restorations are not stock on the inside and that is a good thing. With inexpensive and, more importantly, superior-quality internal parts being manufactured these days, most purists have come around on aftermarket pieces. If you can build more strength, durability, and reliability into your restorations and save money while doing so, it is foolish to rely on inferior, metal-fatigued originals.

Identifying an Engine

The Pontiac V-8's high level of interchangeability did wonders to reduce production costs over the years, and it also went a long way to help shade-tree mechanics get their cars back on the road after a major failure. With an afternoon's worth of work a blown-up 389 could be replaced with a later 350, 400, or 455. This could quickly put an ailing car back in service, but this ease of swapping engines also made for a lot of non-original GTOs. Add to that the fact that many blown-up factory engines were replaced under warranty with service replacement blocks, and finding an original, numbers-matching GTO is not easy. Fortunately for us, this is not a paramount concern but if you are interested in finding out whether the engine sitting between the frame rails of your GTO is the factory-installed original, read on.

Identifying a Pontiac engine is not difficult. What becomes significant to many restorers is whether the original engine is still in the car. How that is determined is by a careful examination of the various codes on the engine's major castings.

The following is information about the casting numbers of engines originally available in GTOs from 1964–1974. Obviously, Pontiac listed many other codes for other applications, but these are the ones that GTOs originally came with. Also, keep in mind that codes were re-used and could have completely different applications assigned to them. This is why these codes all have to be cross-referenced against the date code and the block casting number. Otherwise, you cannot verify the engine's factory configuration. For example, the

Check the engine ID number against the VIN to determine if you have a numbers-matching car. If you do, it's much more valuable. However, even if you don't, that doesn't mean the car isn't worth restoring. A GTO with a replacement service engine, a different Pontiac V-8, or a crate engine is certainly worth restoring, but it's just not going to be worth as much.

CHAPTER 5

code YS could be a base-engine 389 4-barrel used with a 2-speed automatic or a 1970 400 Ram Air III used with a 3-speed automatic.

Block Casting Number

This number is found at the rear of the block. For the 1965 through early 1967 model years, the date code and casting number were both located near the distributor hole. From March 1967 on, the casting number moved to the area between the number-8 cylinder (passenger side) and the transmission/bellhousing mount points. For the purposes of identifying original engines, this book lists the correct block casting numbers for original engine installations for 1964–1974 GTOs. If your casting number does not appear in the list, it is almost certainly not an original engine.

The engine's casting codes provide a lot of information. Casting number 9778789 is used for all 1965 389s regardless of final installation. The arrow on the clock icon points to 2 o'clock, and the arrow just below it points to the "D." The "B205" code is the date; B for February, 20 for the day, and 5 for the year. If it were cast on February 1, 1965, the code would read B15, as no third digit would be used. The date code and arrows are easier to see on the close-up after painting. (Photos Courtesy Scott Tiemann)

Block Date Code

The date code is represented by a letter, followed by two or three numbers. The letter designates the month of the casting—A is January, B is February, etc. The next one or two numbers represent the day of the month. Days before the tenth are usually not given a placeholder zero. The last number represents the year, the year of the casting date, not necessarily the model year. An early 1964 GTO may have a late 1963 build date, and if so, the engine casting date reflects that.

The engine date usually pre-dates the build date of the car (as seen on the cowl tag) by as much as six weeks, though that is certainly not an absolute. In some unusual cases, when bodies were put in storage weeks in advance, the engine casting date could be later than the build date on the cowl tag. Blocks may also tell you whether they were cast during the day or night shift and in some years they also list the hour with a clock cast in.

Block Code and Engine ID Number

Block codes and engine ID numbers are found on a machined pad on the front passenger side of the block, next to the water pump housing, just below the leading edge of the cylinder head. In most cases, the block VIN

Block Casting Number

Year	Engine	Code
1964	389	9773155
1965	389	9778789
1966	389	9778789
1967	400	9786133
1968	400	9790071
1968	400 Ram Air	9792506 (4-bolt mains)
1969	400	9790071
1969	400 Ram Air	9792506 (4-bolt mains)
1970	400	9799914
1970	400 Ram Air III	9799914 (4-bolt mains)
1970	Ram Air IV	979991 (5) (4-bolt mains) *
1970	455	9799140
1971	400	481988
1971	455	485428 **
1971	455 HO	483677
1972	400	481988
1972	455	485428
1973	400	481988
1973	455	485428
1974	350	488986

* The last digit was usually stamped after the cast-in "4" was ground off
** Late-season 455 HO engines also used this casting number

72   HOW TO RESTORE YOUR PONTIAC GTO 1964-1974

ENGINE

and the vehicle VIN were the same, but by late 1967, the block VIN was revised. It started out with a 2 (for Pontiac), the last digit of the year, and a letter for the assembly plant followed by the last 6 digits of the vehicle VIN. The block code is a two or three-character stamping that identifies the engine version, the transmission, and sometimes other information, such as air conditioning, California, or high-altitude delivery zone.

Cylinder Head Casting Number

This number is usually a raised cast-in number or alpha-numeric code located on the center exhaust port of the cylinder head. In the 1965 GTO, the code was on the far right exhaust port, viewing the head from the exhaust side. Date codes are also used on cylinder heads and intake manifolds, following the same coding system. This can be helpful determining whether the heads are original to the block.

Other Information Sources

If your engine doesn't appear on any of these lists, or appears but is in the wrong year, there are other resources that can help you identify them. Wallaceracing.com has a list of engine codes for all years of the Pontiac V-8. I would be remiss if I didn't mention Pete McCarthy's fantastic book on Pontiac engines, *Pontiac Musclecar Performance 1955–79*. If you really want to know about the traditional Pontiac V-8 history, this is one-stop shopping. When I was on staff at *High Performance Pontiac*, my colleague Bart Orlans nicknamed it, "The second book of Pete."

For updated information on modern assembly techniques and components, Rocky Rotella's CarTech book, *How to Rebuild Pontiac V-8s*, is an authoritative guide on the subject.

Choosing a Machine Shop

Selecting a machine shop to handle the preparation of your Pontiac

Engine Block Codes

Year	Code	Carb/Engine, Transmission
1964	78X	4-bbl, manual
	79J	4-bbl, automatic
	76X	Tri-Power, manual
	77J	Tri-Power, automatic
1965	WT	4-bbl, manual
	YS	4-bbl, automatic
	WS	Tri-Power, manual
	YR	Tri-Power, automatic
1966	WW	4-bbl, manual, A.I.R.
	WT	4-bbl, manual
	XE	4-bbl, automatic, A.I.R.
	YS	4-bbl, automatic
	WS	Tri-Power, manual
	WV	Tri-Power, manual, A.I.R.
	YR	Tri-Power, automatic
	XS	Tri-Power, Ram Air, manual
1967	XM	2-bbl, automatic
	XL	2-bbl, automatic, A.I.R.
	WW	4-bbl, manual, A.I.R.
	WT	4-bbl, manual
	YS	4-bbl, automatic
	WS	4-bbl HO, manual
	WV	4-bbl HO, manual, A.I.R.
	YZ	4-bbl HO, automatic
	XS	4-bbl, Ram Air, manual
	YR	4-bbl, Ram Air, manual, A.I.R.
	XP	4-bbl Ram Air, automatic
1968	XM	2-bbl, automatic
	WT	4-bbl, manual
	YS	4-bbl, automatic
	WS	4-bbl HO, manual
	YZ	4-bbl HO, automatic
	XS	4-bbl, Ram Air I, manual
	XP	4-bbl Ram Air I, automatic
	XW	4-bbl Ram Air II, automatic
1969	XM, XS	2-bbl, automatic
	WT	4-bbl, manual
	YS	4-bbl, automatic
	WS	4-bbl Ram Air III, manual
	YZ	4-bbl Ram Air III, automatic
	WW	4-bbl, Ram Air IV, manual
	XP	4-bbl Ram Air IV, automatic
1970	WT	4-bbl, manual
	YS	4-bbl, automatic
	WS	4-bbl Ram Air III, manual
	YZ	4-bbl Ram Air III, automatic
	WW	4-bbl, Ram Air IV, manual
	XP	4-bbl Ram Air IV, automatic
	WA	455 4-bbl, manual
	YA	455 4-bbl, automatic
1971	WT	4-bbl, 3-spd manual
	WK	4-bbl, 4-spd manual
	YS	4-bbl, automatic
	YC	455 4-bbl, automatic
	WL	455 HO, 3-spd manual
	WC	455 HO, 4-spd manual
	YE	455 HO, automatic
1972	WS	4-bbl, 3-spd manual
	WK	4-bbl, 4-spd manual
	YT	4-bbl, automatic
	YC	455 4-bbl, automatic
	WL	455 HO, 3-spd manual
	WM	455 HO, 4-spd manual
	YB	455 HO, automatic
1973	WS, YF	4-bbl, 3-spd manual
	WP, Y6, WK, YG	4-bbl, 4-spd manual
	YS, XN, ZS, YY, XX, Y3, YT, XK	4-bbl, automatic
	YC, XE, ZC, ZA, YA, XL, YK, YD, XM, X7	455 4-bbl, automatic
1974	WP	manual
	YP, YS	automatic
	ZP	automatic, CA delivery

engine is a little easier said than done, though with the addition of some common sense, you will be able to make the right decision. Just because your friend had good luck with a shop that bored out his 350 Chevy, doesn't necessarily mean that it's the shop for you. It also doesn't necessarily rule it out either.

Word of mouth is, in my estimation, the best way to find a good machine shop in your area. In years past, I have had good luck by going into the pits at a drag strip and talking to Pontiac racers about their engine builds and who did their machine work. Time and time again, I was able to pick out one or two good shops within a 100-mile radius.

Today, finding that sort of information is another reason to be on the Internet. Logging onto the various Pontiac message boards and starting a discussion thread like "Looking for a good Pontiac machine shop in Kansas," usually gets the names of companies that can do the job. It's also a good idea to check with Pontiac parts suppliers for their recommendations. Places like Butler Performance or SD Performance also pass along the names of customers in your area who will agree to talk to you for recommendations. This is also one of the great things about the Pontiac hobby that you will come to appreciate—the people are great, and most are more than happy to help out a fellow Pontiac enthusiast and/or owner.

Once a shop has been chosen, be sure to talk to them in detail about what you want done—and what you do not want. Have them walk you through the entire process you are paying for from beginning to end. The idea is to avoid any surprises, such as decking the engine and having all of the factory-stamped information obliterated. If that happens, the block ID that makes your car a numbers-matching example has been ruined and the car is worth dramatically less. Will they be hot-tanking the engine? How many steps does a clean-up overbore entail? How are valve jobs done? Will they be installing hardened valve seats? Will the combustion chambers be cc'd?

Once the ground rules have been laid down and a price is agreed upon, be sure to photograph every marking on every piece that you are sending off to be machined. It wouldn't hurt to mark your pieces on a non-visible and unmachined area and let them know that you did so. Show them the marks so they can keep track of your items.

Repair or Replace?

Just as with the rest of the car, once an engine is apart, some surprises can pop up, even in a running engine. When parts are Magnafluxed, sonic-tested, and pressure-checked, problems can arise. Remember, you are dealing with castings and rotating assemblies that were built during the Johnson and Nixon administrations. Many components and problems could have occurred over the ensuing

Cylinder Head Casting Number

Year	Code
1964	9770716
1965	77
1966	093
1967	142 (2-barrel)
	670 (base engine)
	97 (Ram Air)
	997 (Ram Air)
1968	14 (2-barrel)
	16 (base engine)
	31 (Ram Air 1)
	R (96)
	A (Ram Air II, round exhaust port)
1969	45 (2-barrel)
	48 (Ram Air III)
	16 (base engine and Ram Air III)
	62 (base engine with A/C)
	722 (Ram Air IV, round exhaust port)
1970	11 (2-barrel)
	12 (base engine with manual transmission and all Ram Air III)
	13 (base engine with automatic)
	614 (Ram Air IV, round exhaust port)
	64 (455)
1971	96 (400)
	66 (455)
	197 (455 HO, round exhaust port)
1972	7K3 (400)
	7M5 (455)
	7F6 (455 HO, round exhaust port)
1973	4X, All (secondary casting number on squared-off boss to the left of the exhaust port just below valve cover rail determines application)
	400 3H, 7H
	455 1H
1974	46 (350 GTO with screw-in studs)

ENGINE

years. Maybe it was that overheating back in 1981 or that time it was over-revved in a street race in 1986 that did it in. In any event, the decision has to be made—repair or replace?

If you do happen to have an original, numbers-matching GTO, there is no doubt your overall investment is enhanced by keeping it that way. If that means locating a correct, dated-coded cylinder head to replace the cracked original or tracking down previous owners to see if they still have the original carb, then take the time to do so. You might be surprised with what you find.

There are also enthusiasts who pull out and store the original driveline, then build replacements so they can race the car without worry of risking damage to the original engine. Most competitions, such as the annual Muscle Car Shootout in Stanton, Michigan, or the Factory Appearing Street Tire (F.A.S.T.) Series, do not require an original powerplant. F.A.S.T. allows for a whole host of modifications, while the Muscle Car Shootout requires the cars to be stock and correct. Either way, it is an option that not all builders fully explore.

If the original engine is gone, you actually don't have the burden of keeping it numbers-matching and you can then explore other avenues. There is one point I want to make perfectly clear: Locating a replacement engine does not require it to be an original GTO engine. For example, let's say your original YS-coded engine is long gone from your 1966 GTO. You can get almost the same exact engine in a much less expensive YE- or YF-coded 389 4-barrel out of a 1966 full-size car.

What are the differences beyond the codes and casting numbers? A slightly milder 066 cam instead of the 067, and 1/4 point of compression, the total of which is 10 hp and 2 ft-lbs of torque less—a power level easily recaptured in a performance rebuild and a whole lot more, if you plan ahead.

If you aren't concerned with the fact that a sharp-eyed Pontiac fan might notice that your cylinder heads say "092" instead of "093," it is a much more cost-effective way to go. Where a rebuildable, correctly coded

This 1965 GTO and its 389 Tri-Power were restored in the late 1980s. The classic 389 Tri-Power in this car is correct in most areas, which includes the fasteners, hose clamps, and plug wires. However, there is one glaring problem—the engine is the wrong color! This Pontiac shade of silver blue was first used in 1966 and lasted through 1970. This is a car of pedigree so all of the finishes should be factory correct, especially the engine-block color. Therefore, this 389 should be repainted in the correct 1965 Pontiac blue paint color. While the engine may have been painted this later color for personal preference (and it does look attractive), most purists see it as a waste of effort. But it would be relatively easy to pull the engine, place it on an engine stand, mask off all the parts, and paint the engine the correct color.

Another older restoration, this 1964 has several minor mistakes or non-original equipment items under the hood. These include the belts, hoses, fasteners, and finishes. The block and manifold are also painted. The master cylinder inspection cover was spray painted gold, which is incorrect but generally presentable and fine for a driver-quality machine.

engine for a GTO can run in excess of $3,500, a similar engine from a full-size car may be in the $500 to $750 range. Whether the additional cost of a correct engine is worth it is up to the person footing the bill, and that is you. I'm of the opinion that if you build the car the way you want, you will want to keep it. If you build it "for the next guy," he is the one who will ultimately get the car.

Detailing the Engine

Once the engine is back together, it's time to paint and detail it to give it an authentic, correct appearance. In addition to the paint, other areas to pay attention to are fasteners, wiring, and hoses.

Paint

Ideally, the engine should be painted in the same manner as the rest of the car—in a paint booth using a quality paint gun, proper, and safe equipment. If that is not possible, you can still get very professional-looking results with spray cans. After all, they are simply very compact, one-time use, compressor sprayers. But you need to be sure that the surface of the engine is clean, free of grease, and properly prepared. Make sure your painting area does not have contaminants and air flowing through it, which means do not paint your engine in the driveway.

Whether using a spray can or a spray booth, the secret to satisfactory results is the preparation of the surfaces. Every little sanding scratch or bit of oil will show up when painted over.

Surface preparation is fairly simple, but time-consuming. If you want it to look right, take the time it deserves. If your engine was at a machine shop, it was likely hot-tanked, but still requires chemical degreasing and a thorough rinsing. After that, a primer coat will indicate any imperfections that need addressing. Remove all rust before any degreasing takes place.

One area of Pontiac engines that requires a different approach than other V-8 engines is the exhaust port area of the cylinder heads. This area burns off paint very quickly. The reason is because the port has a 135-degree turn, which puts an immense amount of heat just before the port's exit point—right where the casting code is. At car shows you see that area almost always has the paint burned off and rust is starting to form.

Although it seems like nothing really stops the problem dead in its tracks, many restorers and engine

Original Pontiac engine block colors and other engine bay colors are readily available from a number of suppliers. A professional paint gun provides the best results because of its superior application, but spray paint in rattle cans also provides impressive results.

Pontiac Light Blue Metallic was offered on 1966-1970 Pontiac sixes and V-8s while 1959–1965 Pontiac V-8s are offered in Light Blue. The Light Blue Metallic was offered on so many cars and many businesses offer this color, including Ames, Classic Industries, Krylon-Dupli-color, and PPG. Light Blue is available from Ames, Classic Industries, DuPont, Plasti-Kote, Performance Years, and others. As with any other type of painting, be sure that the block is free of grease, oil, and any contaminants. The cleaner the surface is, the better the paint will be. Apply multiple thin coats for the best results.

When it comes to engine restoration, attention to all the details is necessary when competing in a show. This level of detail work wins gold awards, as with this 1964 Tri-Power engine. The beautiful paint is factory correct. The fasteners are in perfect condition and have the correct finishes. The engine wiring is correctly shrink-wrapped and held down with the factory-supplied tabs, which are held down with the valve cover bolts. Note the finishes on the bare metal pieces. Brilliant work all around. You can find the hardware and apply the correct paint, but you need to follow this book closely and pay close attention to all the details. (Photo Courtesy Scott Tiemann)

ENGINE

Bill Hirsch Automotive Products offers a wide range of high-quality automotive paints, including a high-temperature, high-gloss engine enamel paint. This paint matches the factory cast-iron GTO exhaust manifold finish so your GTO's value benefits from this correct finish. If you are using a spray gun and you want the best results possible, a high-temperature, high-gloss paint, such as Bill Hirsch, does a great job. This paint is safe to 700 degrees F, so it holds up better than other types. (Photo Courtesy Bill Hirsch Automotive Products)

Replicating as-cast finishes in paint helps ward off rust and retains a fresh appearance. These Eastwood paints are specially formulated for that purpose. Eastwood offers paint that mimics the color and gloss level of cast iron, cast aluminum, and even cadmium plating. (Photo Courtesy Eastwood)

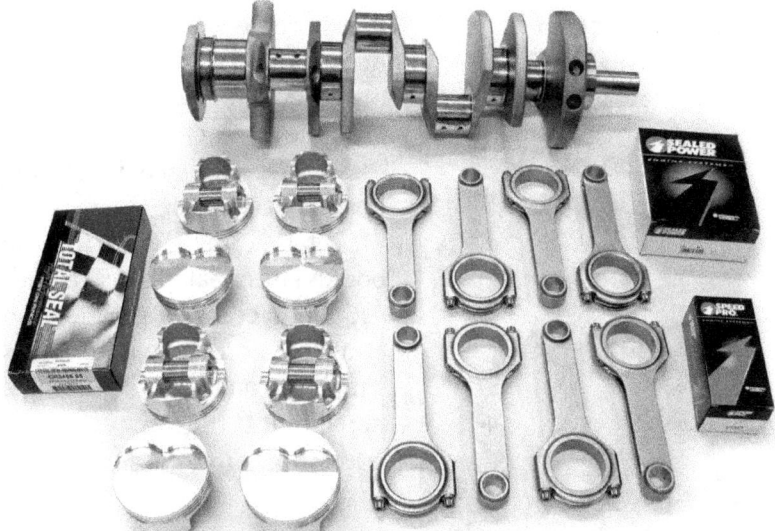

This Butler Performance stroker kit features forged rods, pistons, and a crankshaft. Best of all, it can be slipped into a regular 389 or 400 block and provides a huge increase in displacement and torque, while retaining a bone-stock look. (Photo Courtesy Butler Performance)

builders have had good luck with priming those areas with several coats of VHT header paint. The rough-cast finish of the exhaust port and the flat finish of the paint work provide a good base for top-coat adherence. If you are using a spray gun, look for a high-temperature version of the correct-year engine paint for your Pontiac engine. A product like Bill Hirsch Engine Enamel does a good job.

If you find that your exhaust ports are still starting to discolor after a few weeks of driving, make a template to mask off the surrounding areas of your engine and touch them up. It generally needs to be done once or twice each season. It is just one of the little idiosyncrasies of owning a Pontiac.

For exhaust manifolds, use Eastwood's Factory Gray Hi-Temp Coating. It does a great job of replicating the color of bare cast iron without the threat of rusting like a bare metal piece inevitably does. Interestingly enough, the manifolds don't get as hot as the exhaust port, so this paint holds up fine.

Other Eastwood paints do a great job of replicating bare cast finishes. If you want to retain that fresh-cast look on aluminum and other surfaces, check out its detailing paints.

Fasteners, Wiring and Hoses

Once again, the automotive aftermarket has come to the rescue with many items that have long since been depleted from dealer inventories. Even more importantly, wearable items, such as hoses and belts, should be replaced with newly manufactured items. The reasoning is this: even if you could find one, do you want a 40-year-old radiator hose on your car? Do you want fuel lines not resistant to today's gasolines,

CHAPTER 5

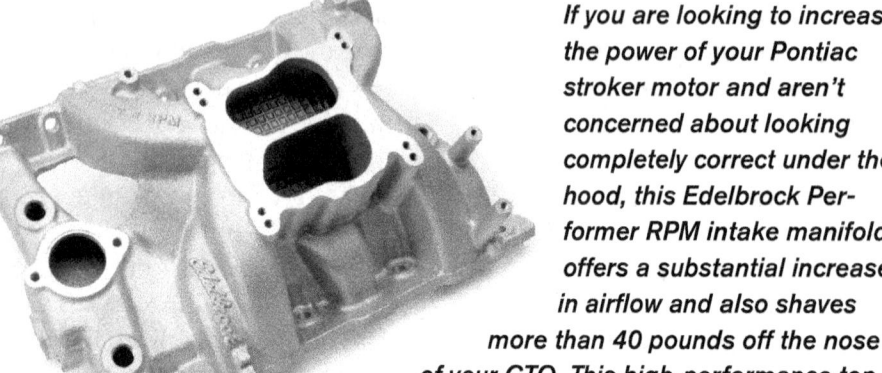

If you are looking to increase the power of your Pontiac stroker motor and aren't concerned about looking completely correct under the hood, this Edelbrock Performer RPM intake manifold offers a substantial increase in airflow and also shaves more than 40 pounds off the nose of your GTO. This high-performance top end can be painted to give a more factory-stock appearance. (Photo Courtesy Edelbrock)

Replacement hoses and wiring should always be new for two reasons: old items crack and fail and old items can be harmed by today's "alcohol-enhanced" fuels. (Photo Courtesy of Ames Performance Engineering)

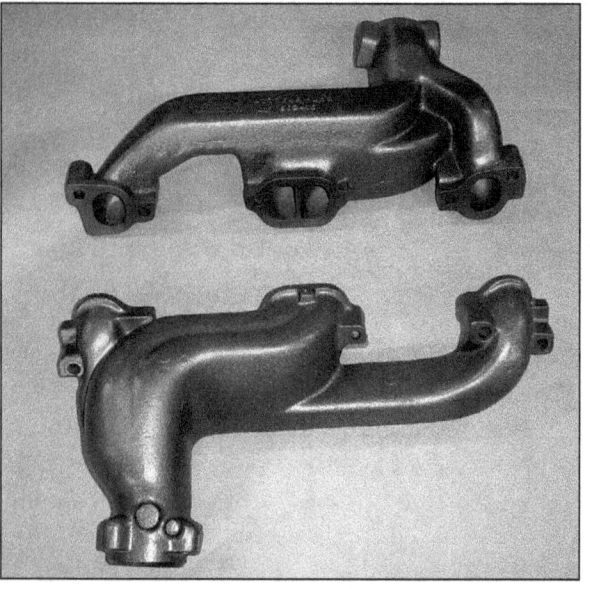

Reproduction Ram Air exhaust manifolds are a great choice for those seeking additional performance but do not want the leaking and ground clearance problems associated with headers. These can be ported or extrude honed for additional flow, though care must be taken to make sure they do not get too thin. (Photo Courtesy Ram Air Restoration Enterprises)

which contain at least 10-percent ethanol? How about old plug wires arcing between each other? No, no, and no.

With companies like Ames Performance Engineering, Original Parts Group, Year One, and Performance Years taking the time and money to invest in the manufacture of quality reproduction hoses, correct clamps, distributor caps, engine wiring harnesses, wire loom separators, plug wires, Ram Air pan gaskets, and other related items, it has become customary in the last decade or so to refrain from seeking out original pieces. Instead, restorers grab the latest GTO restoration catalogs to see who has what and who has the best deals.

Again, the Pontiac message boards are great places to see what supplier pieces are better than others and which ones come from the same supplier. You'd be surprised by how much of it is the same.

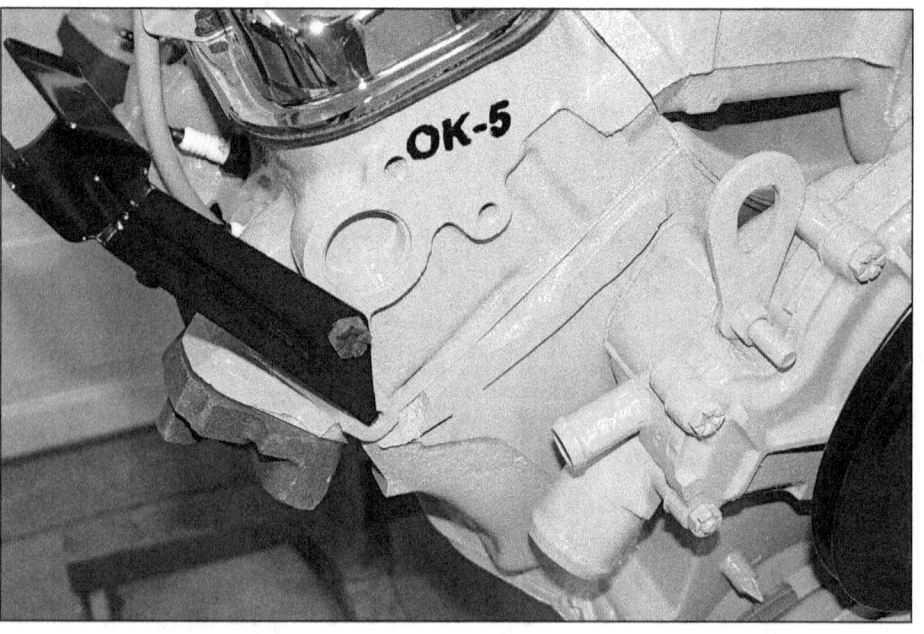

Quality control markings, like this one (OK-5), can be replicated using rubber stamps from companies such as Inline Tube. (Photo Courtesy Scott Tiemann)

ENGINE

Engine Disassembly and Inspection

Remove Carb and Valve Covers

1 You don't know what lurks inside a Pontiac V-8 until you disassemble it and thoroughly inspect all of the components. A crucial part of inspection is not only identifying obvious and not-so-obvious damage, but also determining which component problems, parts failures, and assembly issues caused the problems in the first place. If you don't identify and remedy the core problem that initiated or created the failure in the first place, when you rebuild the engine the core problem will still exist and the engine could likely fail again. There's nothing more demoralizing than tearing down the entire long block, performing a diligent rebuild, only for the engine to grenade again. (Photo Courtesy Butler Performance)

Inspect Cylinder Bores and Block

2 The cylinder bore wear can be seen from both ends but you can see if there are cracks at the bottom of the bores. Also, keep in mind that the number-4 main cap holds the thrust bearing and this is the journal that takes the most abuse. Pay particular attention to this area and look for visible cracks. There may be some that you cannot see but if they can be seen, you likely have a block that is not usable. If it passes a visual inspection, you may still want to have it Magnafluxed to detect other cracks. (Photo Courtesy Butler Performance.)

Inspect Lifter Valley and Block

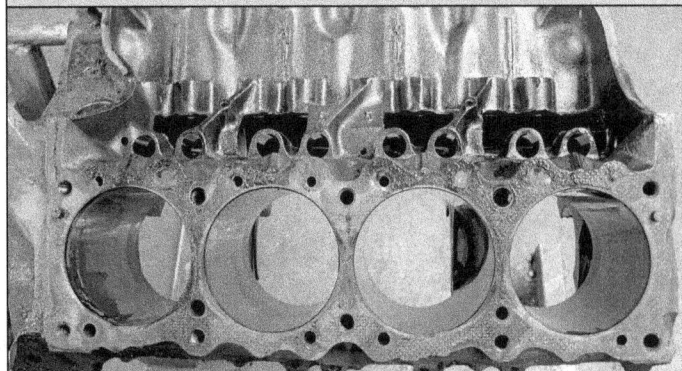

3 Pontiac blocks have an inherent weakness in the lifter bore area. It is largely open and there is not a lot of metal, so if there is excessive spring pressure and/or cam lift, cracks may appear or a lifter bore can break. Extreme high-horsepower cases have seen blocks split down the middle, but it is a rarity with street engines. A worthwhile upgrade for a performance rebuild is an SD Performance Mega Brace, which supports the lifter bores and greatly increases the strength of the block. (Photo Courtesy Butler Performance.)

CHAPTER 5

Inspect Cylinder Walls

4 With any engine that has seen high-mileage and hard use, the cylinder walls show wear and sometimes scoring. This particular block shows extreme scoring and needs an overbore. Feel for a notch or a ridge around the circumference of the top of the bore. One typically develops after many miles and/or hard use. If one has developed, the block needs to be overbored. Any visual damage also requires an overbore.
Use a telescoping micrometer to take precise measurements at the top middle and bottom of the bore. Compare these measurements to the stock specs to determine the amount of overbore required.
A .030-inch boring procedure usually cleans up any cylinder wall damage and allows enough material for a future rebuild. Even so, you need to determine the size of overbore before you order pistons, as another pass on the boring bar may result in pistons too small for your build.

Measure Engine Block

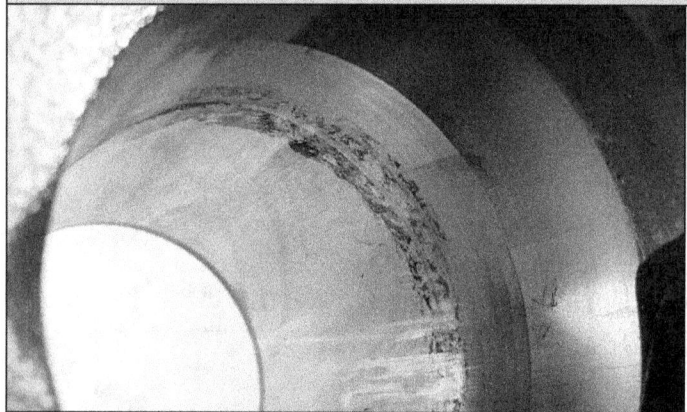

5 This cylinder wall has been deeply scored, which necessitates an engine overbore. Use a telescoping micrometer to measure the bore size at the top, bottom, and middle. If the block wall is too thin and it's been overbored to .060 inch, have it sleeved or replace the block. You can go with an OEM unit or an aftermarket block that supports much more horsepower than stock. But of course, then the engine is not factory correct and the engine package is worth far less.

Inspect Engine Internals

6 This engine has suffered severe engine damage. The entire main bearing is nearly worn away, and when it wore it sent metal throughout the entire engine that damaged the bearings, the connecting rods, crankshaft, and cylinder walls. Main bearings should never look like this, and if they do, expect to see damage throughout the entire engine.

ENGINE

Inspect Crankshaft Journal

7 Crankshaft journal damage is ugly, and this crankshaft may need to be replaced. Use a caliper micrometer to measure the journals near the fillets and also in the center of the journals to determine any variance or unusual wear pattern. The crankshaft main journal spec for a Pontiac V-8 is 3.00 or 3.25 inches. (Photo Courtesy Butler Performance)

8 Another view of this deeply scored crankshaft journal. Pontiac V-8 rod journal diameters measure 2.249 to 2.500 inches. These oil feed holes supply lubrication to the main bearings. Make sure the holes are chamfered to prevent stress risers from developing. (Photo Courtesy Butler Performance)

9 Metal from the main cap bearings have embedded in the crankshaft journals. Note that the oil holes in the crankshaft journal have been slightly chamfered. The crankshaft journals have suffered enormous damage and must be turned down. Oversized bearings must be fitted to the crankshaft. Crankshaft runout must be measured as well.

Inspect Connecting Rod Bearing Caps

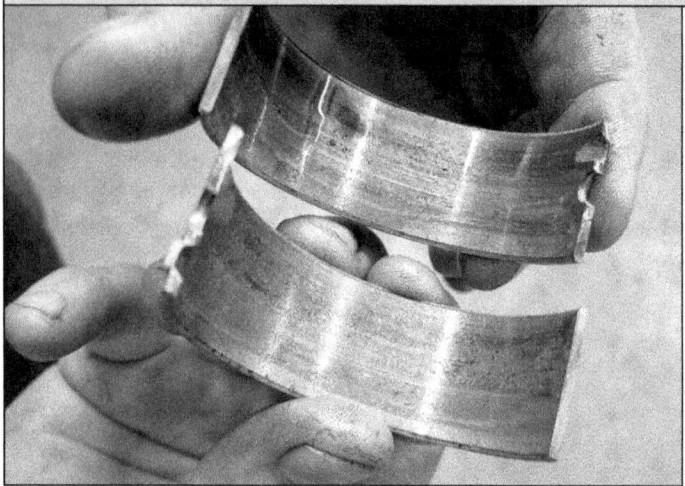

10 The connecting rod bearing caps are severly worn and remind me of the damage caused from debris that's sucked into the engine. On the other hand, if the connecting rod bearings are copper in color, that means the engine has probably suffered detonation. (Photo Courtesy Butler Performance)

Inspect Connecting Rods

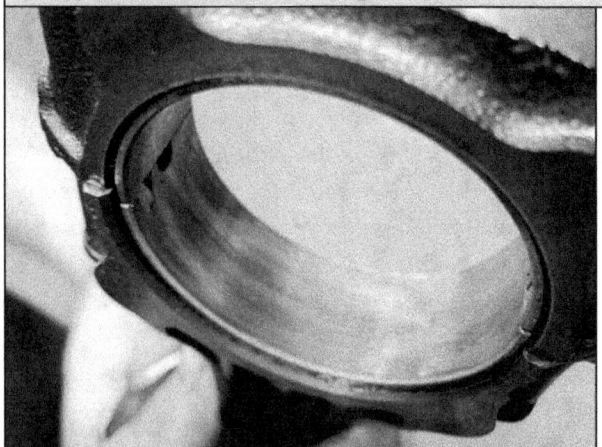

11 The connecting rods have suffered significant wear during their service inside the engine. The original I-beam rod can now be stress relieved and shot peened, but the surface area has suffered extreme wear and must be overbored. In addition, it requires larger rod bearings to accommodate the increased size. Any time you're rebuilding an engine you should invest the money and replace the stock rods with stronger forged rods. Rods are under enormous stress and heat cycling changes the metallurgy of the rods over time and weakens them. Most stock cast rods in a stock engine can last well over 100,000 miles, but if you're rebuilding an engine, buy new rods according to your performance goals. (Photo Courtesy Butler Performance)

Inspect Main Bearing Caps

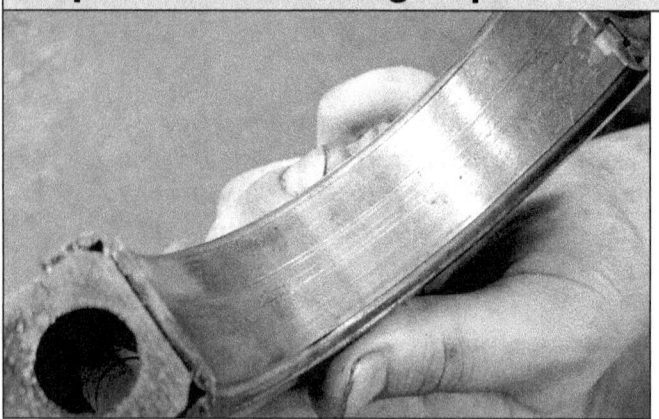

12 The damage to this main bearing cap is plainly evident and deep scratches indicate that debris or other material circulated through the engine and damaged the bearings. (Photo Courtesy Butler Performance)

13 After removing the main bearing caps, inspect the main bearings. As you can see, these bearings are heavily worn and must be replaced. The heavy grooves indicate that contamination at some point crept into the engine and caused this damage, or at some point there was oil starvation and the friction between the crank and the main bearings wore them out. Whenever you rebuild an engine, install new main bearing caps. (Photo Courtesy Butler Performance)

ENGINE

Inspect Bearings

14 The cam bearings on this engine also need to be replaced. This operation should be performed by your machine shop, as it will ensure they are square to the block, which is essential to proper camshaft break-in and longevity. (Photo Courtesy Butler Performance)

Engine Assembly

Install Main Bearing Caps

1 The Pontiac V-8 main bearing caps and connecting rods have been installed. This particular block has two-bolt main bearing caps. In three steps, torque the rear main bearing cap using a 15/16-inch socket. For the rear main bearing cap, torque to 40, 80, and then 120 ft-lbs. The rest of the main bearing caps are torqued to 80 ft-lbs in three steps. Once the main bearing caps have been torqued in place, verify that the crankshaft turns freely and there are no impediments. Turn the crankshaft over and feel for any restrictions. (Photo Courtesy Butler Performance)

Select Rods and Pistons

2 When rebuilding a Pontiac V-8, you can opt for the OEM cast pistons and I-beam rods. However, if you're horsepower target is significantly above stock, you need some high-performance engine internals, and those include forged H-beam rods and forged pistons. This piston-and-rod assembly can cope with up to 700 hp.

Inspect Piston

3 In preparation for installing the pistons in the block, you need to complete the piston and rod assemblies. Use a piston ring tool to install the three piston rings. Once the rings are installed, install the wrist pin and connecting rod to the piston. The pressed pin is stock type and the floating wrist pin uses a bronze bushing. Be sure that correct clearance is achieved for the particular type of wrist pin, which means carefully measuring the small end of the rod and the pin itself. The pistons and connecting rods must match the requirements of the particular rebuild. Therefore, the rod length and big-end diameter must match the crank journal measurements. The piston must have the correct clearance to the valves. If the piston comes in contact with the valves, catastrophic engine damage will occur.

Torque Connecting Rod Bolts

4 The piston-and-rod assemblies have been installed through the bores. And the connecting rod caps and nuts have been installed, so at this stage, it's time to correctly torque the rod nuts to the appropriate torque spec. First, check with the rod manufacturer for the correct torque spec. The OEM and ARP fastener torque specs are often different and incompatible, so if you use the wrong torque spec, you may strip the fasteners. The factory torque spec for connecting rods is 43 ft-lbs. Use a 9/16-inch socket on a click-type torque wrench and torque the nuts to 15, 30, and finally 43 ft-lbs for the OEM nuts.

Measure Piston-to-Valve Clearance

5 Once the pistons have been installed, you need to measure piston-to-valve clearance. Install the dial indicator and then rotate piston number-1 to TDC. At TDC, the dial indicator should measure no less than .080 inch for intake valves and .100 inch for exhausts. If the measurement is less than this, the crowns of the pistons may come in contact with the valves, and catastrophic engine failure can occur. Another way to take this measurement is by using modeling clay. Put the clay between the piston and the valve, rotate the engine, and then measure the depressed clay. Typically, using a stock-lift cam does not have an issue. If you are using an aftermarket cam profile, check with the manufacturer for recommendations on this critical clearance measurement. (Photo Courtesy Thomas A. DeMauro)

Install Dipstick Tube and Oil Pickup

6 Once the connecting rods have been properly installed, install the lower dipstick tube. Insert the tube into the intermediate tube in the block. It is held in place with the windage tray. After coating the threads with thread-lock adhesive, use a 1/2-inch socket to torque the windage tray bolts to 15 ft-lbs. At this stage you also need to install the oil pump. Place the pickup tube in a freezer overnight so it contracts. When it is cold enough, it slips inside the oil pump body. Use a 3/4-inch open-end wrench and a hammer to insert the tube into the oil pump body. Then slot the oil pump shaft into the oil pump drive in the block. Two bolts fasten the oil pump to the block; torque them to 30 ft-lbs. (Photo Courtesy Thomas A. DeMauro)

Prep Heads for Installation

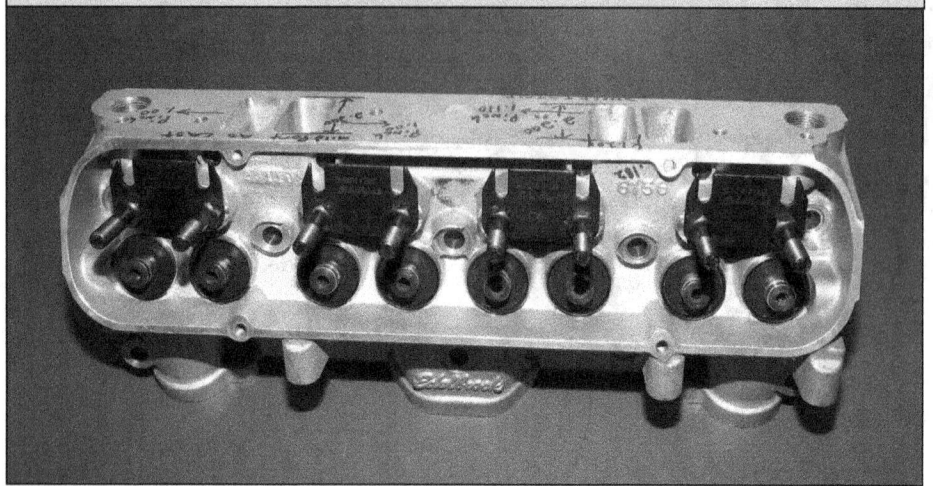

7 Prepare the Edelbrock D port head for installation. (Photo Courtesy Thomas A. DeMauro)

Torque Head Bolts

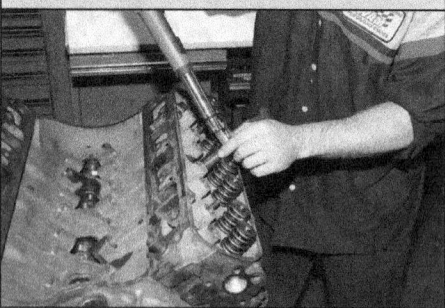

8 Smoothly and evenly apply force when torquing down the head. A jerking motion can cause inaccurate readings. The torque wrench will click when the proper amount of force is applied. (Photo Courtesy Rocky Rotella)

Install Manifold and Carb

9 Once the heads and valvetrain have been installed, you can install the valley pan and intake manifold. Place the intake manifold gasket over the studs and into position. Place a pinch of gasket sealer on each side to hold it in the desired centered position, so it doesn't move around. Lower the manifold into its correct position. By hand, thread all the manifold bolts until they are properly seated. Install the timing covers next and torque these bolts to 15 ft-lbs. Using an alternating torque pattern, tighten the manifold bolts to 40 ft-lbs. Then, place the carb gasket on the intake manifold. Slide the carb over the four manifold studs, and then torque the carb mounting nuts to 5 ft-lbs. (Photo Courtesy Thomas A. DeMauro)

Install Distributor

10 Unless you're restoring a 100-point concours car, you should install an HEI or similar distributor. A modern electronic distributor gives you far stronger and more consistent spark, and it doesn't wear over time and require adjustment like a points-type distributor. The distributor gear needs to be compatible with the cam, and many distributors require a different gear for a roller camshaft. On the compression stroke, place the number-1 piston at TDC. Align the distributor's rotor tip with the cylinder number-1 terminal. Make sure the distributor is sitting flush against the block and rotate the distributor to the right for the first time to run the engine. Then fasten the hold-down clamp with the appropriate socket. With a counterclockwise pattern, install the cap and route the plug wires to the correct cylinders in a 1-8-4-3-6-5-7-2 arrangement. (Photo Courtesy Thomas A. DeMauro)

Inspect Valvetrain

11 As you peer into the lifter valley, you can see the newly installed lifters and pushrods riding on the cam. Be sure to apply a good coat of the recommended break-in lube on the camshaft and lifters because you do not want the cam to prematurely wear on first start up of the engine. Submerge the lifters and rocker arms in 30W engine oil so these parts are thoroughly lubricated and prepared for operation. Flat-tappet cams require coating the face of the lifters and the lifter faces are definitely coated in this photo. The lifters should easily slide and move up and down in the bores. If there is any restriction or slop in the lifter bores, the lifter bores must be resurfaced. In addition, the pushrods should simply slide down through the heads and rest squarely on the lifters. There should be no impediments or restrictions, and the pushrods should match up with the stock stamped rocker arms. (Photo Courtesy Butler Performance)

Perform Final Procedures

12 The engine is near final assembly. A number of procedures must be done before it is completed, such as installing the carb linkages, belts, valve covers, and fuel pump. A factory-correct restoration includes using the correct factory paint, and this V-8 is adorned with Light Blue Metallic. No matter what engine paint is required for your particular Pontiac V-8, be sure that it's an accurate representation of the original paint. Do your research, look at message boards, talk to professional restorers, and best of all get recommendations from judges and club members so you use the best quality and most accurate paint available. If you get the paint wrong and you plan on entering the car in car shows, it will be judged harshly for this particular drawback. (Photo Courtesy Butler Performance)

CHAPTER 6

TRANSMISSION

Pontiac's transmission offerings for 1964–1974 GTOs were similar to the transmissions offered in other Pontiac and GM models. Transmissions were sourced from Muncie, Saginaw, GM's Hydra-Matic Division, and even Dearborn (Ford). In addition to 3- and 4-speed manual transmissions, Pontiac also offered 2- and 3-speed automatic transmissions.

When the GTO arrived in 1964, three manual transmissions were available: the standard Muncie 3-speed manual, an optional wide-ratio Muncie M-20 4-speed, and a close-ratio Muncie M-21 4-speed available only with 3.90:1 gears installed at the factory or with dealer-installed 4.33:1 gears. (There has been speculation as to whether the close-ratio 4-speed was actually installed in any 1964 GTOs, even though it is listed as available.) All manual transmissions used a 10.4-inch clutch featuring a single dry-friction plate, bent-finger diaphragm spring, and a 2,350-pound spring-loaded pressure plate. The clutch assembly was housed in an aluminum bellhousing, which also mounted the transmission.

The sole automatic transmission choice was an upgraded version of the 2-speed Super Turbine 300 that was available in the Tempest and LeMans series. The transmission was mated to the 215 inline six (I6) and the 326 and 389 V-8s in the General Motors A- and B-Body cars. This

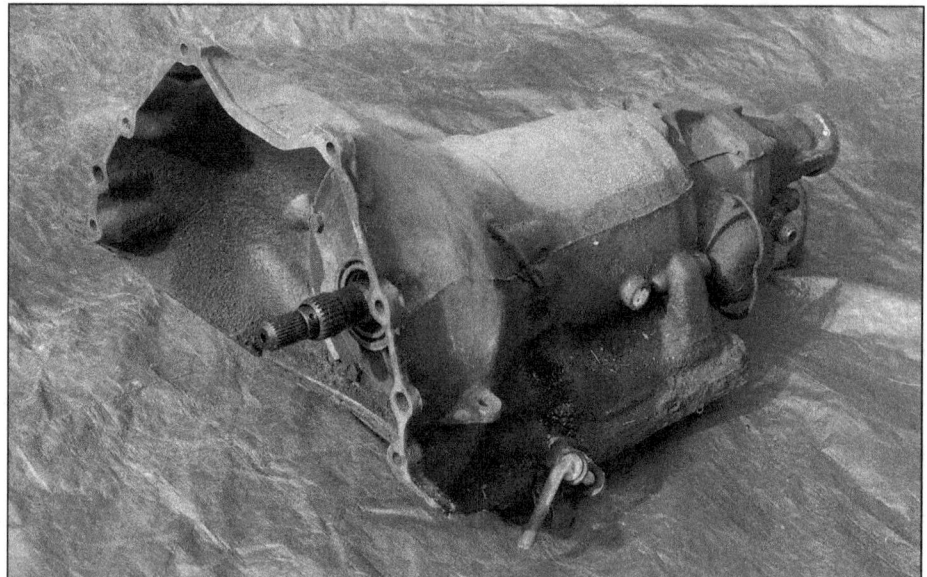

This Turbo 350 was originally installed in a 1975 LeMans, but it somehow found its way into a 1971 GTO. These transmissions have a long history of performance and durability, but of course, it's a non-numbers matching GTO, so it does not enhance the value. Unless you are a concours-style restorer, having a later-model transmission in your GTO is perfectly fine. This transmission will eventually be rebuilt with high-performance internals, given a slightly looser converter and re-installed. If you do decide to put a higher-stall-speed converter in your transmission, consult the manufacturer. Choosing too loose a converter hinders drivability and generates a lot of additional heat, which necessitates an auxiliary transmission cooler to prevent damage.

2-speed transmission was slotted into various models in the Buick, Oldsmobile, and Pontiac lines. The ST300 has a complex multi-angle torque converter and front and rear clutch packs. A planetary gear set, front band, and a clutch pack were dedicated for manual low gear and reverse. The transmission weighed 152 pounds, and it shifted from low to high gear at highway speeds. Though often mistaken for the Chevrolet Powerglide automatic, it is in fact a different transmission. Both transmissions have a certain level of similarity, but they are different designs.

Compared to other transmissions offered by competing manufacturers, such as Ford's C4 3-speed automatic and the clearly superior Chrysler 727 TorqueFlite, the Super Turbine 300 transmission sent performance enthusiasts straight to the manual transmission choices. History has treated the Super Turbine 300 very kindly and because of its design and wide gear ratio, but not many owners opt to rebuild the Super Turbine 300. Instead, many GTO owners install a Muncie or Turbo 400 if using a period-correct transmission, particularly with non-numbers-matching cars.

The transmission offerings were revised in 1965. The Muncie 3-speed manual was replaced with a Ford-built Dearborn Toploader 3-speed. This transmission is the strongest manual transmission ever put in a GTO and required a new transmission bellhousing to mount it. This transmission lineup continued unchanged through 1966.

The manual transmission lineup remained unchanged for 1967, but the performance-sapping Super Turbine 300 was finally dropped from the GTO lineup with the introduction of the legendary M-40 Turbo 400 Hydra-Matic. An extremely strong and durable 3-speed automatic, it was introduced in the 1964 Cadillacs and in the full-size offerings of other GM brands the following year. It featured gear ratios of 2.48, 1.48, and 1.00:1. The Turbo 400 is still regarded as one of the greatest transmissions ever developed, and even nearly half a century after its initial release, GM is still building the 4L85-E, a computer-controlled overdrive version of this transmission.

These basic transmission offerings were retained without changes other than coding until the 1970 model year. It was then that two significant changes were made. First, the introduction of the 455 HO V-8 required the substitution of a larger 11-inch clutch with an effective 2,750-pound pressure plate to handle the additional torque output of the long-stroke engine. It was similar in design to the standard 10.4-inch version. Only the 455 engines received the larger clutch.

The second major change was the retiring of the Dearborn Toploader 3-speed manual transmission. The new base transmission was a Muncie heavy-duty 3-speed manual transmission that was related to the Muncie 4-speeds.

The 1971 transmissions were the same as from previous year, except that the M-21 close-ratio 4-speed transmission was replaced with a stronger version of the Muncie close-ratio gearbox—the famous M-22 "Rock Crusher" 4-speed. It was the strongest 4-speed manual ever installed in a GTO. This lineup remained unchanged in 1972.

If you are looking for a transmission, be sure to get one with the proper Buick-Olds-Pontiac (B-O-P) bolt pattern, so the bellhousing easily bolts to the engine. Fortunately, the B-O-P bolt patterns is very easy to distinguish. The Chevy transmission features a bolt pattern with a triangular-shaped top (right), while the B-O-P version features a concave-shaped (left). Why the difference? The reason goes back to the 1940s, when the GM divisions were much more autonomous. The Powerglide was developed for release in the 1950 Chevys and used the same bolt pattern as the manual-transmissioned cars. Likewise, the Buick Dynaflow and Hydra-Matics were developed to bolt up to the existing Buick, Oldsmobile, and Pontiac engines of the day, which used manual transmissions and shared common bellhousing patterns.

CHAPTER 6

In the interest of fuel economy and emissions, some more restrictive changes were made in 1973. The close-ratio M-22 was dropped, leaving the wide-ratio M-20 as the only 4-speed transmission. Additionally, the optional 455 4-barrel V-8 was available only with the M-40 Turbo 400 automatic.

With the GTO moving from the A-Body platform to the X-Body, the transmission choices mirrored those available in the rest of the Ventura series and continued to use the 10.4-inch clutch system. The Muncie manual transmissions were replaced with lighter-duty Saginaw transmissions. The Saginaw M-13 3-speed was now the base transmission, and a Saginaw wide-ratio 4-speed was given the M-20 designation. The Turbo 400 used in previous years was replaced with the more compact M-38 Turbo 350 automatic.

Rebuild or Replace?

The transmission in your GTO may not be the original one from the factory. Many failed in the line of duty and were replaced under warranty or were swapped out later.

If your car is a numbers-matching example and you are doing a concours-style restoration, then retention and rebuilding of the original transmission is a priority, especially if it is a manual transmission, which not only has the application code, but also the VIN of the car stamped on it. As long as the case is in good condition, everything inside can be replaced without detracting from the car's value or hindering authenticity with regards to judging. Cars equipped with automatic transmissions are not judged as stringently as cars fitted with manual tranmissions, though the application code must be correct for the car to be considered numbers-matching.

If your car does not have its original transmission, it is still worth restoring and certainly it's less of an issue if the GTO is to become a regular driver. If the transmission you have is in good working order or is at least rebuildable, you can save quite a bit of money working with it. For example, if your GTO has a later Borg-Warner Super T-10 out of a Trans Am, or your 1965 Goat has a Turbo 350 instead of the 2-speed automatic, it really isn't a problem and if you don't want to search out a correct transmission that might actually hurt its drivability, it is perfectly acceptable to work with what you have.

Turbo Hydra-Matic 400

The Turbo Hydra-Matic is one of most prolific and highly regarded automatic transmissions of all time and certainly the GTO helped further its performance record. The Turbo 400 offered a breakthrough in performance from its predecessors and became favored among racers and hot rodders. Whether on the street or track, drivers could run larger and stickier tires and put the transmission under more stress, and it kept coming back for more. The Turbo 400 transmitted the power from 400 and 455 GTOs, but this legendary transmission also handled the shifting duties for many Buicks and Cadillacs.

A huge aftermarket offers every component for this transmission including torque converters, gear sets, gaskets, seals and bearings, so this transmission can be set up for virtually any application. You can find a wide range of high-performance parts, such as flexplates, planetary parts, torque converters, bellhousings, cases, and valve bodies. The Turbo 400 can also be rebuilt at home, but there isn't time or space to cover all the specifics here. However, the entire rebuilding process of the Turbo 400 is covered in *How to Rebuild and Modify GM Turbo 400 Transmissions* by Cliff Ruggles. A myriad of businesses offer every kind of performance part for the Turbo 400. Among the many reputable shops is TCI Transmissions and Cliff's High Performance.

Automatic Transmission Upgrades

When you need to upgrade your transmission, you can improve the one you have for better performance or you can swap in a newer, more modern unit for the advantages of better technology, strength, and an overdrive gear.

Most transmission manufacturers and remanufacturers offer shift-improvement kits, high-performance clutch packs, high-strength bands, and other components to increase transmission performance and durability. Additionally, a higher-stall converter can also be added without causing a visually incorrect situation. All of these upgrades can add up to a very noticeable performance gain. If you are restoring a numbers-matching GTO, this is a normal and accepted regimen that won't cause any deductions in points.

If you are not restoring a numbers-matching GTO, or not otherwise concerned with originality, you have many more options. Replacement transmissions are as close as your local rebuilder or a larger company, such as TCI, B&M, or other

Transmission Code

From 1964 to 1974, a variety of transmissions were offered in GTOs. These included automatics of Super-Turbine 300, Turbo Hydra-Matic 350, Turbo Hydra-Matic 400. A number of manual transmissions were also offered, including the Muncie M20, M21, and M22, Muncie 3-speed, Saginaw 4-speed, and Dearborn Toploader.

Year	Code	Transmission
1964	X	Muncie 3-speed
	W	Muncie wide-ratio 4-speed
	9	Muncie Close-ratio 4-speed
	J	Super Turbine 300 2-speed automatic
1965	X	Muncie 3-speed
	W	Muncie M-20 wide-ratio 4-speed
	8 or 9	Muncie M-21 close-ratio 4-speed
	J or 40/NA	Super Turbine 300 2-speed automatic
	T or 40/NB	Super Turbine 300 2-speed automatic with A/C
1966	S	Dearborn Toploader 3-speed
	W	Muncie M-20 wide-ratio 4-speed
	8	Muncie M-21 close-ratio 4-speed:
	J/NA	Super Turbine 300 2-speed automatic
1967	DB	Dearborn Toploader 3-speed
	FO	Muncie M-20 wide-ratio 4-speed
	FT	Muncie M-21 close-ratio 4-speed
		Turbo 400 3-speed Automatic
	PT	2-barrel
	PS	4-barrel early
	PX	4-barrel late
	PQ	Ram Air and HO
1968	DB	Dearborn Toploader 3-speed
	FO	Muncie M-20 wide-ratio 4-speed
	FT	Muncie M-21 close-ratio 4-speed
		Turbo 400 3-speed Automatic
	PT	2-barrel
	PX	Standard and HO:
	PQ	Ram Air
1969	DB	Dearborn Toploader 3-speed
	FO	Muncie M-20 wide-ratio 4-speed
	FT	Muncie M-21 close-ratio 4-speed
		Turbo 400 3-speed Automatic
	PT	2-barrel
	PX	Standard
	PQ	Ram Air

Note: VIN was stamped into transmission case for manual transmissions only.

Year	Code	Transmission
1970	DG	Muncie HD 3-speed
	DJ	Muncie M-20 wide-ratio 4-speed with 3.31 or 3.55 gears (455)
	DP	Muncie M-21 close-ratio 4-speed with 3.90 or 4.33 final drive (400)
	DL	Muncie M-21 close-ratio 4-speed
		Turbo 400 3-speed Automatic
	PY	Standard
	PD	Ram Air
	PR	455

Note: VIN was stamped into transmission case for manual transmissions only.

Year	Code	Transmission
1971	RM	Muncie HD 3-speed
	WT	Muncie M-20 wide-ratio 4-speed
	WO	Muncie M-22 close-ratio 4-speed
	PX	Turbo 400 3-speed automatic 400 w/ 3.08 or 3.23 final drive
	PY	400 w/ 3.55 final drive
	PW	455 D-port w/ 3.07 final drive
	PE	455 D-port w/ 3.31 final drive
	PQ	455 HO
1972	RM	Muncie HD 3-speed 3.23 or 3.55 final drive, 400 only
	WD	Muncie M-20 wide-ratio 4-speed
	WJ	Muncie M-22 close-ratio 4-speed
	PG	Turbo 400 3-speed automatic 400 w/ 3.08, 3.23 or 3.55 final drive
	PR	455 D-port w/ 3.08, 3.31, or 3.55 final drive
	PQ	455 HO w/ 3.07-3.55 final drive:
1973	TD 400 only	Early Muncie HD 3-speed
	RM 400 only	Late Muncie HD 3-speed
	UA 400 only	Early Muncie M-20 wide-ratio 4-speed
	WD 400 only	Late Muncie M-20 wide-ratio 4-speed
		Turbo 400 3-speed automatic
	PG	Early 400
	P2G	Late 400
	PR	Early 455
	P2R	Late 455
1974	TN	M15 Saginaw 3-speed manual
	WC	M20 Saginaw 4-speed manual
	ME	M38 Turbo 350 3-speed automatic

manufacturers. They are also stocked by Summit, Jegs, and other larger performance parts retailers. You can have a transmission custom-built to your specifications and price range, often cheaper than doing it yourself if you figure in the cost of the specialized tools needed to do the job. If you already have the skills and tools to rebuild a transmission yourself, great. Otherwise, it is perfectly acceptable to buy one ready to go. Again, if you are inexperienced in the area of transmission rebuilding, have a reputable builder prepare your transmission.

Super Turbine 300 to Turbo 350

If you have a 1964–1966 GTO that came with a 2-speed Super Turbine 300 automatic and aren't doing a concours restoration, a time-honored, inexpensive, and very easy swap is to replace that substandard 2-speed slushbox with a vastly superior Turbo 350 automatic out of a 1968 or newer Pontiac A- or F-Body. While not quite as beefy as the larger Turbo 400 in stock form, it does have less parasitic drag and it swaps into these early GTOs with minimal effort, using the existing crossmember and driveshaft without alteration. It is an option well worth looking into. If strength becomes an issue with your combination, beefed-up versions take up to 700 hp, so you're not really losing anything by using one.

Overdrives

Another option that makes a lot of sense with street-driven GTOs is to use an automatic overdrive transmission. Even if your car does not have aggressive gears, it is still advantageous from fuel economy, engine longevity, and highway comfort standpoints to have your Pontiac V-8 merrily loafing at 1,500 to 1,800 rpm at common highway speeds. If you have experienced driving a vintage GTO for sustained periods at 65 to 75 mph, you already know that without an overdrive, it tends to rev higher than necessary, negatively impacting gas mileage. If you're used to later-model cars, it's more than a little annoying; it's like you're waiting for the overdrive and lockup to kick in, yet it never does. Using an automatic overdrive transmission often increases the mileage to such an extent that it actually becomes a viable cross-country hauler. It is not unheard of to crack into the low-20-mpg range with an overdrive-equipped GTO, even with 400 or more horsepower.

Conversely, the use of an overdrive allows you to retain a modicum of driveability when using aggressive gears. With an overdrive of .70, a 3.90 becomes a 2.73:1, a 4.11 gear runs like a 2.87:1, and a 4.33 performs like a 3.03:1 final drive, adding a great deal of civility to a car with steep gears from the factory or for a more radical street/strip combination.

If you are going for the ideal combination of fit and beefiness in a factory transmission, look for the 2004R out of a 1986–1987 Buick Grand National or a 1989 Trans Am turbo. Though rare, they can be found from used parts vendors, eBay, racingjunk.com, or even craigslist.org, if you're lucky. These transmissions are desirable for two reasons. First, the Buick V-6 used in those cars and the Pontiac V-8 use the same bolt pattern, so adapting is not necessary. Second, they are strengthened to handle the power output of the turbocharged V-6s, which were actually as strong as most 1960s-era big-blocks. Many aftermarket versions are even further strengthened. If you strike out finding one of those fairly rare units, most automatic transmission builders can build you one that is beefed up to handle just about any power level.

Another option is to use the more common 700R4, used on many performance-oriented GM products from the late 1980s and early 1990s. Avoid units built before 1987, as they are substantially weaker than their later counterparts. They are easily upgraded with high-strength components from the later-model, computer-controlled version, the 4T65-E, which was offered in LT1 and LS1 powered cars. The 700R4 requires an adapter plate to mate it to the Pontiac V-8 and the crossmember must be modified or replaced with an aftermarket unit designed for the swap. The length of the driveshaft also needs to be modified.

Last, I would be remiss if I didn't mention the 4L80-E, the late-model, computer-controlled version of the Turbo 400 automatic. This is a more complicated and more expensive alternative to the 2004R and the 700R4, but it does offer the advantage of a stand-alone computer that is not tied to any engine controls. The twist is that the 4L80-E was offered behind Diesel engines in Chevy and GMC pickups. Because of the Diesel engine's lack of an ignition system, that combination needed a transmission controller that wasn't dependent on any engine electronics. Once this controller is reprogrammed with shift patterns suited to a carbureted V-8, this transmission becomes a very attractive choice, though it is more expensive than the others and

TRANSMISSION

requires an adapter and driveshaft mods to work in a GTO chassis. It may also require some transmission tunnel mods to fit, as it is physically a very large transmission.

Manual Transmissions

Owners of manual-transmission GTOs enjoy a great deal of aftermarket support, with rebuilding and exchange services available for Muncie, Saginaw, and Dearborn transmissions on both local and nationals levels. Additionally, several companies restore Hurst shifters. Rather than recommend specific companies to do these operations, this is a good area to get the opinions and recommendations of local club members. The reasons are twofold. One, it is likely that you will find someone right in your local club chapter or your area who can do a great job for not a lot of money, or may be willing to trade out the job for parts or other non-cash consideration. The other reason is that the cast of characters is constantly changing, especially in the Hurst shifter rebuilding world. Some of the best guys only do a few each year or are not consistently available. Hurst rebuilds shifters as well, so that is an option.

Muncie 4-Speed

The regular productions codes identify an M-20, M-21, and M-22. Of the regular production codes, one particular Muncie 4-speed type appears. A properly set up M-22 Rock Crusher transmits up to 700 hp, so this stout transmission is a wise choice for high-performance applications as well as authenticity. But that is not a definitive method for positively identifying the transmission.

On the edge of the main case is a number stamping that identifies the Muncie gearbox as well as state the year and month it was made. For Muncies, the serial number starts with the letter P. The serial number sequence from 1963 to 1966 started with the month and then the day of the month. For August 16, 1963, the serial number is P0816.

However, from 1967–1968 the year designation was first in the serial number sequence followed by the letter for the particular month. The third digit represents the month. The first month in the year is A, so the third month in the year is C. The third day in the month is represented as 03 So, this gearbox reads P7C03.

Several businesses offer high-quality rebuild kits for the Muncie 4-speed transmissions, including 5speeds.com and T&B Transmission & Gear. These businesses offer a full range of gears, synchros, gaskets, mainshaft bearings, and even a full case, so you can build a Muncie 4-speed from the ground up or you can rebuild one from your GTO. T&B and 5speeds.com offers the M-22 Rock Crusher Supercase. T&B offers a complete Muncie 4-speed and it features the new Masiero Italian gearsets, Muncie Supercase, super tailhousing, iron midplate, and roller bearing sidecover. Medatronics Corporation at 5speeds.com offers M-22 complete transmission with the finest components from Autogear. Like the T&B M-22, the Medatronics sold M-22 exclusively uses Masiero gears. When buying a rebuild kit or an entire gearbox, be sure to buy these components from a reputable source. Some of the Muncie components you see Online are made to substandard tolerances and are of inexpensive materials. You put yourself at risk of failure if you build your gearbox with these components.

Muncie 4-Speed Torque Specifications

Component	Torque (ft-lbs)
Bearing retainer nut	40
Input shaft retainer bolts	20
Side cover bolts	18
Upper tailshaft to main case bolts	20
Lower tailshaft to main case bolts	30
Filler plug	30
Speedometer gear retainer bolt	4

Required Tools

- SAE wrench or socket set
- Various flat-blade screwdrivers or prybars
- Soft-face mallet
- Standard hammer
- Gasket scraper
- 3/16-inch-diameter punch
- Hydraulic press
- Length of 1 3/4-inch-diameter steel pipe
- Length of 1 5/8-inch-diameter steel pipe
- 3/4-inch diameter steel dowel
- Bearing, race, and seal driver set
- Bearing separator tool
- Snap-ring pliers, external, notched tip
- Clutch-gear bearing retainer tool

CHAPTER 6

This 1969 Muncie M-20 4-speed was located and purchased for use in a non-numbers-matching 1969 GTO and was treated to a rebuild kit from Midwest Transmission Supply. The kit retails for about $110 and once installed provides the M-20 with like-new operation and a 100,000-mile service life. The input shaft goes to the cluster gear. The cluster is mated to all the speed gears, first, second, third, and fourth. The speed gears are independent of the mainshaft. A Muncie 4-speed works best when the synchro assemblies are precisely assembled and work in harmony with the gear cone and slider. The disassembly and assembly of the M-20 is similar to that of the M-21 and the M-22 Rock Crusher. The big difference between the M-22 and the other Muncie 4-speeds is that the first, second, and third gears are helical cut so that the gearbox makes its signature whine. Remove the side cover by using a hammer and a punch to drive out the pin that retains the reverse shifter shaft. Once the pin has been driven out, lift off the cover. (Photo Courtesy Rocky Rotella)

The transmission rebuild kit carries PN BK116WS and is designed to work with 1967–1974 Muncie 4-speeds. This synchro-and-bearing kit includes bronze blocker rings, high-quality roller bearings, and all necessary gaskets and seals. (Photo Courtesy Rocky Rotella)

Whenever restoring a GTO, have a shop manual to refer to, as it contains diagrams and exploded views of the transmission that greatly aid in transmission disassembly and re-assembly. In addition to original versions being available on eBay, Craigslist, Amazon, and other similar sources, check with restoration parts houses for paper versions. Also, digital versions of the GM shop manual from Detroit Iron also cover your particular transmission. (Photo Courtesy Detroit Iron)

Muncie 4-Speed Disassembly

Place Shift Shafts in Forward Position

1 To begin the rebuild, use a 9/16-inch wrench to remove the four bolts that secure the clutch gear bearing retainer. The bearing-retainer nut, which is a left-hand thread, follows both shift shafts on the case cover. The shift shafts are placed in the forward position, locking the transmission into gear. Midwest Transmission Supply offers a J-tool (PN WT297-W) to facilitate the job. It retails for about $40. (Photo Courtesy General Motors. Used with Permission, GM Media Archive)

Remove Case Cover

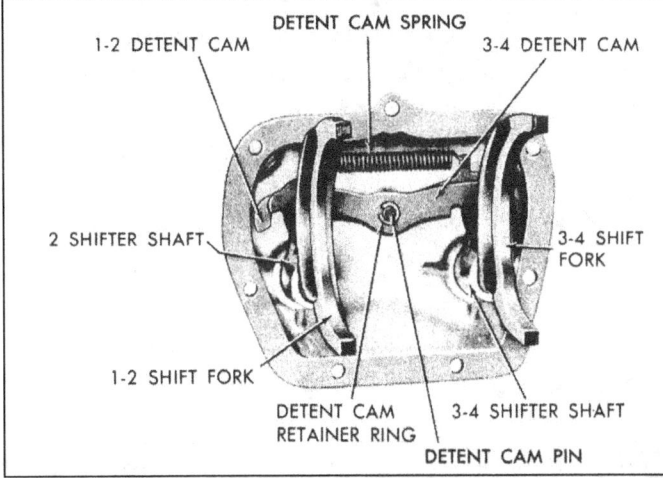

2 Before removing the case-cover assembly, place the transmission into second gear by leaving the rear shift shaft (on the case cover) in the forward position and moving the front shaft to the center. Remove all seven case-cover retaining bolts with a 1/2-inch wrench, lift the assembly away from the unit, and set it aside. (Photo Courtesy General Motors. Used with Permission, GM Media Archive)

Remove Speedometer Gear

3 Remove the speedometer gear fitting using a 7/16-inch wrench, which is required to take off its retaining bolt. Pull it out of the case and examine it. Make sure the nylon gear is in good condition and is not damaged. Set it aside for the re-assembly process. (Photo Courtesy Rocky Rotella)

Remove Reverse Gear Lock Pin

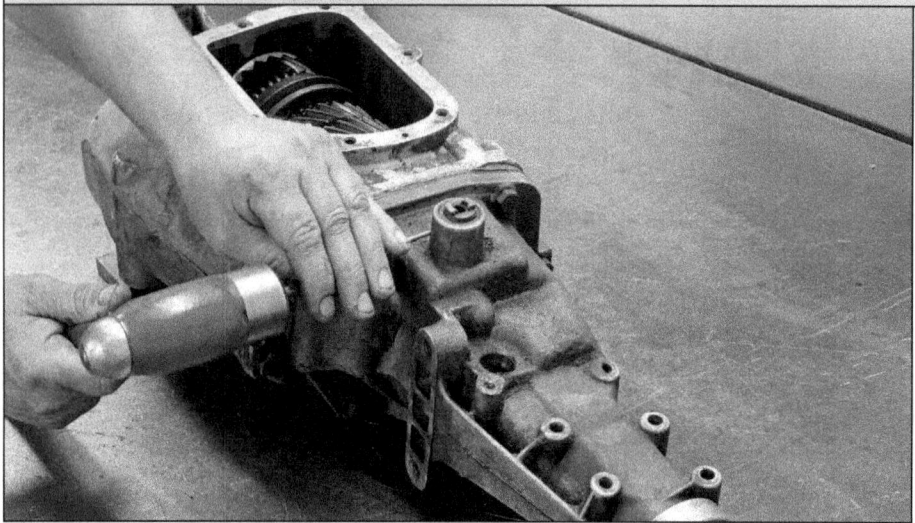

4 Look down inside the case at the mainshaft gear and the counter gear. If there has been a gear box failure and it's locked up, you can see the damage to the gear sets. Use a 3/16-inch-diameter punch to drive the reverse-gear lock pin upward and out of the rear extension (tailshaft). *(Photo Courtesy Rocky Rotella)*

Place Transmission in Neutral

5 After removing the case cover, place the transmission in neutral by manually positioning the rear synchronizer sleeve so the teeth of all four bronze synchronizer rings are visible. *(Photo Courtesy Rocky Rotella)*

Separate Main Case and Tail Case

6 Thread a bolt into the reverse shift shaft and pull the reverse shift shaft outward about 1/2 inch, freeing the reverse shift fork from the reverse gear. The rear extension is attached to the main case assembly by six bolts, all of which must be removed with either a 9/16- or 5/8-inch wrench. A few blows from a soft mallet separates the main case assembly and the tail case, which is rotated away and set aside. *(Photo Courtesy Rocky Rotella)*

Remove Mainshaft from Case

7 Extract the rear-bearing retainer and mainshaft assembly, including the reverse idler gear, from the main case. Though still intact here, the main drive gearshaft (or input shaft) simply pulls away from the mainshaft, but most likely remains in the main case, where it can be gently tapped out of its main bearing and into the main case. It can also be tapped outward, along with its bearing, and be removed as a unit. (Photo Courtesy Rocky Rotella)

Remove Steel Drive Gear

8 The speedometer's steel drive gear is pressed onto the mainshaft and must be pulled off for complete disassembly. Use a bearing separator tool (available from Mac Tools and other sources) to complete the task. Slide the mainshaft reverse gear off the mainshaft and pull the reverse idler shaft straight out. (Photo Courtesy Rocky Rotella)

Inspect Mainshaft Gears

9 The mainshaft and gear cluster are seen here. Inspect the gears for chipping, excessive wear, or other visible imperfections. It is a lot easier to replace any necessary parts at this time, than take the cluster out of the case a second time. (Photo Courtesy Rocky Rotella)

Remove Rear Bearing Snap Ring

10 To disassemble the mainshaft, use a pair of external snap-ring pliers to remove the rear-bearing retainer snap ring located on the rear end of the mainshaft. (Photo Courtesy Rocky Rotella)

Press Mainshaft through Bearing

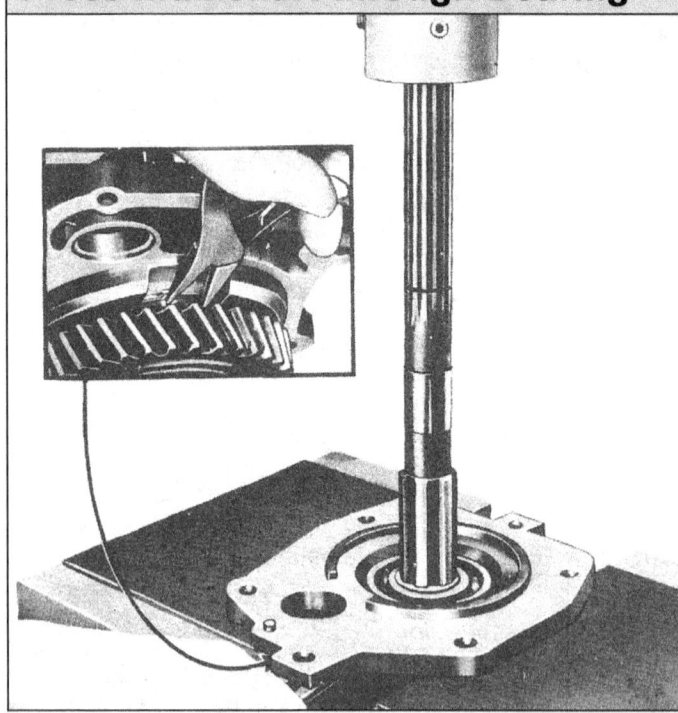

11 Insert the mainshaft assembly into a hydraulic press; while supporting the rear-bearing retainer, spread the snap ring, and press the mainshaft through the rear bearing, separating the two. The procedure is the same as the one illustrated here from the service manual. (Photo Courtesy General Motors. Used with Permission, GM Media Archive)

Disassemble Mainshaft

12 Using snap-ring pliers and working front to rear, remove the front snap ring that retains the third- and fourth-gear synchronizer sleeve and third gear. (The synchronizer sleeves and hubs are matched pairs, so be sure to keep them oriented correctly.) (Photo Courtesy Rocky Rotella)

TRANSMISSION

Disassemble Mainshaft (Continued)

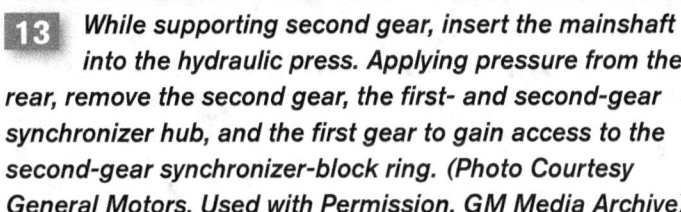

13 While supporting second gear, insert the mainshaft into the hydraulic press. Applying pressure from the rear, remove the second gear, the first- and second-gear synchronizer hub, and the first gear to gain access to the second-gear synchronizer-block ring. (Photo Courtesy General Motors. Used with Permission, GM Media Archive)

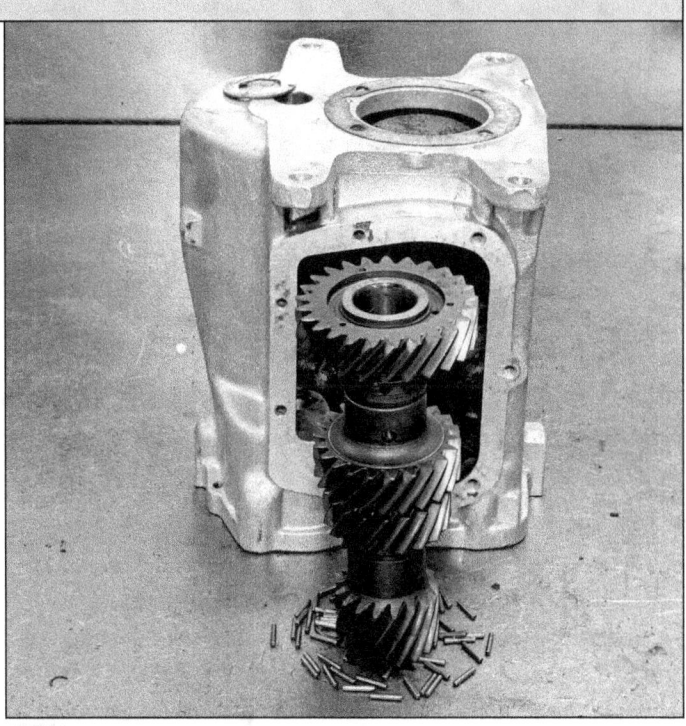

14 Using a 3/4-inch-diameter metal dowel and a hydraulic press, remove the countershaft gear pin by applying pressure from front to rear. This allows removal of the countershaft gear, its 112 roller bearings, and its thrust washers, as well as the front reverse idler gear and its thrust washers. Set all parts into a parts washer for a thorough cleaning. The main drive gear and its bearing were already removed from the main case. (Photo Courtesy Rocky Rotella)

Decode Transmission ID

15 Here is an example of the coding found on a manual transmission: P9E01A. It breaks down as follows: P=Muncie Plant; 9=1969; E=May; 01=1st day of the month; A=M-20 wide-ratio. (Photo Courtesy Rocky Rotella)

16 The original vehicle's VIN is typically stamped on the top of the main case in Muncie applications and, in this particular case, it's broken down as follows: 2=Pontiac Motor Division; 9=1969; R=Arlington, Texas, assembly plant; 175134=vehicle identification number. This unit appears to be from a 1969 Pontiac A-Body, most likely from a GTO, but possibly from a Tempest, Custom S, or LeMans. (Photo Courtesy Rocky Rotella)

Muncie 4-Speed Assembly

Press On Second Gear

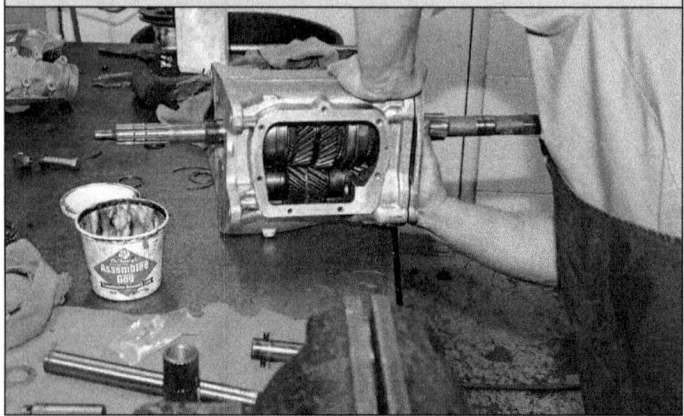

1 After visually inspecting all the parts that could be reused for signs of excessive wear or fatigue, cut a suitable length of 1¾-inch-diameter steel pipe to help press the second gear, its bronze synchronizer-block ring, and the first- and second-gear synchronizer clutch assembly (synchronizer hub and sliding sleeve) onto the mainshaft. (Retain the shifting keys on the synchronizer hub with heavy bearing grease.) Once that is completed, install the retaining springs. (Photo Courtesy Rocky Rotella)

Press On First Gear

2 Continue with the first-gear synchronizer-block ring and first gear. Use lightweight engine oil for lubrication. (Photo Courtesy Rocky Rotella)

Install New Rear Bearing

3 Tap a new rear bearing in place using a 1⅝-inch-diameter pipe and then install the rear-bearing retainer. Spread the front snap ring, sliding it over the rear of the mainshaft and fully seating it against first gear. Select a rear-bearing retainer snap ring that reduces clearance between the snap ring and the rear-bearing face to a maximum of .005 inch. This limits mainshaft endplay when under load, much like an engine's thrust bearing. (Photo Courtesy Rocky Rotella)

Install Third and Fourth Gear Synchro

4 The third gear and the third- and fourth-gear synchronizer clutch assembly and snap ring follow. Set the completed mainshaft assembly aside for the time being while the main case is attended to. (Photo Courtesy Rocky Rotella)

Install Countershaft Roller Bearings

5 Use a liberal amount of heavy bearing grease to retain the countershaft gear's roller bearings and bearing washers. This procedure includes loading a .050-inch washer in one end, followed by a row of 28 roller bearings, another washer, 28 more roller bearings, and the last washer. (Photo Courtesy Rocky Rotella)

6 Perform the same steps on the countershaft's opposite end until a total of 112 roller bearings are installed. (Photo Courtesy Rocky Rotella)

Place Countershaft Gear in Main Case

7 Set the countershaft gear and thrust washers into the main case. Using a hydraulic press, gently press the countershaft pin into the case from the rear. (Photo Courtesy Rocky Rotella)

Insert Pin in Main Case

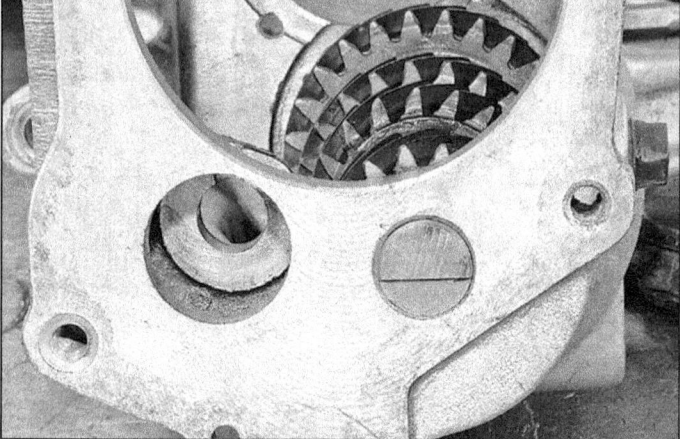

8 The pin should be flush with the front of the case, and its stepped portion should face downward to clear the rear-bearing support. Check the countershaft gear endplay with a dial indicator if old thrust washers are reused. It shouldn't exceed .025 inch. If it does, replace the washers. (Photo Courtesy Rocky Rotella)

Install Roller Bearings in Mainshaft

9 In this diagram from the service manual, heavy bearing grease is used to retain 17 new roller bearings and a retaining cage into the main drive gear cavity before installing the unit onto the nose of the mainshaft. (Photo Courtesy General Motors. Used with Permission, GM Media Archive)

Install New Gasket

10 Install a new gasket onto the front of the rear-bearing support, placing the fourth-gear synchronizing ring on the main drive gear, sliding the 3-4 synchronizing clutch sleeve forward into the fourth-speed detent position, and insert the entire mainshaft assembly into the main case. This positions the main-bearing retainer so that the guide pin in it aligns with the hole in the case. Tap it into place. (Photo Courtesy Rocky Rotella)

Install Front Reverse Idler Gear

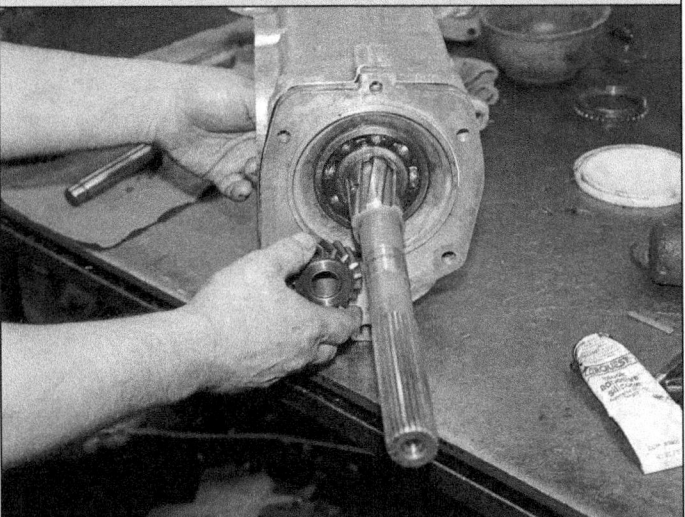

11 With the unit loosely assembled, install the front reverse idler gear (its tanged thrust washer into the main case) and insert the rear reverse idler gear through the rear-bearing support. (Photo Courtesy Rocky Rotella)

Orient Front Reverse Idler Gear

12 This photo was taken prior to the installation of the front reverse idler gear on the mainshaft assembly. It shows the correct orientation of the front reverse idler gear's forward thrust washer. (Photo Courtesy Rocky Rotella)

Insert Reverse Idler Gear

13 Insert the rear reverse idler gear thrust washer and reverse idler shaft. Note the position of the shaft's lock pin; it corresponds with a notch in the rear extension. (Photo Courtesy Rocky Rotella)

Install Reverse Shift Shaft Seal and Parts

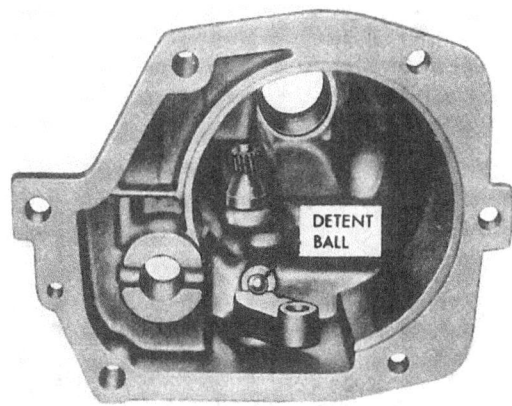

14 During disassembly, you removed the reverse shift fork and drove the reverse shift shaft into the extension housing (the reverse shifter shaft detent ball and spring fell out). Replace the reverse shift shaft seal before reinstalling the spring-and-detent-ball assembly back into the housing (shown is the assembled housing). With a small flat-blade screwdriver, reinstall the reverse shift shaft and shift fork, then remove the existing bushing in the rear extension and tap the replacement into place with a race driver. Next, install the rear extension oil seal. (Photo Courtesy General Motors. Used with Permission, GM Media Archive)

Install Reverse Gear and Speedometer Drive Gear

15 Slide the reverse gear onto the mainshaft and drive the speedometer drive gear into place using a length of steel pipe. According to the Pontiac service manual, the drive gear's proper location is roughly 6.15 inches from the rear of the shaft. Also install the rear extension gasket at this time. (Photo Courtesy Rocky Rotella)

Install Tail Case

16 Pulling the reverse shifter shaft outward, slide the rear extension over the mainshaft while aligning all the internal components. Give the six retaining bolts a coating of blue thread locker and tighten them to the suggested torque spec. Apply torque evenly to the case during tightening. The upper three bolts receive 20 ft-lbs of torque, and the lower three receive 30 ft-lbs. (Photo Courtesy Rocky Rotella)

Install Reverse Shaft and Speedometer Gear Fitting

17 Install the reverse shift shaft lock-pin and speedometer gear fitting. Use a new O-ring to ensure proper sealing. (Photo Courtesy Rocky Rotella)

Install Roller Bearing

18 Install a new roller bearing and snap ring onto the main drive gear. *(Photo Courtesy Rocky Rotella)*

Install Case Cover

19 With the shift shafts and shift forks in place, slide the third-and-fourth gear synchronizer sleeve into the neutral position while leaving the first- and second-assembly in the forward position. From there, position the case-cover gasket and lower the case cover into place. *(Photo Courtesy Rocky Rotella)*

Install Case Cover Bolts

20 Tighten the case cover's seven retaining bolts to 18 ft-lbs of torque using a crisscross pattern. *(Photo Courtesy Rocky Rotella)*

Install Bearing-Retainer Nut

21 After sliding both mainshaft synchronizer sleeves forward to lock the transmission into opposing gears, thread the bearing-retainer nut onto the main drive gear. Although using the correct tool (shown earlier) is preferable, a flat-blade screwdriver and hammer, or a pipe wrench, can also be used to gently walk it around the main drive gear to tighten. Remember, it's left-hand thread, and the correct torque spec is 40 ft-lbs. The nut can also be staked with the corresponding holes in the main drive gear to securely lock it into place. *(Photo Courtesy Rocky Rotella)*

Install Clutch Gear Bearing Retainer

22 *Install a new gasket on the clutch gear bearing retainer before sliding it over the main drive gear. Note the machined hole points toward the bottom. This ensures that the retainer's internal oil drain is positioned correctly. Apply thread locker to the four retaining bolts and tighten each to 20 ft-lbs of torque. (Photo Courtesy Rocky Rotella)*

Install Seals on Case Cover

23 *The forward shift forks and shifter shafts have been removed from the case cover during disassembly. Use a ballpeen hammer and a socket that matches the diameter of the new seals. Then tap the new seals into place on the shift fork cover. (Photo Courtesy Rocky Rotella)*

Manual Overdrives

If you are looking for a fifth or sixth gear for your GTO, there are two main options available. The first is the Tremec 5-speed transmission, which is an aftermarket transmission designed to be a bolt-in replacement for a 3- or 4-speed GM transmission. It bolts up to a factory bellhousing and is the same overall length as a factory transmission, so this transmission is a viable candidate for a street-driven GTO.

The other option is the Tremec T-56 6-speed manual transmission. This is an expensive upgrade for a GTO, or any A-Body for that matter. The most desirable version is from the Dodge Viper and most aftermarket versions use the Viper internals for higher strength. The T-56 should be considered only for a Pro-Touring style of build, as it requires extensive transmission tunnel modification. Really, a new tunnel needs to be fabricated and truth be told, you're cutting the car up pretty well at this

Fill Case with Fluid

24 There are some transmission builders who feel that synthetic lubricant was never intended for use with vintage manual transmissions. Conventional lubricants, such as this 75W-90 product from Valvoline, seem to be the choice of those professionals. The M-20 Muncie's capacity is 2.5 pints. (Photo Courtesy Rocky Rotella)

Place the transmission into each of its four forward gears as well as reverse and turn the main drive gear to ensure the unit is free of any internal binding. With a day's work and about $150 in parts, this completely rebuilt Muncie is ready for service. It now operates quietly and shifts as it was intended. As mentioned earlier, if this procedure seems too dificult, it is acceptable to have this portion of your restoration farmed out. (Photo Courtesy Rocky Rotella)

point. Add a custom bellhousing/scattershield, as well as a new crossmember, and you're talking about a big-ticket upgrade.

Adapting this transmission to a traditional Pontiac V-8 is possible, but if you are seriously considering it, please re-evaluate your restoration mission statement, as this is a pretty serious investment and the course of your project will change significantly.

A T-56 becomes a much more viable alternative if you are re-powering your GTO with a GM LS-series engine, like the original LS1 used in the 1998–2002 Firebird/Camaro or the later LS2 used in the 2005–2006 GTO. You can buy the engine and transmission together, along with the computer system, and do it as a complete conversion. I don't mean to upset any traditional Pontiac V-8 fans who would be against a corporate V-8 transplant, but this information is included in the interest of providing a complete description of the options available. If the idea of an LS-powered GTO is appealing to you, there are other books out there that describe this path more completely.

CHAPTER 7

SUSPENSION

The 1964–1974 GTO, though offered in three distinct generations, used a front suspension system that was very similar in design and componentry. The conventional independent front suspension design featured upper and lower control arms with coil springs and tube shocks. The steering system used a recirculating ball mechanism and hydraulic power assist was optional. The 1964–1972 cars used the same basic system, varying only in spring rates, shock specs, and steering gear-ratios. All used common upper and lower control arms and the spindle designs varied only by the braking systems offered.

The 1973 GTO used an upgraded version of the GM independent front suspension system, which was shared with the second-generation Firebird and the 1971-and-up full-size cars, differing only in spring rates, bushing hardness, and shock valving. The newer design offered improved bump-steer performance and was engineered from the beginning for use with disc brakes and radial tires, though radials weren't used across the board right away.

A properly rebuilt suspension, such as the one in Sam Ranalli's 1969 Judge, shows how form and function can merge into a visually-pleasing system that performs just as it did on a new car fresh from the factory. The bushings are new and the finishes are correct, but in this case, originality was the goal, so factory-installed items that might be simply replaced in a driver restoration were rebuilt. Determining how much should be kept and reused and how much needs to be replaced varies by the car, the level of restoration, and the intended use. For a daily driver or a weekend car, newer or reproduction pieces are suitable because most parts have a stock appearance and generally cost less than rebuilding the original parts. However, if it is a concours restoration, originality is needed for the highest point totals in competition and factory-supplied parts are needed.

SUSPENSION

Of all the A-Body GTOs, the 1973 is easily the best handling, especially if the optional heavy-duty suspension was ordered. Even by modern standards, these cars were very capable handlers and were on par with the Trans Ams of that era. If you have one of these cars, you really do not need to do much more than add stiffer bushings and performance-oriented shocks; they really were that good.

The 1974 GTO used a front suspension system that was similar in design to the 1967–1969 Firebird, which shared the same basic floorpan and firewall. That system was in turn similar to what was used on the 1964–1972 GTO, in terms of control arm design and basic dimensions.

The rear suspension on the 1964–1972 GTOs was shared with other GM A-Bodies. The trailing-arm-design suspension featured upper and longer lower control arms, coil springs, and tube shocks locating a solid rear axle. The upper arms are triangulated to keep lateral axle deflection to a minimum. This rear suspension was very capable in terms of getting the abundant torque of the Pontiac V-8 to the ground. In fact, very little was needed to prep it for drag-racing duty. To this day, many 10-second GTO drag cars employ a stock suspension, except for springs and shocks.

The 1973 rear suspension, similar to the front, was an upgraded version of the previous generation. Owing to its very stout design, this basic suspension was used in A-Bodies through 1977 and under the 1977–1996 full-size GM cars such as the Buick Roadmaster and Chevy Caprice and Impala SS.

The 1974 GTO, based on the X-Body platform, was the sole unibody version of the original GTOs. It shared its parallel leaf-spring rear suspension design with its GM siblings, Chevy Nova, Olds Omega, Buick Apollo, as well as the 1967–1981 Camaros and Firebirds. As a benefit, there is a lot of commonality, so the highest-performance rear-suspension components from a late Gen II WS6 Trans Am can easily be integrated into a 1974 GTO and still look authentic. It's a point to keep in mind.

Restore Safety, Functionality and Appearance

The proper restoration of the suspension of your GTO is an important safety and performance consideration. Making sure all systems are working as designed is an important step but you cannot ignore the effects of 40 or more years of exposure to the elements. Rust-belt cars can experience heavy enough corrosion to where upper and lower control arms become too rusted to re-use. Even Southwestern cars experience deterioration.

In dry climates, items such as bushings, suspension stops, and rubber mounts dry up, crack, and deteriorate, and the suspension no longer works as it is designed. You hear things like squeaks, groans, and clunking sounds that come from suspension components not properly isolated from the frame. While these items are important from safety and performance standpoints, the good news is that returning your suspension to its original condition and operation is not terribly difficult but requires quite a bit of disassembly.

If the restoration is a concours type with originality and correctness a top priority, you have the responsibility to retain as much of the original suspension componentry as possible. The rebuilding of the original pieces

A freshly-rebuilt and correctly-date-coded steering box wins points with the concours judges, but there could be more going on here than a stock rebuild. Companies, such as Power Steering Services, can rebuild your steering box to exactly new and correct condition, or they can upgrade the internals with faster ratios from later, high-performance GM offerings such as a WS6 Trans Am or Impala Super Sport. Best of all, these changes do not hinder collector value because they go completely undetected, so even a concours judge wouldn't be the wiser. It is an option that is highly recommended if the restoration is for a car that will be driven.

HOW TO RESTORE YOUR PONTIAC GTO 1964–1974

CHAPTER 7

is also necessary, and replacement of components is to be limited to those items that were too damaged or worn to refurbish. Those pieces must be replaced with correct, original NOS pieces or used items in rebuildable condition. In cases where the parts in question are date-coded, properly dated replacements are necessary.

None of that criteria is necessary with a driver-type restoration. If it is more cost-effective to rebuild what you have, then that is what you should do. If a reproduction item is available, it could be a financially viable alternative. Last, a better-performing, later-model component, such as a steering box, could be used with little, if any, loss of visible authenticity. When it comes to suspensions, there are a lot of minor modifications that can be made to greatly improve handling, overall performance, and safety. If originality and authenticity are secondary to performance, these relatively minor tweaks can reap large benefits and make your GTO handle much like a later-model relative, such as a 1994–1996 Impala SS, as there is a lot more commonality under the skin than you may realize.

Inspection and Evaluation

If possible, take the time to drive your GTO and make notes on its handling qualities. Are there any obvious problems? Is there vibration, noise, or other undesirable qualities? Do you feel or hear any clunking? Does the car track straight or does it pull excessively to one side? Is there a lot of play in the steering? Does the car bounce around when going over bumps? These behaviors are indicators of specific problems.

For example, clunking sounds are usually from suspension bushings that have failed. Rattling sounds going over bumps or excessive body lean could indicate broken sway-bar mounts. Steering play (turning the steering wheel without a corresponding change in the car's direction) could indicate a worn steering box, steering-arm damage or wear, or a combination of both. Porpoising indicates worn-out shock absorbers. Evaluate your GTO's driving traits to get an idea of what it needs and get a head start on any surprises that might pop up.

After driving the car and taking notes on its handling, it is time to go a bit deeper. With your car on a lift, begin by checking the ball joints for excessive play and wear. Most shops just stick a crowbar between a control arm and the steering knuckle

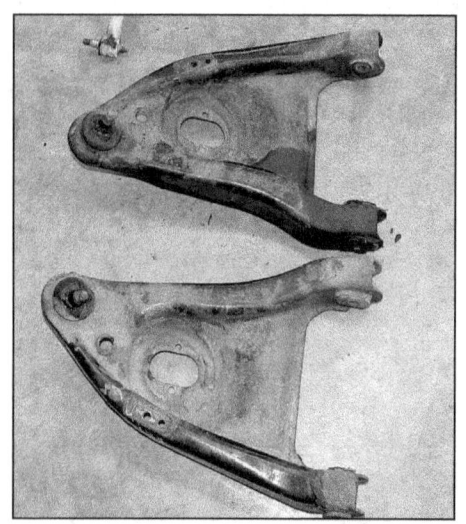

Once the main suspension components, such as the upper and lower control arms, are off the car and disassembled, cleaning and painting can commence. Depending on the amount of corrosion, a wire brush, sandblasting, or even electrolytic rust removal can be used to remove rust, but I recommend that you do not acid dip these components. Acid can make the metal brittle, which could lead to stress cracks. Once free of grease and rust, they can be painted, much like the bolt-on outer sheet metal. Then the replacement of bushings and other items can be accomplished. (Photo Courtesy Scott Tiemann)

This 1964 GTO frame is ready for the installation of the rebuilt suspension systems. The frame, like the rest of the chassis has been painted with a semi-gloss black paint to resist rust and to present an authentic finish. The procedure for metal surfaces is the same, whether it is a frame rail, oil pan, or outer body panel. Once the metal has been sandblasted or otherwise stripped, use PPG's DP-40 epoxy primer to seal the metal. Then place any body filler (frame rails can become pitted) on top of the DP-40. This encapsulates the filler between two layers of primer. After block sanding, prime it with PPG's K-38 primer. Sand with 180-grit sandpaper and then wet-sand with 220. Apply the top coat. In the case of the frame, use either PPG's DCC 9348 single-stage urethane, which comes pre-flattened, or DCC 9300 high-gloss paint with flattener added. (Photo Courtesy Scott Tiemann)

SUSPENSION

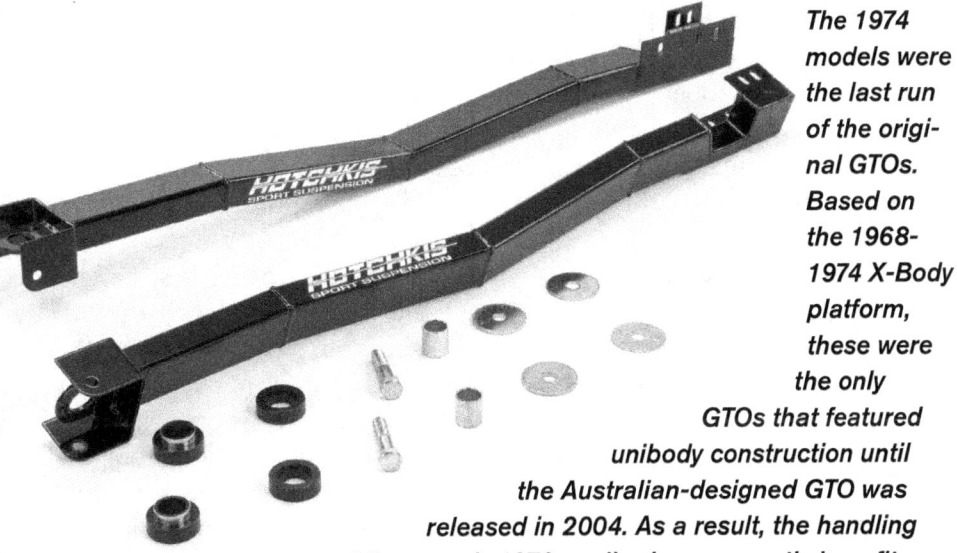

The 1974 models were the last run of the original GTOs. Based on the 1968-1974 X-Body platform, these were the only GTOs that featured unibody construction until the Australian-designed GTO was released in 2004. As a result, the handling of these early 1970s unibody cars greatly benefits from the addition of front-to-rear subframe connectors. Subframe connectors add a lot of strength to the vehicle's structural rigidity. This not only helps with performance and handling, it also helps preserve the body structure because the frame/body is subjected to less torsional stress and therefore you shouldn't see stress cracks or distortion. Different types are available for bolt-in or weld-in installation. Bolt-in units are suitable for street-driven cars and can easily be removed, if desired. (Photo Courtesy Hotchkis Performance)

and start rocking back and forth. If there is excessive free play, then the ball joint needs to be replaced.

Unless the ball joints are perfect, with no play at all, it makes sense to replace them—it is easiest to replace them with the control arms off the car. It can be done at the same time that new control arm bushings are installed. These two operations do a great job of tightening the front end and returning the original feel to the car. Again, your shop manual is the best source of information on this topic.

When ball joints fail, it is usually at low speeds, with the wheels turned to a locked or near-locked position. This is when the most stress is being exerted on them. They generally do not fail at highway speeds, which is a good thing because the driver would have a tough time keeping the car under control.

Control arm bushings give you plenty of warning before they fail. Clunking sounds, the binding up of suspension movement, as well as the creaking and scraping sound as the suspension moves through its travel range are clear indicators that a rebuild is in your future. My first Pontiac restoration made all of those noises as well as a few others that elude explanation to this day.

Suspension and chassis restoration is straightforward mechanical work, and most first-time restorers are well equipped to perform this kind of work. You need to simply remove the suspension arms, springs, bushings, and ball joints, then you need to inspect and evaluate each component. If each major suspension arm is in sound condition, it needs to be sandblasted or stripped, primed, and repainted. Then it should be carefully set aside for reassembly.

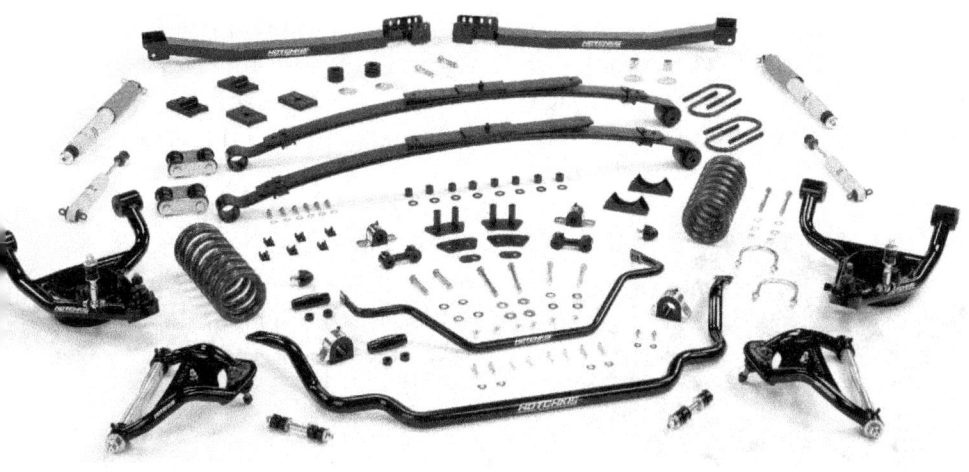

Many aftermarket manufacturers offer handling kits that run the gamut from mild to wild, depending on your intent and budget. (Opting for a suspension kit other than stock rebuild is beyond the scope of this book.) It is not difficult to take your 45-year-old Goat and bring it up to modern handling standards with the addition of a balanced blend of shocks, springs, sway bars, and bushings. This is an area where a driver-quality car can really make some huge strides in drivability. Even concours-style restorations can benefit from harder bushings and other small changes not readily visible. This kit is for a 1974 GTO; similar kits are available for A-Body GTOs. (Photo Courtesy Hotchkis Performance)

HOW TO RESTORE YOUR PONTIAC GTO 1964–1974

CHAPTER 7

Paint Finishes

To restore the luster of your car's underbody, most components must be stripped to the bare metal, primed, and have factory-correct paint applied. Most components, such as the control arms, fit into a bead-blasting cabinet. For larger components, use a sand blaster or soda blaster to remove the former finish, grease, rust, and grime.

If you're restoring a concours car or restoring to factory-correct finishes, pay attention to the type of black paint applied to the suspension parts. Eastwood and other companies offer spray paints, such as Ceramic 2k Satin Chassis black, but some of these are just close and not spot-on. With most GM chassis, the chassis parts are 30-percent gloss. To apply the highest quality finish to your suspension, first strip it down to the metal. Use a professional spray gun with non-sanding primer to shoot the parts. Once done, let it dry and then apply the correct tint of black paint. For most but not all components, use 30-percent gloss-black enamel. To arrive at that tint, add the requisite amount of flattening agent to the paint and properly mix. PPG, DuPont, Eastwood, and Valspar all offer suitable enamel paints to apply to the suspension.

Upgrades

Upgrading your GTO's suspension for improved performance can run the gamut from increased spring rates and better shocks to heavier front and rear sway bars to complete C5 Corvette IRS conversions for a full Pro Touring experience. Here, the discussion of upgrades is limited to bolt-on components, as suspension conversions of that type go well beyond the scope of a restoration.

While rebuilding your suspension, you may consider harder bushings to eliminate the "slop" found in factory systems. If you are willing to give up a little ride quality for a tighter feel, this is a good way to go. The choices are harder rubber or urethane. Harder durometer bushings are good for mild upgrades and help retain ride quality. Urethane bushings greatly enhance handling and road control but transmit more harshness. If you use urethane bushings, use the graphite-impregnated versions or some other means to prevent squeaking or binding like regular urethane units do.

Sway bars are the best bang for the buck for improving the handling of your GTO. Rear sway bars were offered from 1970-on and really helped with cornering stability (keeping the car flat through the corners). In addition to retrofitting factory sway bars, even beefier aftermarket versions are available from Global West, Hotchkis, H-O Racing, and others. It is usually not necessary to increase the spring rate for improved handling, though some may want to, depending on the use of the car. Larger aftermarket sway bars control body roll while maintaining a relatively low spring rate for ride. It is a philosophy generally credited to Herb Adams, the Pontiac engineer who did much of the suspension development for the first two generations of Trans Ams.

Steering

Another area that can be upgraded without significant visual change is the substitution of the stock steering box with a newer, quicker version. Early GTOs are hampered with slow steering boxes, especially the manual steering boxes, which were an agonizingly slow 24:1 ratio, which worked out to more than four turns lock to lock. Variable-ratio power steering became optional equipment in 1970.

Though still of the "low-tech" recirculating-ball type and not of the more modern rack-and-pinion variety, there are some factory GM steering-box choices that provide

Boxed rear lower control arms came from the factory on some high-performance GM cars and can be added to your GTO if it's not already equipped. They are less prone to flex under high-horsepower loads, extreme street use, and racing. If you are handy with a welder, you can modify your existing units with steel plate or you can purchase new ones from most suspension parts manufacturers. These units fit a 1973 GTO. (Photo Courtesy Hotchkis Performance)

SUSPENSION

improved feel, faster ratios, and improved steering response, so much so that converting to rack-and-pinion isn't really necessary. Look for steering boxes from a 1983–1987 Chevy Monte Carlo SS, 1986–1987 Buick Grand National, 1982–1992 Trans Am, or 1994–1996 Impala Super Sport and 9C1 Caprice police car. These all fit, though things like removing the internal stops on F-Body versions must be done in order to preserve the turning radius. Additionally, flex couplings and hoses may need to be exhanged for later-model equivalents, due to the implementation of different sizes and/or metric sizes.

Another option is to have your existing steering box rebuilt with all of the "good stuff" installed, giving you all of the advantages of a late-model box without any conversions needed. Externally, it looks exactly like a stock unit, so the concours would have a tough time detecting the change without actually driving the car. Companies such as Power Steering Services in Missouri can do the conversion for little more than a stock rebuild.

Lower Control Arm Installation

Owners of 1974 GTOs are in a unique situation compared to other model years, as this was the only year of the original run of GTOs to use unibody construction. In actuality, this particular car was more closely related to the 1967–1969 Firebird than it was to any other GTO. As an X-Body platform, it shared much with the Chevy Nova, Buick Apollo, and Oldsmobile Omega. As result, a restorer of one of these cars actually has many options. Reproduction and high-performance items engineered for those vehicles generally work on a 1974 GTO, giving a wide variety of choices.

Another point to consider is that since the front subframe unbolts from the body like a Camaro or Firebird, it makes sense to remove it as part of the restoration. This gives you additional access to the floorpans for cleaning and repair. It also gives you the opportunity to inspect the mounting points and make any repairs. In addition, it makes the rebuilding of the front suspension much easier, since the stub design is much more compact than a full frame, allowing for easy maneuvering, disassembly, and cleaning.

Another item to seriously consider for a driver-quality restoration is the addition of aftermarket subframe connectors. Unibody cars from this era can suffer from a lack of torsional rigidity (resistance to the twisting force of an engine and irregular road surfaces). Pontiac engines are particularly torquey; even the little 350 had much more torque than other V-8s of similar displacement due to its long stroke. This torsional twisting can cause problems with twisting, even going so far as to cause distortion of roof panels and stress-induced cracks throughout the body structure.

Most aftermarket suspension manufacturers offer subframe connectors that join the front stub subframe with the frame-rail sections that mount the rear suspension. There are bolt-in units for street-driven cars and weld-in versions for racing applications. You have to make a decision as to which is right for you. Is the added strength of a welded-in connector worth the added trouble and permanence? Or is a removable version more in line with your mission? Generally, bolt-in connectors are fine for street and street/strip cars and they don't hurt originality.

Adding subframe connectors is a low-cost and very effective way of stiffening the unibody structure, and is recommended for any driver-type restoration. Even if you are not planning on racing or doing a high-performance engine build, it still makes sense to install a set. Ride and handling improve, and you also help preserve the unibody structure and prevent stress cracks and work hardening of the metal.

In this project, we are replacing the lower control arms with units from Hotchkis Performance. While this is a high-performance upgrade, the procedure is essentially the same for a stock control arm replacement, so the sequence illustrated here appplies to installing stock or aftermarket arms. Be sure to properly use protective eyewear and exercise caution. Anytime you are dealing with a compressed spring, you must be extremely careful. If you're removing a spring, be sure that the spring compressor is properly in place and does not slip. If it slips and the spring is ejected, you can be seriously hurt or worse.

CHAPTER 7

Lower Control Arm Installation CONTINUED

Jack Up Car

1 To begin the procedure of replacing the lower control arms, use a floor jack to lift the car and place jackstands at the four corners of the chassis. A hydraulic two- or four-post lift is the most convenient and safest method for lifting and working on a car. Safety is paramount and the last thing you want is to have your 2-ton GTO fall off a lift with any part of you under it. After you have verified that the car is secure, remove the front wheels and set them aside.

Remove Sway Bar

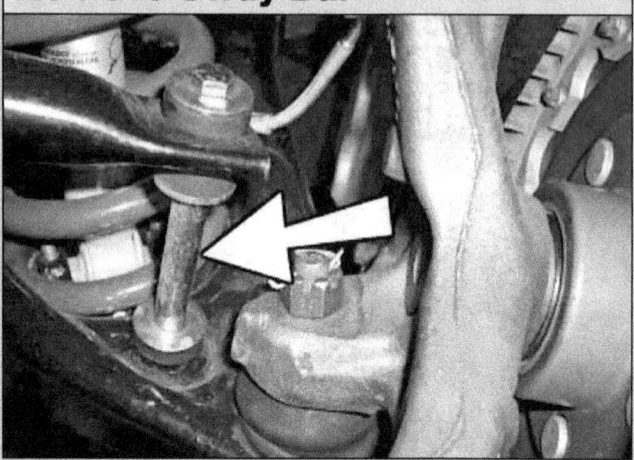

2 Several bolts fasten the sway bar to the chassis. Remove the sway bar end links using a 5/16-inch socket or wrench. Set all of the hardware aside so it doesn't get lost. Remove the sway bar and be sure that it's completely disconnected from the lower control arms.

Remove Shock Fastener

3 The suspension is subjected to all kinds of weather and road conditions. After years of service, suspension fasteners are typically rusted and difficult to remove. Before you start, douse the fasteners with WD-40, Liquid Wrench, or some other lube so that these bolts and nuts are easier to remove. In some extreme cases of corrosion, you may have to use a propane torch to apply heat to the fasteners to remove them. Use a 3/8-inch wrench or socket to undo the top shock absorber mount. Use a combination of wrenches and/or Allen keys to remove the top shock mounting nut. Save all shock bushings and hardware for reinstallation.

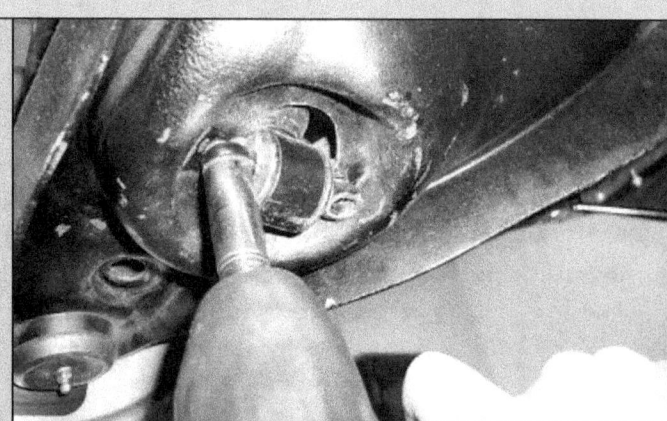

4 Remove the two 5/16-inch bolts that secure the bottom shock mount and remove the shock from the vehicle. Examine the bushings and the hardware. If the bushings are worn, cracked, or otherwise damaged, you need to find replacements. Likewise, if years of use have damaged the bolts, replace them. However, if all parts are in good condition, keep them for reinstallation later.

114 HOW TO RESTORE YOUR PONTIAC GTO 1964–1974

SUSPENSION

Disconnect Outer Tie Rod Ends

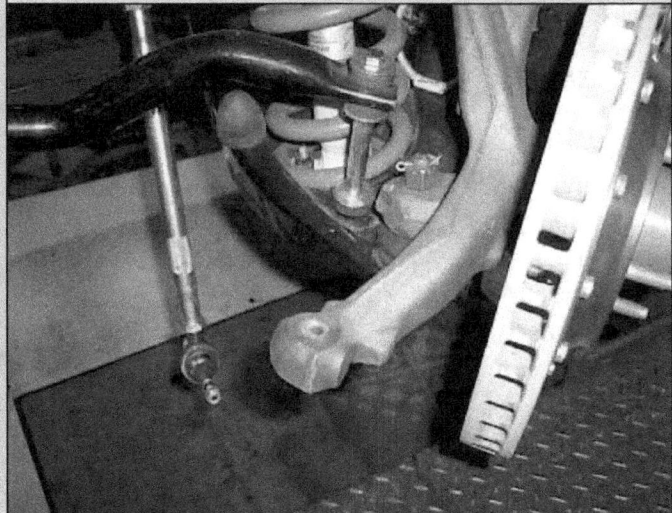

5 Locate the outer tie rod end and remove the cotter pin using a pair of diagonal cutters (dikes). Use an 11/16-inch wrench to remove the tie rod end castle nut. Tap the steering arm with a hammer to knock out the tapered stud. Allow the tie rod to hang down.

Loosen Lower Ball Joint Nut

6 Locate the lower ball joint nut near the outboard end of the A-arm and remove the cotter pin using a pair of dikes. Use a 7/8-inch wrench to loosen the castle nut, but do not completely remove it. Leave three or four threads on the nut.

Break Loose Lower Ball Joint Stud

7 Use a hammer to tap the spindle until the stud pops loose. The castle nut keeps the spring in place and prevents it from launching the lower control arm. Be sure the castle nut is properly secured. Exercise caution during the procedure and make sure to wear eye protection in case of flying debris.

Loosen Lower Control Arm Bolts

8 Hold the nut on the inside of the control arm with a box-end wrench, and use a ratchet or breaker bar to loosen the bolt. Do not remove the two 1/2-inch inboard lower control arm bolts at this stage. Leave three to four threads in the nut. Removal comes later.

HOW TO RESTORE YOUR PONTIAC GTO 1964–1974

CHAPTER 7

Lower Control Arm Installation CONTINUED

Remove Lower Control Arm

9 This is a critical stage in the procedure and one that demands the utmost caution and safety. A suspension spring compressor or floor jack is required to remove the front coil springs. If the engine is installed in the car, you can remove the front suspension springs by using a floor jack. However, if the engine has been pulled from the car, the front suspension is extended and a spring compressor is needed to remove the front coil springs. When working on the lower control arm, place a jack underneath it and jack up the arm until you start to see the ball joint castle nut start to rise. Remove the ball joint castle nut, but be sure that the jack does not slip because the spring is under tension and it must be decompressed slowly. If the jack or the spring compressor slips, serious injury could result.

10 Slowly lower the jack to relieve the tension in the spring. Be well aware that there is a tremendous amount of energy here, enough to hold up one corner of a 2-ton car. If you are removing OEM springs, be extra careful because this type of longer spring has more pre-load than shorter lowering springs. Release the tension as slowly as the jack allows.

11 Lift out the spring once the control arm has been lowered and the control arm is at the bottom of its travel. If these springs have been in service for many years, they need to be inspected for cracks or any damage. Springs lose their rate over time, the ride height drops, and they don't provide the same ride characteristics because they are weaker. Therefore, if you're installing reconditioned stock arms or aftermarket arms, replace the springs while you're performing this procedure. Make sure that there is no longer any tension on it and it is free of obstructions.

SUSPENSION

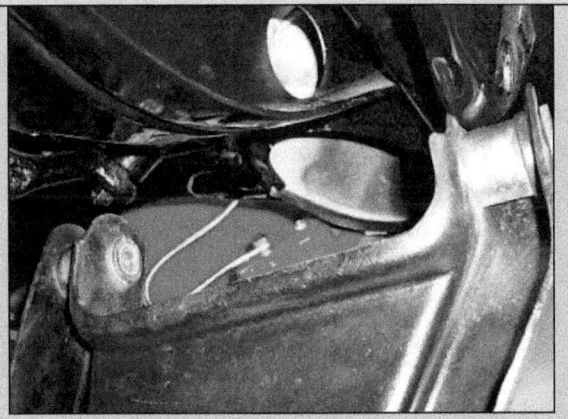

12 Take the two inboard bolts that you previously loosened and completely remove them. Hang onto the control arms while you are doing this, as it otherwise falls to the ground. If reconditioning the stock arms, thoroughly inspect them for cracks, bends, and other damage. Use a chemical stripper to remove all the grease, grime, and dirt. Then the arms can be sandblasted and repainted OEM GTO suspension color and put aside for re-installation later. In addition, replace the ball the joint in the lower arm. To do that is a little tricky. You need to rent a ball joint removal tool or take the arms to a machine shop and have the ball joints installed with a shop press or with a special C-clamp, as shown in the photo. Keep in mind that GTOs have either round- or oval-type bushings for the lower control arm.

Now you have full access to the upper A-arms. Start by removing the nuts on the upper inner shafts. The upper arms often have spacer shims for alignment. Be sure to keep all of these for re-assembly. With the upper A-arms out of the car, the inner cross shafts and bushings need to be removed. To do that, secure the shaft in a bench vise and then use a ratchet or wrench to remove them.

The upper A-arm bushings can be stubborn to remove. Air tools are extremely helpful for this procedure. Rivets secure the ball joint to the control arm. Plant the air chisel on the head of the rivets and drive the rivets out of the control arm. If you will be re-using the stock control arms, thoroughly inspect them at this point. Look for broken welds, cracks, and other damage. If the arms can be reused, strip them of all grease and contaminants. Strip them down to the bare metal for repainting by bead blasting them in a cabinet. Once this has been completed, select the correct suspension paint and spray them.

Install Suspension Arms

13 Install the 1/4-inch spacer and the lower spring isolator onto the Hotchkis lower control arm. At this time, it's not necessary to index the clocking of the isolator. With the 1/4-inch spacer, the stock ride height remains the same. In some cases, such as with a change in spring rate or change in engine, the ride height is changed. Therefore, it is necessary to raise or lower the driver or passenger side to get a uniform ride height. If you need to lower or raise the vehicle you can order 1/8-inch (PN 11990014) or 1/4-inch (PN 11980014) spacers from Hotchkis. No spacer is equivalent to 1/2-inch lower than stock arm. Using a 1/8-inch spacer provides 1/4-inch lower than stock arm. Using a 1/4-inch spacer is the same as the stock arm (default setting). Using a 1/4- and a 1/8-inch spacer is equivalent to 1/4-inch higher than stock arm. Using a 1/4- and a 1/4-inch spacer is equivalent to 1/2-inch higher than stock arm.

CHAPTER 7

Lower Control Arm Installation *CONTINUED*

Align Arms in Brackets

14 Align the new or reconditioned control arm with the mounting bracket and align the bolt holes. Slip the bolt through the bolt holes from the outside. Use a box-end wrench to hold the nut securing the bolt on the inside of the arm and apply torque to the bolt on the outside. Use a click-type torque wrench to verify that the inboard bolts have been tightened to 85 ft-lbs.

Index Suspension Spring

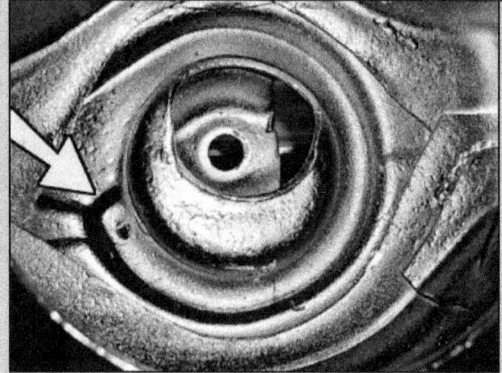

15 With the control arm hanging down, grab the coil spring and place it in the upper pocket. Some model years need to be clocked at a certain angle to match the index. Use a dab of white enamel paint or paper correction fluid (otherwise known as "white out") to mark the frame and the coil. This gives you a guide when you are ready for the final installation. If your car does not have the upper indexing, you can skip this step.

Install Ball Joint into Control Arm

16 Rotate the control arm upward and place a jack underneath it. Place the spring into the upper pocket and index it using your white-out guide. Clock the control arm isolator, so the end of the coil matches up with the index of the isolator. Slowly jack up the arm while pushing the bottom half of the spring inboard into the isolator pocket. This step is easy with aftermarket lowering springs and difficult with OEM stock springs. For OEM stock springs, you may need to use a series of pry bars to pop the bottom end into the pocket.

Once the bottom has been popped in, line up the lower ball joint stud with the bottom of the spindle. Continue to lift the control arm with the jack and insert the ball joint stud into the spindle. Once the stud is in all the way, install the supplied castle nut to 40 ft-lbs or enough to expose the cotter pin hole, whichever is more. Fully tighten this nut and install the new cotter pin. Once the castle nut has been torqued to its proper specification, you may release the jack to relieve the pressure on the control arm.

Install Steering Tie Rod

17 Install the steering tie rod in the same manner as it was removed, torqueing the bolt to 20 ft-lbs or enough to expose the cotter pin hole, whichever is more. Don't forget to install the cotter pin. Once you have the steering linkage pieced together, installing it in the car is easy. Start by bolting on the steering arm and idler arm, then attach the tie rods to the spindles. After the bolts are tightened, be sure to add the cotter pins used to retain the nuts.

Install Shocks

18 At this stage, the lower control arms and the coil over springs have been installed. Therefore, the spring compressor and the floor jack have been tucked away and you have full access to the control arms. Simply guide the shock upward from the bottom and attach the bolt to the top shock mount and let the shock hang. Guide the bottom shock eye into the right position on the bottom control arm, feed the bolts through the shock mount, and fasten the nuts to the bolts. Tighten the upper 3/8-inch bolt to 8 ft-lbs and the lower two bolts to 20 ft-lbs.

Install Sway Bar

19 Attach the sway bar to the control arm with the sway bar end links and tighten to If the roll bar is original and has been subjected to years of use, strip it by sandblasting and then repaint it with the correct factory Pontiac paint. In addition, upgrade to polyurethane bushings for improved handling. Reinstall the wheels and lower the vehicle.

Aftermarket Control Arms

Many advancements in suspension technology, aside from tires, have been in the area of suspension geometry. For example, if you bolt a set of wide wheels and low-profile tires on an otherwise stock early GTO, you notice that as the steering wheel turns from lock to lock, the tire's tread does not remain perpendicular to the ground. Instead, the wheels camber in. This was an acceptable situation in the past, as the narrower tire tread stayed flat on the ground when the body leaned over. With today's wide tires and low profiles, that situation is no longer acceptable.

The addition of aftermarket control arms brings a new level of road-holding and cornering force—they keep the cambering effect under control, providing just the right amount for today's wheel/tire combinations. Though the cambering situation improved somewhat with the the introduction of the suspension design of the 1973 GTOs, it can be upgraded even further. Companies such as Hotchkis, Ride Tech, and Global West offer tubular control arms that improve camber and steering geometry, are stronger than factory arms, and reduce unsprung weight.

Upgrading the factory upper and lower control arms on your Pontiac GTO is probably as deep as you can go with suspension upgrades and still stay in the realm of a restoration. Anything more and you're into a pro-touring build. Some actually say that they are over the line, and while they are entitled to their opinion, I respectfully disagree, here is why.

Over the past 20 years or so, adding a second-generation Firebird spindle to an otherwise stock 1964–1972 suspension layout has been a popular upgrade that improves handling and facilitates the addition of disc brakes at the same time (if the car was not already so equipped). While this mixing of early and late front suspension components does help with cornering and overall handling, it also introduces a bump-steer situation that is not desirable. Bump steer is the phenomenon where the wheels involuntarily turn as the suspension moves through its travel range. The "mix-and-match" aspect of swapping pieces between the two generations is the culprit. The handling improvement does come at a cost.

Aftermarket control arms corrects that particular handling flaw and feature much stiffer bushings, which greatly improve road feel and eliminate any "sloppiness" found in a stock suspension. Hotchkis Performance, Ride Tech, and others build their own versions. While the car doesn't look stock underneath the hood, it isn't an obvious visual red flag as you walk past it. This is a modification for driver-type restorations and makes a dramatic difference in handling, especially when coupled with proper springs, shocks, sway bars, and a wheel/tire combination that makes use of the new technology.

I have spoken with owners of GTOs using aftermarket control arms and all have praised the car's newfound handling prowess. One owner who lives near me combined them with a set of 15-inch Rally II wheels and conventional-size radial tires. It has provided him with a car that looks nearly stock but corners as well as many late-model vehicles. This one car sold me on the idea of including them in a driver-style restoration without it turning into a pro-touring build. These upgrades truly bring the handling of your vintage Pontiac into the twenty-first century.

CHAPTER 8

BRAKES

Whether a stock restoration, a weekend cruiser, or modified for maximum performance, the vehicle's braking system is hands-down the most important system. When I brought my first Pontiac restoration project home many years ago, my dad said, "I don't care how fast this car goes; it damn well better be able to stop." With that, we rebuilt the braking system. It ran and stopped, but before the repairs were made, I almost crashed into my parents' house, relying on emergency brakes when I was moving it in our driveway with rotted-out brake lines and frozen wheel cylinders.

We laugh about it now, but it was one of the scariest experiences of my life—the accelerator became stuck and I was hurtling toward the house at full throttle without any brakes. I did get it stopped without damage to anything other than some rather deep tracks in the front yard. A quarter of a century later, dad's advice still holds true and my parents' house escaped injury, no thanks to me!

In the case of Pontiac GTOs, especially the early ones, the braking systems were not nearly as high-performance as the engines were. The factory-supplied Delco-Moraine drum brakes were the norm back then, and fortunately, replacement parts are available from a variety of sources. By today's standards, they are barely adequate at best and dangerous at worst, not exactly the epitome of a well-balanced performance machine. Even back then, road testers complained about the braking performance, and that there was not

This 1964 GTO brake drum is correct for the application and features a long spring wrapped around its circumference. This was added at the factory to help dampen harmonic vibration and help keep the wheels in balance. Some GTO drums are painted 60-percent gloss black. However, the 1966 GTO carries factory red paint. (Photo Courtesy Scott Tiemann)

HOW TO RESTORE YOUR PONTIAC GTO 1964–1974

CHAPTER 8

If you are restoring a very original car or are planning a concours-style restoration, you need as much of the original componentry as possible. Thus, you need to rebuild and refinish these pieces to their as-delivered condition. If you are restoring a GTO as a driver or are not as concerned about originality you have the benefit of replacement parts with better metallurgy, as well as higher-performing brake pads and shoes. Here, the rear drum brake system appears to be in good operating condition and there doesn't seem to be any obvious problems. When evaluating your GTO's braking system, look for leaks, damage, and excessive and uneven wear. Fittings can leak due to loosening or damage during previous brake jobs. Uneven wear can happen due to a frozen wheel cylinder in a drum system or a brake caliper piston in a disc-brake system. The self-adjusters on this rear drum brake are mounted backward, which means that they were accidentally swapped side for side. (Photo Courtesy Ron Panzer)

With this 1964 GTO front drum brake system completed and ready for installation of the drum, you can see the correct silver cadmium finish for the backing plate, as well as the color-coded springs and the natural-metal backing of the shoes. (Photo Courtesy Scott Tiemann)

an optional braking system that was any different from what could be had in a six-cylinder Tempest sedan. The idea of hauling down a 3,500-pound car from triple digits while relying on a single master cylinder and four fade-prone 9.5-inch drum brakes is mind-boggling, yet that was all that was available for the 1964–1966 model years.

Sure, there were some upgrades available, such as semi-metallic linings and aluminum drums but they were more Band-Aid solutions and didn't offer enough of an improvement to be considered problem solvers in anyone's mind. That situation continued through the 1966 model year, even as optional horsepower levels continued to climb and GTOs became heavier.

It was not until the 1967 model year that the braking situation was improved in a significant way. That year, a dual-chamber master cylinder was added to prevent total brake loss if a brake line broke, and front disc brakes were made optional.

The new braking system was a huge improvement over the previous four-drum setup and featured four-piston calipers and 11.12-inch two-piece rotors. Disc-brake-equipped cars also received a larger 1.125-inch master cylinder bore size, compared to the smallish 1.000-inch size still used on drum-braked cars.

For the 1969 model year, the braking system was revised somewhat. To help correct leakage problems and the resulting warranty costs, Pontiac came out with a new, simpler, front disc-brake system, which was optional in the GTO and other A-Bodies. It featured a new single-piston caliper and a slightly smaller 10.9-inch vented rotor. The pistons were also less prone to cocking and getting stuck in the bores. This system remained pretty much unchanged through the 1972 model year.

The A-Body was completely redesigned in 1973 with a heavier frame, a new Colonnade body style for increased rollover protection, and revised front and rear suspension systems. The brakes were upgraded as well, owing to increased safety concerns and a significantly heavier overall curb weight. While the 9.5-inch rear drums remained from the previous generation, the standard braking system now featured 11-inch front disc brakes; the front drums were finally put to bed. The extra weight of the new platform was obviously beyond any consideration for using them.

When the GTO option package was shifted over to the smaller and lighter X-Body Ventura platform, the braking system once again returned to four-wheel drums as standard equipment. They were 9.5-inch units and the optional front disc brakes were the 11-inch units used on the A-Bodies. All the listed systems were shared with various GM A-Body and X-Body offerings, as well as other platforms.

Repair or Replace?

It is reasonable and customary for much of the braking system to be replaced in the restoration process. While it may be possible to save certain items for the sake of originality, it is usually desirable to have fresh, new, and undamaged pieces going back on the car because the brake system is the most important safety system on the car and it shouldn't be compromised. It makes sense to save the backing plates and perhaps rebuild the calipers and master cylin-

The front disc-brake system of this 1970 Judge convertible uses the later single-piece rotors. Both early two-piece rotor and later single-piece units are now being reproduced and are available from The Parts Place and other outlets. The correct finishes for this system include a 60-percent gloss-black caliper and a gold cadmium mounting bracket. The caliper bolts are torqued to 35 ft-lbs. In many cars, the seals on the pistons have deteriorated over time and are leaking. You can rebuild the calipers but it takes some time and patience to seat the new pistons without damaging the seals. If you do not need to re-install the existing calipers, you should select factory replacements and simply bolt them to the mounting brackets then bleed the system. (Photo Courtesy Scott Tiemann)

der if they aren't too corroded, but beyond that, everything should be replaced with new items. If your budget can include correct calipers and a master cylinder, go for it. Most restoration parts houses have replacement brake parts in stock.

If you are restoring a car for a points-judged show competition, there are a couple of areas where you are probably going to be stuck with used parts where a better performing new part would otherwise be preferable. For example, the two-piece rotors used on 1967 and 1968 GTOs only recently began being reproduced. A single-piece replacement rotor was available that fits the application, but it is not factory correct. For a driver, this is a non-issue, but if you are going for the gold, you need the correct pieces to avoid having points deducted. In the past, it was necessary to re-use existing pieces or, if needed, find better examples. Though it appears that the problem has been rectified with this new release, I have not seen the reproductions, and therefore cannot verify that they are indeed correct enough looking to satisfy judging requirements.

Fortunately, the sheer number of GM A-Bodies still on the road today, and the large market that exists for these cars, the aftermarket offers a variety of parts that restore and even upgrade these vehicles for daily-driver or high-performance use. From brake lines to drums, rotors, pads, shoes, master cylinders, wheel cylinders, and even front and rear disc brake conversion kits, just about everything you need is available. These replacement parts also benefit from improved metallurgy, and while authentic looking, they also perform better and last longer than the original equipment.

One of the most complete catalogs of reproduction and aftermarket brake parts can be found at Inline Tube. Owner John Kryta has had an obsession with correct restoration products for many years. This has driven him to start and run a very well-respected business with top-quality parts. He began his business by offering perfect reproduction

CHAPTER 8

Brake lines are frequently rusted out on Northeastern cars but cracking and other damage can occur no matter where the car spent its life. Replacements are available in the original steel as well as in stainless. If replacing the brake lines, you need to ensure the stock rubber or aftermarket stainless-steel lines are correctly routed from the master cylinder all the way to the back of the car. Make sure the lines do not get chafed or crimped. When installing the banjo fitting on the calipers, be sure to install all the hardware, including the copper washer. Once all the lines have been installed, complete the bleeding procedure to make the system operational. (Photo Courtesy Scott Tiemann)

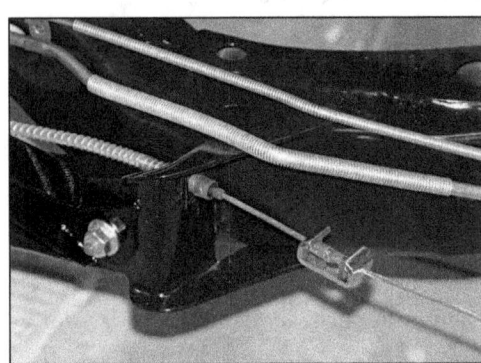

Emergency brakes often need to be reconditioned; the return springs wear out and need to be replaced. This is a mechanical backup system, as opposed to the hydraulic design used in the primary braking system. Correct cables and fittings are available from a variety of restoration parts outlets. (Photo Courtesy Scott Tiemann)

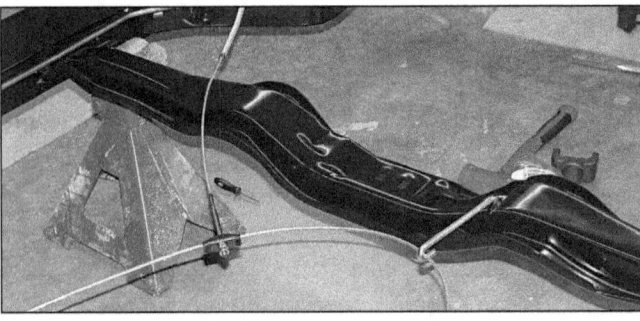

In order for the emergency braking system to work correctly, all of the fittings, hangers, and related hardware must be in sound condition; otherwise there won't be enough tension on the cables for them to operate the brake. To recondition the brake, remove the cable clip then slide the barrel out of the parking brake to remove the cable. Remove the parking brake retainer in the firewall. Remove the bolts that hold line behind the fenderwell. Then get under the car and remove the cable from the equalizer. Pop off the clip that holds the line to the frame. Pull the cable out and thoroughly douse it with cable lubricant and work the cable back and forth until it is freed. Now it can be re-installed. The hooked cable guide holds the cable on one side and fits through a hole in the crossmember. All contact points on the brake cable should be lubricated with bearing grease to avoid binding and excessive wear. (Photo Courtesy Scott Tiemann)

brake lines and he expanded from there. Year One, Ames Performance Engineering, Original Parts Group, and The Parts Place also do a very good job with brake parts but for the really hard-to-find items, Inline Tube is one-stop shopping.

Check for Condition

When it comes to evaluating your GTO's braking system, start by focusing on some of the more common problems and typical repair and replacement required for overuse or simple age. Wear items, such as brake pads, shoes, rotors, and drums, should be replaced. New brake lines should also be part of the program, preferably in stainless steel to avoid further corrosion problems.

If the braking system is working properly, the wheels spin with very little resistance and do not make any noises that would indicate damage or frozen components. The actual contact surfaces—the rotors and drums—appear smooth, with very little in the way of imperfections. The surface may have a slightly wavy appearance, but there should be no discoloration, grooves, or gouges. Rust on the contact surface indicates improper seating of brake linings.

Additionally, there should be no wet spots on any of the brake lines and no seepage from the master cylinder or wheel cylinders. Any brake fluid puddles under the car need to be addressed before the car is driven.

The three main things to be looking for are leakage, uneven wear, and outright damage.

Leakage

Following the path of the brake fluid from the master cylinder to the wheels likely shows some leakage of

BRAKES

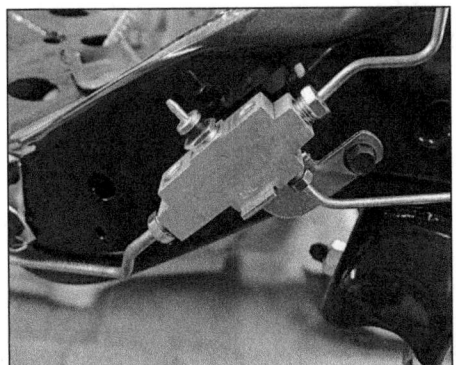

The distribution block is mounted on the frame rail below the master cylinder. This block was used on all cars, whether they had disc or drum brakes. (This is not a proportioning valve because it does not modulate pressure.) If there is a loss of pressure in either the front or rear braking systems, it activates the brake warning light in the dash. To replace the distribution block, simply remove the lines, install them on a new block, and bolt the distribution block to the frame rail. If you replace the distribution block, you're opening the brake system, so you have to bleed it. Reproductions are available from Inline Tube. (Photo Courtesy Scott Tiemann)

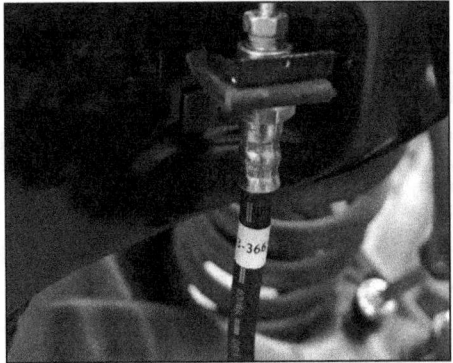

Reproduction brake hoses with the correct markings are available from Inline Tube and other manufacturers. Whether you use them or another type, make sure that the fittings are not damaged, there is no leakage, and they are securely fastened to their frame mounts. (Photo Courtesy Scott Tiemann)

This rear brake drum from the Royal Bobcat 1964 GTO is correct for the application, as evidenced by its casting number D-50325. The "D" stands for developmental, which sometimes shows up on a pilot line and early production vehicles. While they typcially are reserved for experimental pieces, the developmental casting numbers can remain if no changes are needed for production. Since the car was an early build, November 2, 1963, it is more than likely the original drum bolted to the car. (Photo Courtesy Scott Tiemann)

brake fluid. Obviously, this is not a good situation, as hydraulic pressure pushes the brake fluid out with great force. Eventually, there is not enough brake fluid to operate the brakes and the car no longer stops. Typical leakage spots are found around the fittings joining two assemblies, such as the master cylinder to the brake line and the brake hose to the wheel cylinder. The lines themselves can corrode and leak from pinholes, and lines weakened by corrosion sometimes break under the pressure. The early cars with a single master cylinder are especially vulnerable (they lose pressure and braking force to all four wheels sometimes), and cars equipped with a dual master cylinder do not suffer a full loss of brakes (either the front or rear pair still functions).

Repairing leaks is typically taken care of in a total brake system rebuild and/or replacement. New lines, master cylinder, and wheel cylinders replace defective items as long as they are properly installed.

Uneven Wear

When inspecting your brakes, look for uniformity of wear. Though your rotors may look fine, it is possible that the brake pad on one side of the rotor may have worn more than on the other side. This is actually a pretty common situation and can be felt by the car pulling to one side or the other.

The problem is usually caused by one of the pistons being frozen in the bore and not applying pressure to the rotor, though other rusted/broken/stuck hardware can cause similar problems. The car still stops, but braking force is significantly reduced.

Damage

Drums and rotors are exposed to extremes of heat, cold, torsional stress, and pressure, but they are designed to handle those conditions, within common operational constraints. When typical operating conditions are exceeded, specific types of damage can occur. Excessive heat from repeated high-speed bursts, towing, and racing can manifest itself in the way of bluing of the metal and cracks. Additionally, galling of contact surfaces is also a common consequence when the linings become damaged by the intense heat.

In all cases, regardless of the type of restoration, these damaged items should be replaced whether or not correct replacements can be found. If you have this level of damage and are restoring a car for points-judged

CHAPTER 8

This is a shot of the rear brake assembly for a 1970 Judge convertible. It is complete and ready to be bolted on the end of the axle tube. As with the 1964 front drum system, you can see the color-coded springs and correct finishes. (Photo Courtesy Scott Tiemann)

competition, find used parts in better condition or use possibly incorrect reproduction items until you can find more correct examples. Any rotor or drum that is gouged, blued, cracked, or similarly damaged needs to not only be replaced but properly disposed of so it is not re-used at some point in the future.

Aftermarket Systems

With the current popularity of pro touring, many owners want their older cars to perform on par with or better than a new high-performance vehicle. Even if you are not looking to build your GTO into a competitive road racer, chances are that you want your car to be able to stop at least as well as a modern passenger car.

Fortunately, the aftermarket has come to the rescue with a variety of options. Kits are available from most restoration outlets that bring your drum-braked GTO up to 1973-and-up specs, and you can even upfit those items from your auto parts store, though the kit approach is more attractive from the parts and completeness standpoints. If you are more adventurous, other kits are available from places like Baer Racing, Stainless Steel Brakes, and Wilwood Engineering that can outfit your car with options from high-performance street to a truly race-ready system. The only limitations are your preferences and budget; there is an amazing amount of brake options for these cars in the aftermarket. Keep in mind that depending on the system you choose, you may not be able to use OEM wheels.

Master Cylinders, Proportioning Valves and Lines

As part of a brake system upgrade, you are left to sort out the many options in the areas of master cylinders, proportioning valves, and brake lines. Every case is likely to have unique requirements. Depending on the year of your particular GTO and the configuration of the front brakes, you may be able to work with what you have or you may have to upgrade. Either way, it is imperative that the front and rear brakes work efficiently and in harmony with each other, and it's your job to make sure that happens.

For safety's sake, make sure your brake lines are in good condition. Replace whatever is needed to ensure they are all up to snuff. A modern master cylinder should be used. If your car came from the factory with a disc/drum setup, you can reuse the stock unit, provided that the egg-shaped pressure booster in the rear lines is removed. Its job is to increase the line pressure to the drums, as they require more pressure to use than the discs. It is not required with rear discs.

Next, installing an adjustable proportioning valve helps tune the proper front-to-rear balance. You don't need to remove the proportioning valve at the master cylinder, though an adjustable proportioning valve must be downstream of the distribution block. A Wilwood unit costs between $40 and $80, depending on whether you want a lever (PN 260-8420) or more economical knob style (PN 260-8419). A popular mounting point is on the frame, near the front of the side rail.

If you have a four-wheel-drum system, are upgrading to discs up front, and want to go the aftermarket route, Stainless Steel Brakes, Wilwood, Baer Racing, and countless others market affordable, high-quality master cylinders that generally run around $200.

1964 Rear Drum Brakes

The 1964 10-bolt rear ends have additional issues to overcome. Since there is no separate retainer plate to hold the bearings in the rear, you must take the old drum brake backing plate and cut out the material that mounted up against the axle. This material can then be used as a shim behind the new backing plate. Slide all the parts over the axle in reverse order of final assembly and press on the bearing. Other than this particular bit of cutting, everything else is the same.

Rear Disc-Brake Conversion

Pontiac GTOs have a lot going for them—great looks, powerful engines, and instant street credibility, especially for the performance versions of each series. The only real drawback is that they don't really drive like new cars. By modern standards, the handling is only so-so, and the brakes are several feet short of spectacular. True, the addition of disc brakes in 1967 did help quite a bit, but they still are not up to what you find in a minivan with a base engine. They certainly aren't adequate if even modest gains in horsepower are achieved.

Bringing performance up to modern standards is the whole idea behind the pro touring movement. Making an early GTO accelerate like a new one is not difficult—several are already there in stock form. Getting one to handle and stop like a new car, well, that's a little more of a challenge. But it's one that many are taking up and finding worth the effort. Sometimes, effective upgrades for earlier cars can come from inexpensive factory components.

Whether you're building a corner-carving GTO or just want something that stops shorter than your current disc/drum setup, I have a solution that costs less than $500. You will also be able to run a factory-style, 15-inch wheel on your car, though a 14-incher does not quite clear the caliper. Also, keep in mind that with this swap the rear track increases approximately 1/4 inch on each side, so check your tire clearance.

Install Upgraded Brakes

1 *Imran Chaudary's 11-second 1969 GTO now stops as well as it goes, thanks to a cleverly designed four-wheel disc-brake system conversion that uses boneyard and over-the-counter parts, available at any parts store or GM dealer. This system uses brake equipment from a Chevy S-10 truck.*

Visit Salvage Yard for Parts

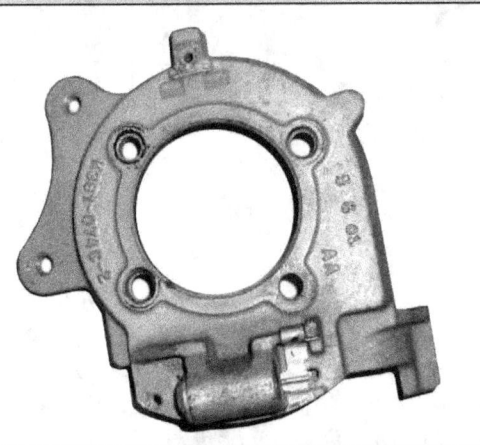

2 *Go to your local salvage yard or to GM and find a pair of rear disc brake backing plates for 1998–2002 S-based two-wheel-drive trucks and SUVs. Rear disc brakes were an option in those years. These brackets also have an integrated parking brake. It works by expanding a brake shoe against the inner portion of the rotor. When disassembling the bracket at the salvage yard, take special care to salvage the parts for the parking brake assembly. You should be able to pick them up for around $50 or less per pair. Some salvage yards have already removed the parts from the vehicle; if not, be sure to have a shop manual to outline the removal procedure if you have to take it off yourself.*

Rear Disc-Brake Conversion CONTINUED

Ontario-based GTO restoration expert Imran Chaudary has developed an affordable and relatively simple rear-disc-brake conversion for 1960s- and 1970s-era GM cars that uses parts originally designed for 1998–2002 two-wheel-drive compact GM pickups (Chevy S-10/GMC S-15) and SUVs (Chevy Blazer/GMC Jimmy and Envoy). The system works for 8.2- and 8.5-inch 10-bolt and GM 12-bolt differentials. Imran has installed this system in his street-driven 11-second 1969 GTO and has racked up four years of trouble-free performance. Keep in mind that even though these are considered compact trucks, they can easily tip the scales at more than 4,500 pounds, so these brake systems are not overtaxed with even the weight of a late-1960s Bonneville.

This setup is also used on Andy Pooni's pro touring 1965 GTO. Other Pontiac owners in the Niagara Falls area have used this combination for their own cars and have recorded similar results. Best of all, the conversion won't break the bank and is fairly simple to accomplish.

"It's really amazing how well these new parts go together with the older rear ends," Pooni says. "I guess that when it comes to pieces like rear ends and axles, there is a lot of carryover from year to year and even generation to generation. When you have the critical dimensions laid out and tooling to pay for, it doesn't make sense for GM to change things if they don't have to."

The S-10s were designed to use the same front suspension pieces as the Chevy Caprice, and the Caprice is an outgrowth of the 1973–1977 A- and G-Bodies, which were closely related to the 1964–1972 A- and G-Body platforms. It's now easy to see that these seemingly unrelated vehicles actually share some vital DNA.

For this particular setup, most of the components can be purchased at any late-model salvage yard. The parts that Chaudary or Pooni purchased new were the wear items in the system such as rotors, calipers, hoses, brake pads, and dust shields, which were available from a local dealer.

When searching through your favorite salvage yard, look for two-wheel-drive S-based compact pickup trucks and SUVs between the years of 1998 and 2001. Rear disc brakes were available on some as an option and as standard equipment on higher-end vehicles. "When Andy and I searched our yard, we removed parts for his 1965 GTO from a 1998 Envoy, and I removed mine from a 1999 Jimmy SUV," Chaudary says. "The yard had already taken off the rotors and calipers."

Find Brake Retainer Cages

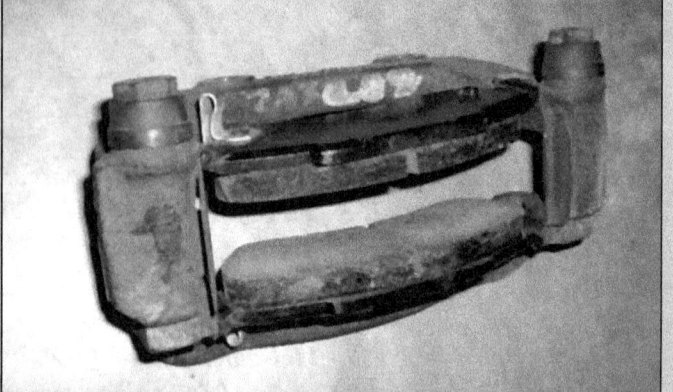

3 While at the salvage yard, also look for a set of brake pad retainer cages (GM PN 18026155), which are shown with the pads installed. These items can be difficult to find, though they are available new from GM for $87.95 each.

Buy New Brake Dust Shields

4 A new dust shield from GM costs only $19.70, so it makes sense to discard the old ones. Before you do, be sure to compare them to the new ones, as there are two different designs, depending on whether the backing plates locate the calipers at the 11:00 or 2:00 position. They work equally well; base your choice on what you think looks better.

Once you've found the appropriate donor vehicle, the first thing to do is to remove the rear axle cover to drain the fluid, so you can slide the axles out. Keep in mind that these differentials have C-clips, so you must remove the small bolt holding the axle pin. Once the pin has been removed, rotate the carrier until you can get at the C-clips. Push the axles in to remove the C-clips.

This allows you to remove the four nuts on the end of the flange and take off the backing plate and disc-brake dust shield. The backing plates are the most important pieces in the conversion, because even though everything else can be purchased fairly inexpensively from your local GM dealer or parts retailer, the plates are quite expensive new, listing at $74.06 each. And it's one of those situations where used versions for $50 or less per pair at your favorite salvage yard work just as well. These backing plates also have an integrated parking brake.

"Our dust shields were almost toast," Pooni said. "So we opted to get new ones from our local GM dealer parts department ($19.70). Keep the old dust shields you get from the yard to match them up with the new ones from GM."

Why? They made two different versions. On the S-15 the calipers are at the 2 o'clock position, and on the Jimmy and Envoy they are at the 11 o'clock position. They work equally well, so there really isn't a more desirable location, though aesthetically one may appear better than the other, depending on your preference.

The rotors are a really nice design, measuring 11.625 inches in overall diameter. They also feature an integral parking brake drum that lends itself well to adaptation to earlier cars. The calipers are a fairly conventional full-floating, single-piston design that may not be as exotic as some aftermarket units, but are very effective and light-years ahead of the drums you're replacing.

Install Backing Plates

5 Inspect and regrease the cam for the parking brake mechanism (rubber piece on the bottom of the plate). Line up the dust shield and backing plate and bolt up to the flange. Place a new parking brake shoe (also available at your local parts store or dealer) over the backing plate, ensuring that the open end lines up properly with the piston mechanism on the bottom of the mounting bracket.

Properly Orient Parts

6 This is how the backing plate and the dust shield should be oriented to mount onto the right-hand axle. Since the axle tubes of the S-series trucks and the GTO are the same, it is a matter of bolting them on the GTO in the same manner as they were on the truck. (Parts shown from the axle side.)

CHAPTER 8

Rear Disc-Brake Conversion CONTINUED

Install Caliper

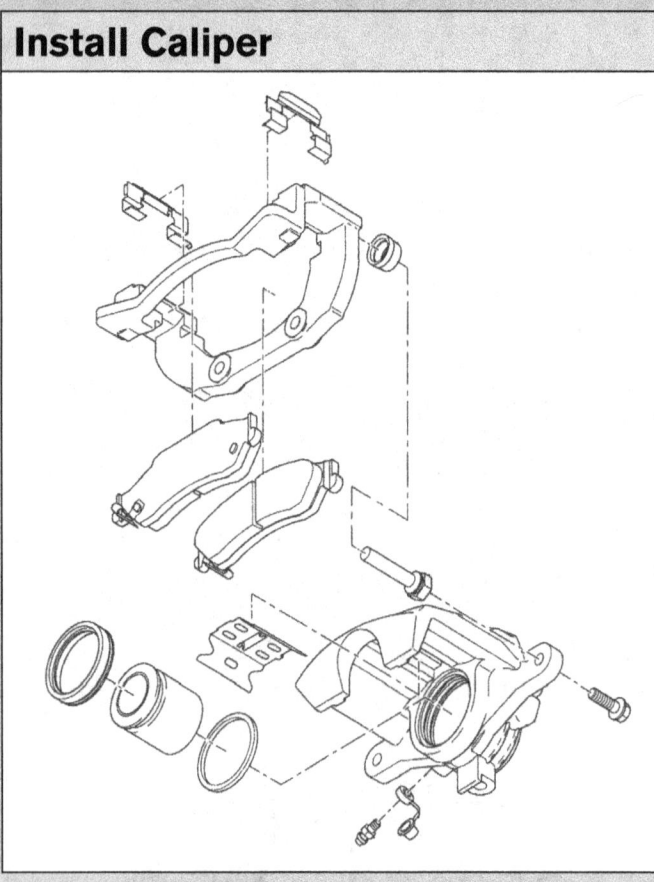

Acquire New Rotor Parts

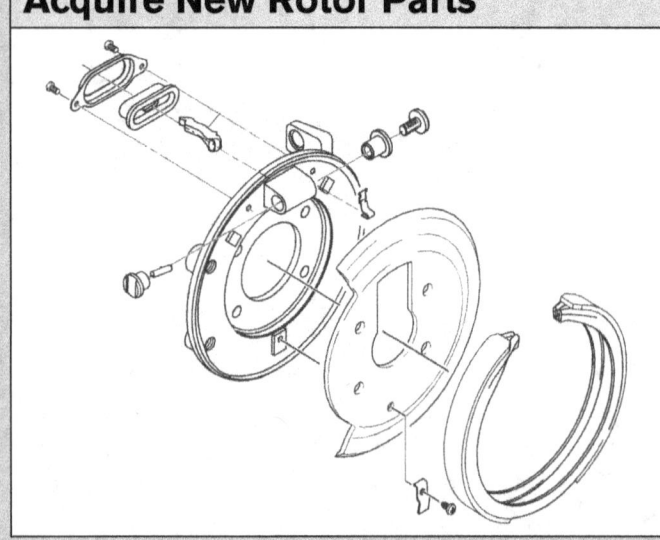

7 This exploded view of the S-based truck caliper shows the single piston, O-rings, pads, retaining cage, and various fittings and fasteners. These are available new from GM or a remanufacturer, and the price difference is substantial. (Diagram Courtesy General Motors. Used with Permission, GM Media Archive)

Install Mounting Flange

8 This diagram of the entire S-based truck rear end shows a partial view of the braking system. You can see how easily the backing plate can be adapted to an older rear end, as the mounting flanges are actually the same. This is what makes the entire swap so straightforward. (Diagram Courtesy General Motors. Used with Permission, GM Media Archive)

9 Though the design in this exploded view is slightly different, it shows what you see after removing the rotor. The rotor's integral parking brake drum hides the shoe. GM sells all of these pieces as a kit for $164.23 per side. (Diagram Courtesy General Motors. Used with Permission, GM Media Archive)

Remove Axle Shafts

10 After removing your current drum brake components, the new parts simply bolt onto any 1965-and-newer 8.2-inch, 8.5-inch 10-bolt, or 12-bolt differential. The drum housing is unbolted from the axle tubes in the same fashion as the disc brake backing plates were removed from the truck axle. You need to remove the axle shafts. To do this, drive out the cross-shaft pinch bolt with a punch, and then remove the C-clip by sliding the axle into the housing. The C-clips may fall out on their own or you may need to use a screwdriver to pry them out. Replace the stock S-10 studs with 1-inch-longer wheel studs.. Use a mallet or hammer to pop out the old wheel studs and clean the holes with a wire brush. Lubricate the splines on the studs and push them through the back of the hub. Then torque down the lug nuts on the front of the hub so the heads of the lug nuts are fully seated on the hub. Next, slide the bearing retainer, backing plate, and dust shield onto the axle for the driver's side (left), and slide the axle into the rear end. Use stainless steel grade-8 bolts with lock washers, and bolt the axle to the axle flange. Shim as necessary to center the caliper, and torque the axle flange bolts to 35 ft-lbs. (Photo Courtesy Imran Chaudary)

Position Brake Pads

11 After you place the rotor on the wheel studs, position the brake pads into their retaining cage and place them over the rotor. Use a ratchet and socket to bolt down the retainer bracket to the backing plate using lock washers. (Photo Courtesy Imran Chaudary)

Slide Caliper over Brake Pads

12 Slide the new caliper over the pads and bolt it to the retainer plate. At this point, you are ready to install new brake lines, an adjustable proportioning valve, and if needed, a new master cylinder. (Photo Courtesy Imran Chaudary)

Rear Disc-Brake Conversion CONTINUED

Purchase Brake Parts

13 The dust shields, calipers, rotors, and pads can be purchased from your local dealer or parts supplier, and I strongly recommend that these particular parts be new.

The caliper I purchased at a local dealer was a remanufactured unit for $36. It is a single-piston, full-floating unit that is a huge improvement over the factory-installed drum.

Install Brake Line Bracket

14 Chaudary used a brake line bracket from the front of a Chevy 3/4-ton truck for his conversion. He slid the line through the hole in the bracket and used a retainer clip at the coupler to hold it to the bracket, just like the factory does for front brake lines. Next, he drilled holes and bolted the bracket to the shock mounts on the rear end. He then hooked up the lines and bled the brakes. Then he clipped the original GTO front parking brake cable to an S-10 rear parking brake cable and checked for proper operation. (Photo Courtesy Imran Chaudary)

Parts List

- 1998–2002 two-wheel-drive Blazer, Jimmy, and Envoy SUVs, and S-10 and S-15 pickup trucks with rear disc brakes
- LH caliper (AC Delco) 19141678
- RH caliper (AC Delco) 19141679
- Rotor (2 required) 15733196
- GM DuraStop rotor (GM Replace Series) 18039567
- Brake pad cage (2 required) 18026155
- Brake pads (pair) 18038569
- LH backing plate 88935985
- RH backing plate 88935986
- Shoe kit (2 required) 12376595
- LH backing plate kit 15047014
- RH backing plate kit 15047013
- Brake fluid 12377767
- Dust shield (2 required) 88935987
- Flexible brake line
- Wheel studs 1-inch Longer
- Axle bolts 1-inch longer

Once everything has been bolted to the rear end, a few things are left to do. To finish, cut the existing brake line, install a threaded coupler, and flare the line. Finally, attach a flexible brake line to the coupler. Here you may want to fabricate a bracket to hold the flex line to the rear end. Next you can set up the parking brake.

CHAPTER 9

INTERIOR

The interior portion of your restoration is as much about perception as it is about reality. How well the interior turns out reflects on the quality of the rest of your GTO's restoration. The good news is that this is one portion of the restoration that you can likely do yourself, and just about everything you could possibly need is available in high-quality reproduction.

Most of the restoration parts available are quite authentic looking and work well. There is not as much difference in quality of interior parts as there is with other restoration parts, such as die-stamped versus hand-formed quarter panels. However, owners seeking the most authentic interiors can spend a little more and get a bit more quality and correctness.

Like the rest of the car, the components of the interior are subjected to wear, tear, aging, and deterioration. While it is indeed possible for an interior to survive in near-mint condition for the life of a vehicle, it is far more likely that its overall condition is consistent with the condition of the rest of the car. Therefore, if the interior is original or more than 20 years old, it needs help.

As with other major systems in need of attention, the choice to do this portion of the restoration yourself hinges largely on your skill set, but this is one area where you can save yourself some money and do most, if not all, the work yourself. The disassembly requires little more than regular hand tools and with the possible exception of headliner installation, you probably have all the skills necessary to complete the job.

The truth be told, the interior of our 1969 GTO Judge coupe was pretty worn out and needed pretty much everything, which is a common situation. Forty-plus years of sun, heat, and wear take their toll. The seats and door panels were cracked, faded, and musty and the carpeting actually had holes in certain areas. Fortunately, replacements are readily available. (Photo Courtesy Scott Tiemann)

CHAPTER 9

Disassembly and Evaluation of Components

As you unbolt and unscrew the original interior pieces, keep in mind that you may be able to re-use more than you realize. Restoration technology has advanced significantly in the last decade or so, and items that were once relegated to the scrap bin can now be saved and re-used because original finishes and textures can now be replicated, sometimes even at home. NOS or reproduction parts might not be available, or too costly for the budget, so refurbishing an otherwise serviceable item offers a solution.

A good example of this advancement is in the area of rechroming plastic. Twenty years ago, the technology was just starting to creep from the model car hobby into the restoration world, but now it is a cost-effective and viable alternative that can return dash inserts, armrests, knobs, and other items to their original splendor. Even if your item is not in perfect condition, it can most likely be repaired prior to the rechroming process. Even large damaged areas can be saved, further extending the budget.

As you remove door panels, unbolt seats, and peel back old carpeting, make mental notes. You

If most of your interior is in great shape, it still is a wise investment to replace all of the seat upholstery when one seat is in need of recovering. No interior manufacturer is going to be able to compensate for the aging of the original material and no matter what you do, the seats will not have a consistent color or wear match. By replacing all of the seat upholstery, the interior has a "just-built" look that positively reflects on the entire restoration. (Photo Courtesy Scott Tiemann)

When removing carpeting for replacement, make sure that you remove the insulation and padding underneath. These items are notorious for holding moisture and likely are musty smelling and deteriorating. This is also an opportunity to add some aftermarket sound deadener, such as DynaMat or Eastwood Thermo-Coustic sound deadener. This insulation adds weight to the car but the difference it makes in interior acoustics is really amazing. Best of all, once installed, it is invisible and also insulates the cabin from heat and cold. If you are adding a louder-than-stock exhaust system or a high-end aftermarket stereo system, sound insulation is an inexpensive and worthwhile investment. Fat Mat (shown here) is popular with many in-car entertainment installation companies and has many comparable qualities to DynaMat at roughly half the cost.

INTERIOR

are sure to notice items that are in obvious need of replacement, such as threadbare carpeting, ripped seat covers, and water-damaged package-shelf cardboard, but other items may just need a good cleaning and/or repainting. For example, are the interior kick panels still in good shape? Can they be reused and brought back to new condition with a simple repainting? Can the window crank knobs be polished and returned to service? Can the steering wheel be cleaned, repaired, and re-used?

You can really save money by figuring out what is still good in your interior. By retaining original pieces, you also have a leg up on authenticity. While the impulse may be to grab a reproduction parts catalog and order everything in sight, it might not be the best way to go, budget-wise.

Authentic Reproductions

Once you have figured out what can be re-used and what has to be replaced, you can start ordering parts. The next question is, "Which products are better than others?" When it comes to soft parts, such as seat upholstery and door panels, Legendary Auto Interiors is consistently recognized as producing the best reproduction interior components available. Of course, this comes with a price. Legendary's interior pieces are consistently 30-plus percent higher in price than from its competitors, but in the end, it boils down to whether you want to pay the premium price for the superior quality.

The other main interior parts supplier is Parts Unlimited, Inc. (PUI).

Inspection of the dash and gauge cluster shows the effects of 40-plus years of use and the elements. When disassembling the dash, keep in mind that the more careful you are, the better the likelihood of being able to use most of the original pieces. The major components of this dash cluster look like they can be re-used after some cleaning. (Photo Courtesy Scott Tiemann)

It is amazing how much of a difference fresh gauge lenses make in the overall look of a gauge cluster. If yours are cracked or yellowed, replacements are readily available. Sometimes, just a thorough cleaning and polishing restore their clarity—and saves some money in the process. (Photo Courtesy Scott Tiemann)

CHAPTER 9

While Legendary is the choice for the concours, points-judged crowd, PUI also offers some high-quality components at more affordable prices. The main difference is in the finishing—the vinyl PUI uses is correct, the contours are good, but in many cases, additional work is needed to get them to work correctly.

For example, PUIs door panels holes for window cranks, armrests, and door handles are not pre-cut into the vinyl, though some holes are cut in the cardboard base. Those have to be opened up by the installer. Of course, that negates their returnability.

In some cases, more assembly is required, such as with interior quarter panels, and seat covers may need some additional effort to position correctly. If you are pinching pennies and don't mind a little extra work, PUI interior parts are more than acceptable.

In order to show you how to cut the holes and do the extra work involved, we are using PUI interior parts in this book.

Mix and Match?

Soft items, such as seat covers and interior door panels, must be of the same condition and from the same company to maintain a consistent appearance. If one seat needs recovering, do them all. It does not make sense to recover one bucket seat and not the other, or have front and rear bench seats not match. While it might appear to save money, it quickly reveals itself and the seats do not look uniform, harming the overall appearance of the restoration. The perception of the entire restoration is reflected in the interior—skimp here and some may wonder what other shortcuts were taken elsewhere.

Vapor Barriers

Whether you call them vapor barriers or water shields, they are the paper shields installed between the metal door shell and the interior upholstery panel. Factory units were made out of tar-covered paper, and they become deteriorated after decades of use. When that happens, the cardboard backing of the door panels becomes wet and distorted, becoming warped and moldy, requiring replacement. Moisture can even move into the carpeting and damage the floorboards, causing rust problems. Wet footwear bringing moisture to the carpeting and water leaking from the doors into the cabin are the main causes of floorpan rust damage.

The water shields work in conjunction with the water drains in the door shell to keep water out of the interior. When rain collects at the base of the door glass, the water shields are part of the routing system that moves water into the drain holes. If they are not present or not working properly, water seeps into areas it is not supposed to and causes damage.

While the original-style paper units are available, it makes sense to use plastic replacements, as they are much more resistant to the elements. These are available commercially, though you can make them yourself out of clear or translucent polyethylene sheeting for just a few bucks. Use the original units as templates and simply cut out new ones with a scissors. It makes sense to use water shields made of a non-biodegradable material and further protect your investment.

Attaching vapor barriers to the door shell is accomplished with trim adhesive or strip caulk. Using transparent plastic shields has the added advantage of allowing you to see whether your installation is actually sealing off the elements.

Carpet and Sill Panels

Factory carpeting was a rayon/nylon blend molded to fit the contours of the floorpans. Depending on the model year, assembly plant, and supplier, some minor variations did occur, but these don't affect performance. The carpets were a two-piece design with the rear installed first and the front section fitting over it at the trailing edge.

While carpet replacement is not brain surgery, there is a more to it than pulling the old one out and sticking the new one in. The seats must all be removed, along with the seat tracks, console, and sill panels. The factory-installed insulation should also be removed at this time—chances are it is deteriorated, damp, and smells bad.

The carpet installation also assumes that any repairs to the floorpans have already been performed at this point in your GTO restoration. If you find rust holes or rust damage that weakens the floorpan integrity, refer to Chapter 3 for instructions on floorpan replacement.

As for the quality of reproduction carpets, most restorers report that there is not much, if any, difference in quality in the offerings of various manufacturers. Auto Custom Carpets, Ames Performance Engineering, Performance Years, Original Parts Group, and Year One offer suitable replacement factory-style carpets.

With the advancements made in materials since these cars were new, it makes sense to use some

INTERIOR

modern sound-deadening insulation, though replacement-type materials are available. There are many good products available, such as DynaMat, Eastwood Thermo-Coustic, or Fat Mat. You can also get creative and use suitable radiant barrier as found at many home improvement stores. The upshot is that whatever you use, it is invisible, so appearance is not affected, though having a quieter, more solid feeling interior enhances the overall quality of your project.

Door-sill panels are one area with a slight difference in authenticity. If you are looking for the most authentic reproductions available, make sure that the Fisher Body tag is correctly riveted onto the sill, rather than simply glued on. If you find yourself with glued-on panels, you can get the correct panels from Original Parts Group.

The inside of our 1969 Judge is as empty as a tin can. There is actually a bit of work to do before the carpet installation, most notably, the installation of the seat tracks.

Test fitting all the parts ensures a smooth final installation.

Carpet Installation

Inspect Carpet

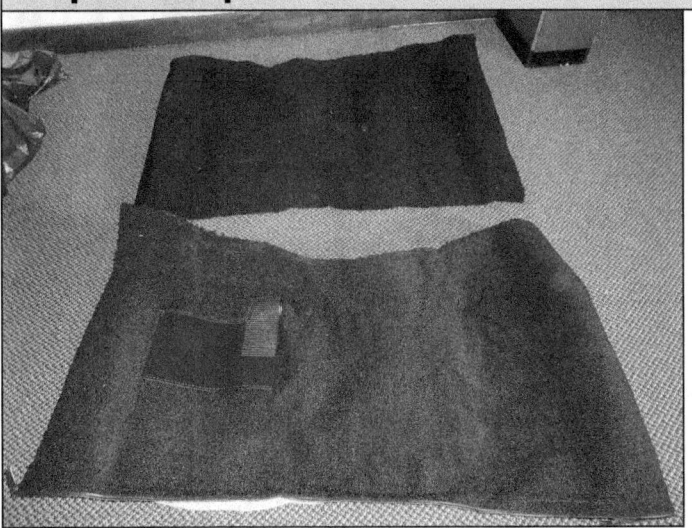

1 *Be sure to roll out the new carpet flat and look for wrinkles or imperfections. The wrinkles can be steamed out at installation time, but damage or a manufacturing defect doesn't go away. At this point, the carpet is still returnable; if it is altered in any way, it's yours.*

CHAPTER 9

Remove Wrinkles

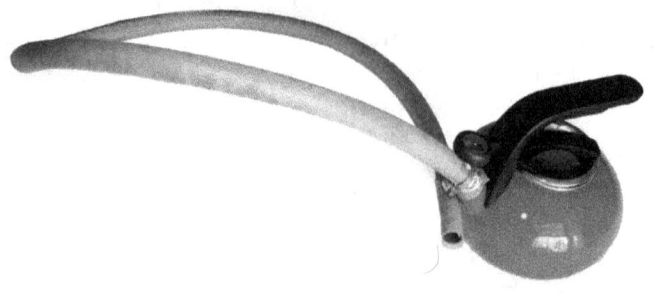

2 *While some installers have exotic and expensive steamers to do the job, you can use a low-buck, low-tech alternative. It is nothing more than a tea kettle with a long length of heater hose clamped to the spout. Using a hot plate or camping stove as a heat source, the steam passes though the tube and exits at the far end. Total cost was less than $15. If you want to be a hero, buy a nice new tea kettle for your wife/girlfriend/mother and take her old one in trade.*

Test Fit Carpet

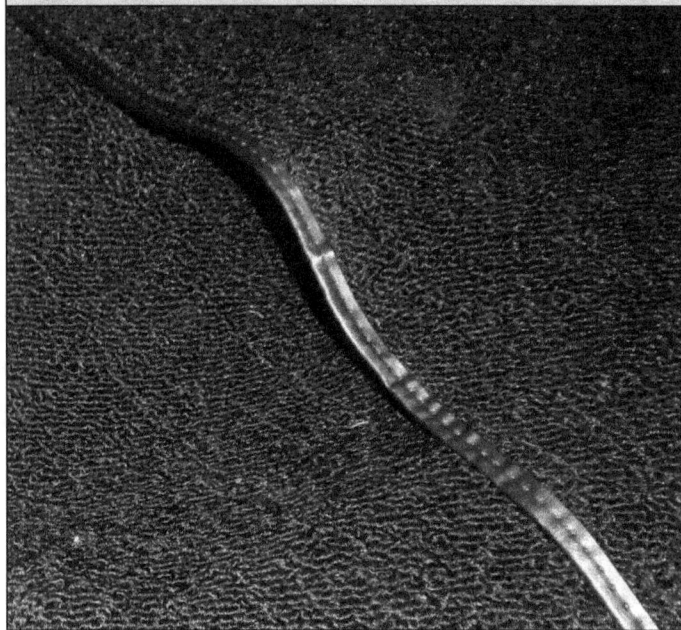

3 *The test fitting begins with laying the rear carpet first and then the front. The trailing edge of the front should lay over the leading edge of the rear.*

Cut Out for Seat Frame

4 *Use a knife to make cutouts for the rear seat frame so that the seat can lock into the mount without interference.*

INTERIOR

Cut for Seat Belt Anchors

5 The seat belt anchor areas need to be opened up in order to install the bolts. Cut holes rather than Xs. This way, the bolt threads are not cut into the carpet causing it to unravel.

Cut for Floor Shifter

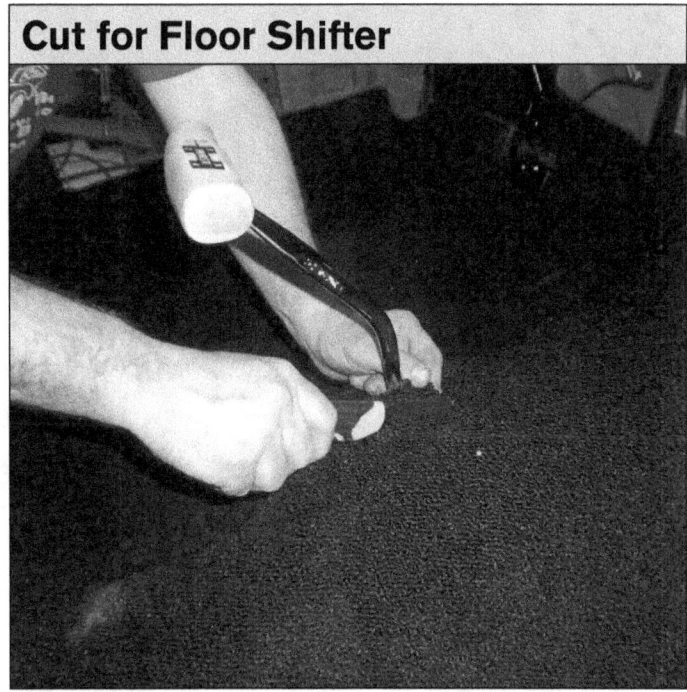

6 Cut away the floor shifter area to allow for its proper operation. If your car doesn't have a console, use the boot trim as a template for the cut. You can be a little more liberal with the cutting if you have a console, but be careful not to cut away more than is necessary.

Cut for Seat Anchors

7 Uncover the seat anchors, cutting small circular holes.

Trim for Sills

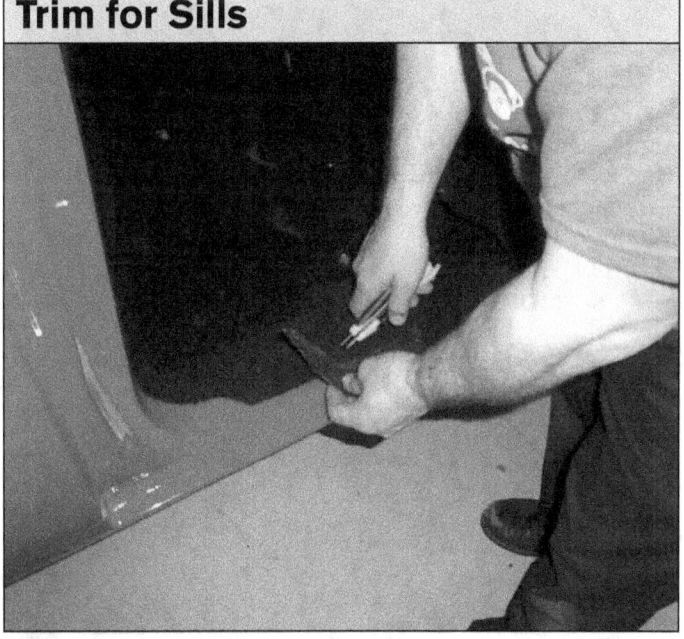

8 If your carpet is significantly wider than necessary, hanging over the rocker panels, cut it back to make it easier to work with the door sill panels. After the excess is cut away, use the sill panels as guides to make the final cuts.

HOW TO RESTORE YOUR PONTIAC GTO 1964–1974

CHAPTER 9

Door Panel Installation

Inspect Door Panel

1 The PUI interior door panel looks very authentic and correct but lacks some of the holes needed for a proper installation. Some are pre-drilled in the cardboard backing and not in the vinyl and some are not there at all.

Cut Door Panel Holes

2 The upshot is that the holes are easy to cut and the cost of the panel is significantly less than the Legendary equivalents. Both look correct after proper installation.

Inspect Armrest

3 If your original armrests are in good shape, you can clean them up with Simple Green and reuse them.

Remove Window Hardware

4 If your restoration uses all new glass, pull out the original windows and transfer the hardware to the new side glass. The difference it makes to the overall appearance of the car is nothing short of amazing.

Bolt Glass to Window Track

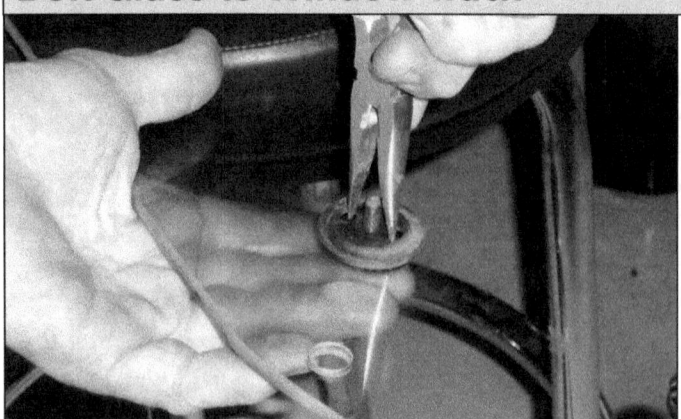

5 This replacement door glass is an exact reproduction, even down to the date-coding etched into the surface. Bolt the glass to the window track to allow it to go up and down. Even though there are rubber grommets that go between the glass and the metal track, there is no need to tighten the bolts to anything more than snug. The last thing you need to do is put a stress crack in the new and expensive door glass.

INTERIOR

Loosen Window Tracks

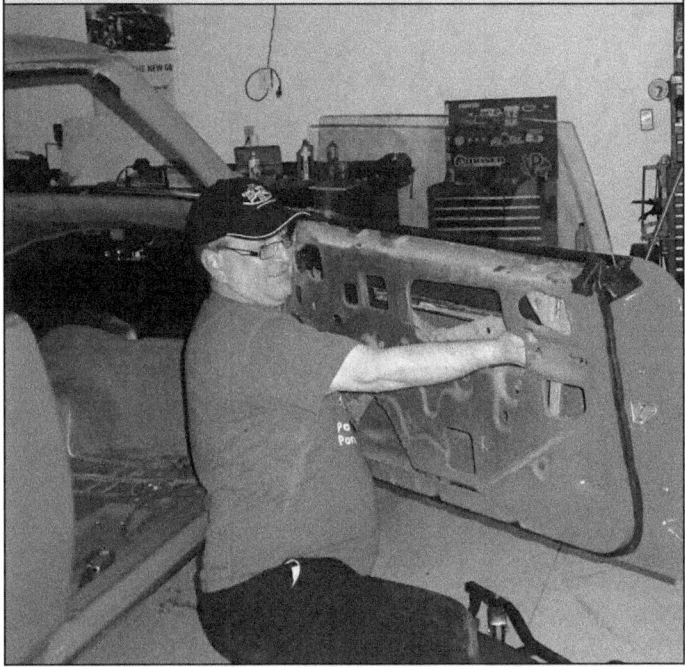

6 Loosen the window tracks in the door in order to install the new glass. Carefully slide it in and test for up-and-down clearance.

Inspect Tabs

8 This cloth-covered tab puts tension on the window to hold it firmly in place as it travels up and down. Be sure to check the tabs for condition, as they can scratch the glass over time if the protective cloth is damaged. Make sure they are still flexible and able to keep the glass in the track. If not, remove them and replace them; it's a simple bolt-on.

Inspect Glass Tensioners

7 When realigning all of the pieces, take note of the cloth-covered glass tensioners. These keep the window moving smoothly in the track and help the glass contact the window seals to provide a watertight fit.

Install Door Lock Clips

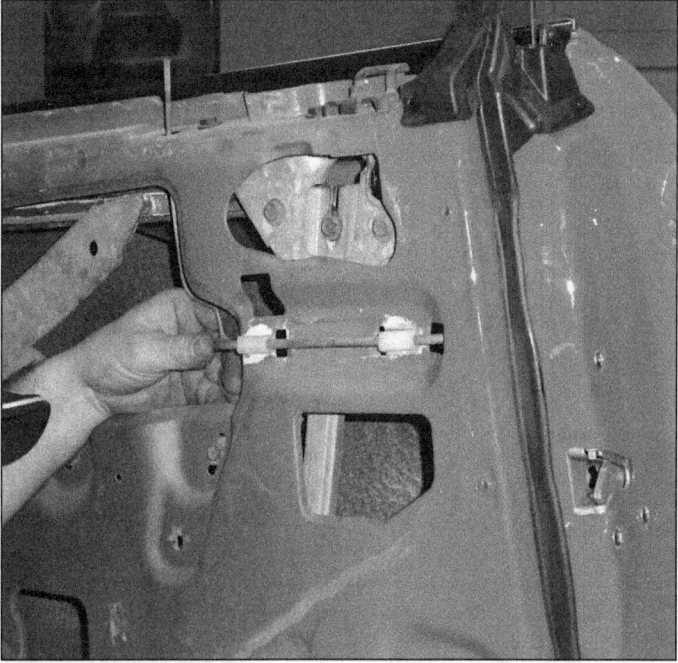

9 The door lock mechanism requires the two plastic clips that locate and retain the metal rod assembly be intact to prevent binding, which would hinder the up-and-down movement necessary to operate the lock. These clips snap into the door shell without tools, but if they are broken, they need to be replaced.

Reinstall Door Lock Linkage

10 Reinstall the linkage for the door lock button. Add white lithium grease, both to allow the plastic holder to slide into the door easily and to prevent sticky operation of the door locks. The homemade plastic vapor barrier goes on with stick caulk.

Reinstall Armrest

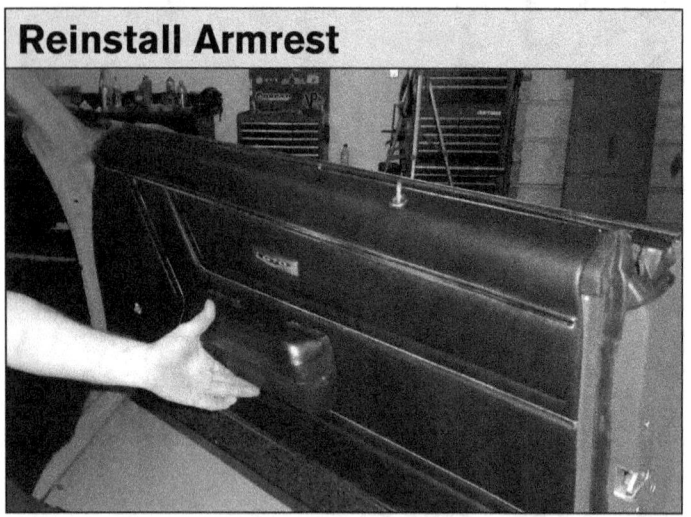

12 Once the door panel, window crank, and door handle are installed, the last part of the procedure is to reinstall the armrest. If yours are usable, a cleaning is likely all they require. If you need new ones, they are available from most of the restoration parts houses. It is advisable to replace all of them if one is bad in order to keep the look consistent. This original armrest was in near-mint condition and went back on using the stock screws.

Reinstall Door Handle

11 After the holes were opened up with a scissors and were trimmed to match the hole punched in the cardboard, the doorhandle and window crank, both were re-installed with the ring clips.

Completed Door Panel

13 The door panel installation was completed and it looks great. As mentioned, the PUI door panels did require more finishing work for a proper installation, compared to their Legendary Interiors counterparts, but they are quite a bit less expensive. If you are willing to do a little more work, it is an opportunity to save some money, which could go elsewhere in the restoration.

Deck Package Installation

Test Fit Rear Deck Package

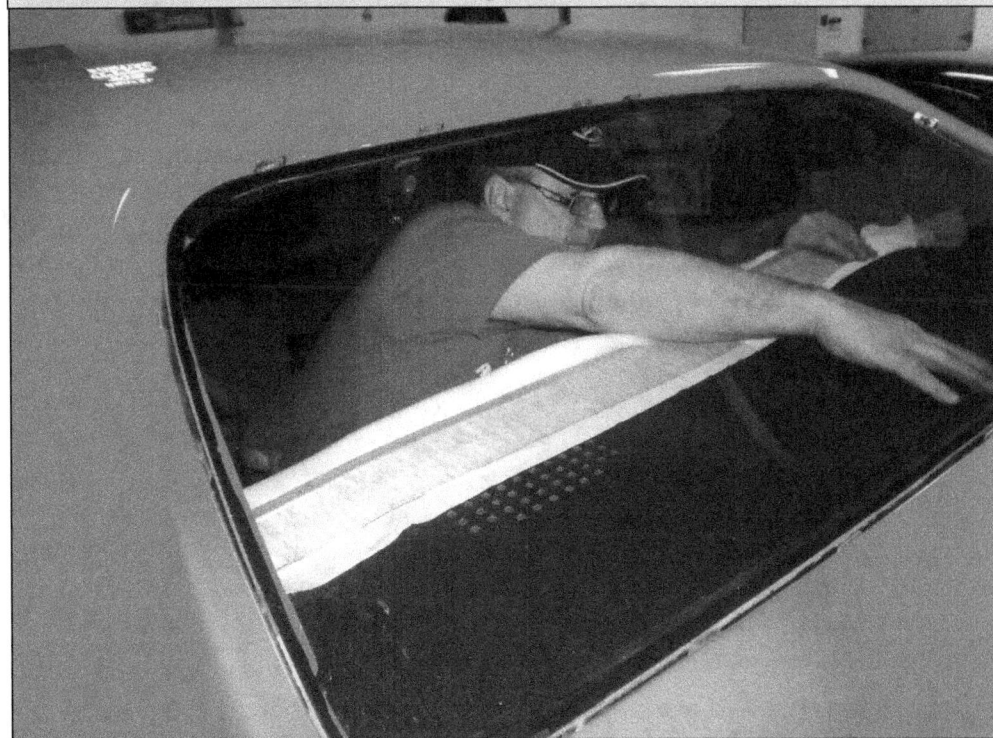

1 The installation of the rear deck package is one of the easier operations. It can be finished in minutes. Start by test fitting it and sliding it into place without. Ideally, it should slide under the base of the rear window. The upholstered flap is left up as shown.

Apply Glue

Smooth Flap

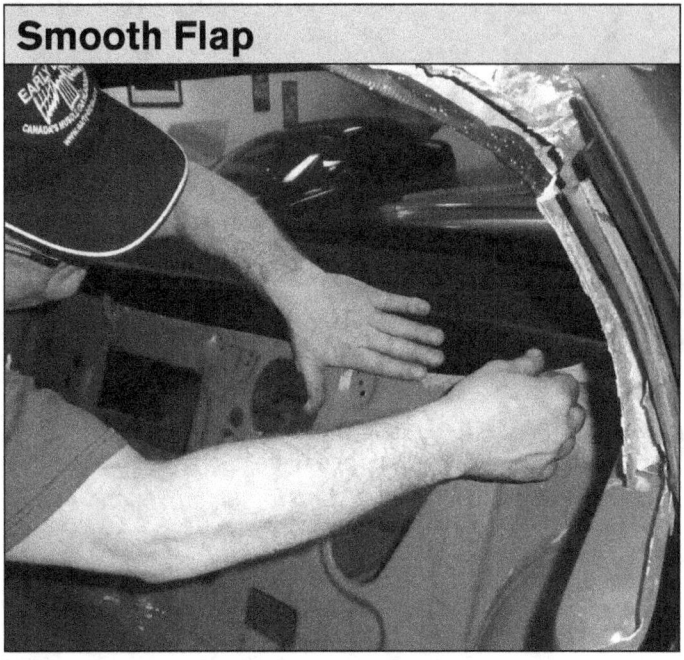

3 Carefully spread the upholstered flap over the top of the bulkhead and smooth it down. That's it!

2 Spray a light, but even, coat of glue over the top of the rear bulkhead panel, just enough to see a light beading.

CHAPTER 9

Dash Pad Restoration

Dash pads are an area where you spend a lot of money for absolute authenticity or sacrifice a bit of correctness for huge savings. When performing a concours-type restoration, it is standard operating procedure to take any less-than-perfect dash and send it to a company such as Just Dashes or Dashboard Restoration USA for a complete remanufacture of the original dash to as-new condition.

It is a costly and time-consuming procedure that can run more than $1,000, depending on the year of the car, the condition of the original unit, and who is doing the work. In a "worst case scenario" dash restoration, the unit is completely stripped of the vinyl cover and foam. From there, new foam is installed and shaped to provide the perfect fit for the new vinyl cover. Adhesive is then sprayed over the foam.

From there, the part is placed in a vacuum-forming machine, where it is heated until pliable. Then a sheet of correctly-grained vinyl is sucked over the foam, replicating the original shape of the dash. It is cooled, excess material is trimmed off, and the edges are glued into place. The process is completed when the correct color is applied to the dash.

While it sounds simple, it is an involved process that is time-consuming and, thus, costly. The end result is a restored dash that cannot be distinguished from an original piece—it really is that good.

For many restorers, the cost of a high level of authenticity cannot be justified, particularly if the car is going to be a driver. If you're restoring a car that's destined to be a points-judged car, you have to invest in a top-quality interior. But if you are a home-restorer building your car on lunch money, it's most likely a bit too much.

Fortunately for bargain-hunters, an alternative is available in the form of a vacuum-formed dash cover that fits directly over the cracked, nasty original. While the quality can vary from year to year and manufacturer to manufacturer, there are good ones that when properly installed, are difficult to detect. They usually come in black and can be painted to match any interior.

Best of all, they can be installed without removing the dash and they glue into place using 3M Trim Adhesive or an equivalent product sometimes supplied with the kit. The

Replacing the dash pad is a time-consuming job, but in many cases necessary because the existing dash has been sun-faded and cracked, and for all intents and purposes, it's worn out. To remove the dash, first remove the pedals, defroster assembly, ashtray, radio, and steering column. Once this is done, you have access to the dash and are able to remove it in one piece. Once the dash is removed from the car, you have full access to the gauges and the wiring harness. Remove the gauges, lights, and wiring from the dash panel. If the wiring is original, it may be brittle, cracked, or frayed. If this is the case, the wiring must be replaced.

Often, the metallic bezels for the speedometer, tach, and gas gauge need to be refinished and you need to send the dash out for this to be done by a professional. If the gauges themselves are functional, you can re-install them. However, for a factory-new appearance, you should send out the gauges for reconditioning. To restore the finish of the dash, professionals apply a metallic material to the various areas of the dash. Once that has been completed, the walnut veneer is applied to the dash.

INTERIOR

cost can run between $80 and $300, the dashes from earlier model years running quite a bit less due to their simpler design.

The downside is that they often are a harder plastic than original, and while they usually look fine, they do not have the same feel. This might be offset somewhat by the feeling of having $800 left over in your pocket to put elsewhere.

Pedal Assemblies

Fortunately, the floor pedals of your GTO do not require a tremendous amount of attention. Aside from replacing any parts too damaged to use, they do not need anything more than painting and replacing the rubber pedal pads.

Steering Wheels

Original standard steering wheels feature steel rims with a plastic outer layer. In the early years, the wheels were a hard plastic, which tended to crack with extended use and exposure to ultraviolet rays. You can restore them with a repair kit, such as ones offered by POR-15 and Eastwood. From these kits, a plastic putty is carefully spread into the cracks and sanded smooth. Then the rim is prepped for paint with cleaning agents supplied in the kit and repainted. The chrome trim is polished or replaced.

This method is great if the wheel isn't too badly damaged, and there aren't any missing pieces of plastic. However, if the wheel is substantially damaged or worn, you won't be able to correctly repair it on your own. Therefore, you should buy a wheel in better condition at a swap meet, from classified ads, or on eBay.

If you have a seriously damaged original steering wheel and want to bring it back to concours-level condition, companies such as Quality Restorations or D&D Automobilia can help. They strip all of the plastic off your steering wheel and recast it, so it is exactly as new. This procedure can run north of $1,000, so like the dash recovering, it is a costly process.

In 1969, the standard GTO steering wheel was a vinyl-cushioned three-spoke design with a matching vinyl center. These wheels, while softer, proved to be very durable, and as long as they are not cut, can usually be brought back to like-new condition by disassembling and thoroughly cleaning. Never use a petroleum-based cleaner on any plastic steering wheel, as it severely damages the finish. Instead, use a biodegradable cleaner such as Simple Green. The stuff is amazing, removes years of dirt and grime, and rejuvenates the wheel's appearance.

Of course, there is also the possibility of adding a wood wheel to spruce up the appearance of your interior. While originals can

The standard steering wheels on early GTOs are made of opaque plastic over a steel rim and they sometimes crack. Eastwood Company has a line of fillers and primers that remove the cracks and prep the wheel for final painting. If the steering wheel is missing or you just want the optional and highly sought-after wood wheel, quality reproductions are now available.

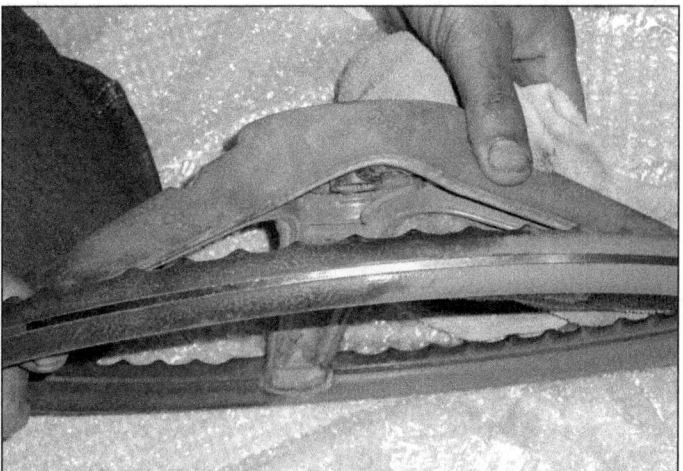

Later GTO standard steering wheels are steel rims covered with flexible vinyl. If they aren't damaged, they can be brought back with a thorough cleaning. Never use anything petroleum-based such as paint thinner to clean the steering wheel, as it destroys the plastic. Instead, use a cleaner such as Simple Green, which does a fantastic job of removing years of dirt and grime. Allow to dry thoroughly and reassemble.

sometimes top $2,000, depending on year, reproductions are now on the market that look very authentic and cost significantly less. Most years cost in the $300 range, though the rarer 1964 version is now available for about $500. Admittedly, that is a lot of money, but it's more affordable than a recast of a standard wheel, and it looks better.

Restoration of an original wood wheel is even more complex than that of the standard wheel. The reason is because the wood isn't really wood but wood-grained plastic. Actual wood was rejected from production due to the possibility of splintering in a collision.

Again, the process for restoring them is expensive, but some have had good luck at home restoring them. The procedure is similar to restoring a standard wheel—using putty, surface prep, and paint. It is difficult, but not impossible to recut the wood grain in the wheel. There are several companies, such as Gary's Steering Wheel Restoration, experienced in the process and can do the job for a reasonable price and guarantee it. My advice is to have a pro do it because the time you spend to complete the restoration could be better used elsewhere.

Seat Belts

As with any safety device, this is an area where corners should never be cut. Reproduction seat belts are available from most restoration parts suppliers. Additionally, restoration services for originals are available from companies such as Snake Oyl Products and Morris Custom Classics. They disassemble the originals, re-plate the buckles, and replace the original webbing with new equivalents, authentic down to the date-coded labels. If your seat-belt hardware is in good enough condition, these companies add new belt webbing to your existing belts. It is more cost effective than a full restoration, yet it returns full functionality to your safety restraint system.

Whatever you do, resist the temptation to re-use the original belt material. I know that some restorers just clean them with Simple Green, let them dry, and call it a day. This is, in my opinion, an unwarranted safety risk. In any restoration project, the belt webbing should be replaced, as it can be a safety hazard due to aging, deteriorating fabric. If you want to use more affordable reproductions, fine—just don't risk disaster by re-using the original belt webbing. You and your family deserve better.

Kick Panels

Kick panels came by their name naturally, and as a result, are not always treated well. On non-air-conditioned cars, the kick panels house vents, which are operated by a cable with a knob on the end. These cables can become bent, which greatly hinders their operation. As a kid, I remember trying to shut the vent on my dad's car by pushing the cable with my foot and bending it badly. Of course, I got in trouble for it. After my father repaired it, I remember the chewing out being severe enough to never attempt it again!

The panels themselves are prone to rough usage and can sometimes be damaged in the process. Remove them by pulling them away from the body once all of the screws are removed. Getting your fingers behind the outer edge of the vent hole or the bottom gets the process started. The passenger side should be fairly easy, but the driver's side sometimes requires the emergency brake pedal to be removed. The panels are fairly flexible, so it is a matter of maneuvering them to clear the bottom of the dash. Once they are out, they can be painted with vinyl paint or replaced. Be consistent—paint them both or replace them both.

More importantly, once the kick panels are out, clean out the ducting. Over the years, leaves, twigs, pine needles, and other assorted debri get in there, retains moisture, and cause rust damage. GM designed its Astro Ventilation system to use these ducts as a primary source of fresh air, and they have built-in water ducting and drains that keep water out of the interior. They work together with the drains in the cowl sides, rockers, doors, and quarter panels. When they become clogged, they retain water and rusting begins.

Console

If bucket seats were installed, consoles were available on any GTO. Over the years, the designs changed, though a cast-plastic base was used throughout the GTO production run. The 1964–1966 versions featured a ribbed, chrome-plated, pot-metal top surface. In 1967, woodgrain appliqués were used. In 1968, a new design featured a grained plastic outer body and a padded-and-upholstered storage compartment door.

Consoles take quite a bit of abuse, particularly the storage compartment door, which can become damaged, as well as the mounting points for it on the base. Once the base is broken, it is quite difficult to perform a satisfactory repair—the combination of aging plastic and the stress point at the mounting bracket ensures any repair is a temporary repair.

Most pieces necessary to put your console back in tip-top shape are available from the aftermarket, including storage compartment lids, wood-grain inserts, trim pieces and fasteners, lamps, wiring harnesses, shift selector indicators, among others.

Reproduction bases are available for all applications from 1964 to 1972, except for the automatic 1968 version. There are differences in the shifter bezel area and though a 1969-up version fits, it is not correct. Additionally, a complete reproduction console kit for 1965–1966 models is available. If you plan to add a console to a car that didn't originally have one, you must drill holes to mount it to the transmission/driveshaft tunnel and add the proper wiring harness for the lighting.

Seat Installation

Disassemble Seats

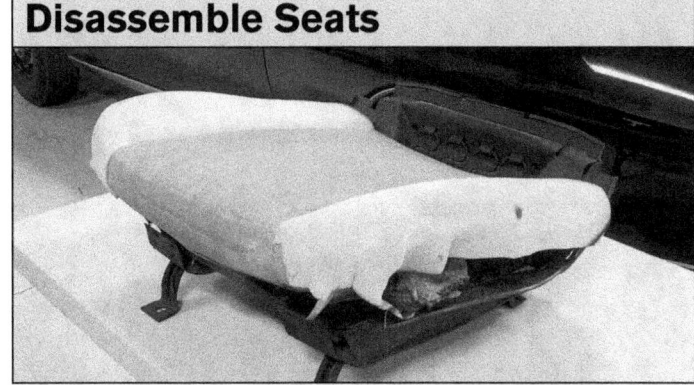

1 On this project, the original seats were disassembled and relieved of their original covers. The springs were not broken and had not sagged. Though the seat frames and springs were originally left as bare metal by the factory, these were shot with semi-gloss black paint to prevent rusting. The original seat cushions, sometimes referred to as buns, were still firm and supple, without any drying out, so they were retained. If yours are dried out or otherwise unusable, reproductions are available. In order to fill the seat covers and compensate for any settling, thin sheets of foam can be glued on the outer edges of the cushions.

Load Hog Rings

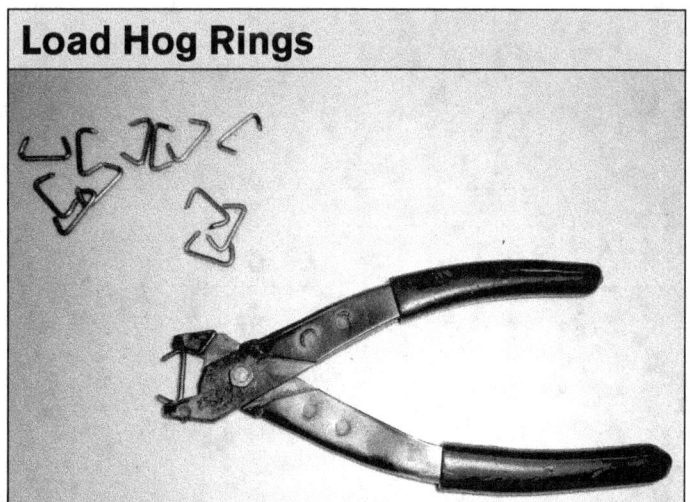

2 Use hog rings to fasten the seat cover to the frame. Load them into a special set of pliers and bend them into shape. Hog rings pierce the upholstery along a seam reinforced by a metal rod. The rods are not usually included in a reproduction seat cover kit. If the rods are not usable from the original covers, new ones can be fashioned out of sections of a brass coat hanger. The brass does not rust away like steel does.

Insert Extra Foam Blocks

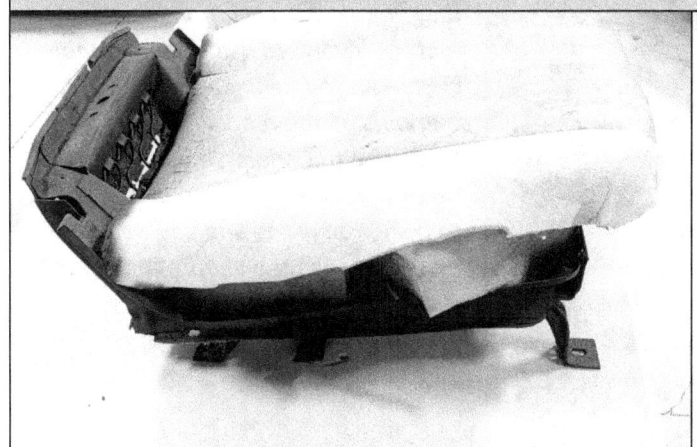

3 Blocks of foam can also be stuffed into the void between the bottom of the seat bun and the frame to quiet the metal springs. This area is hidden by the bottom seat cover.

CHAPTER 9

Test Fit Seat Cover

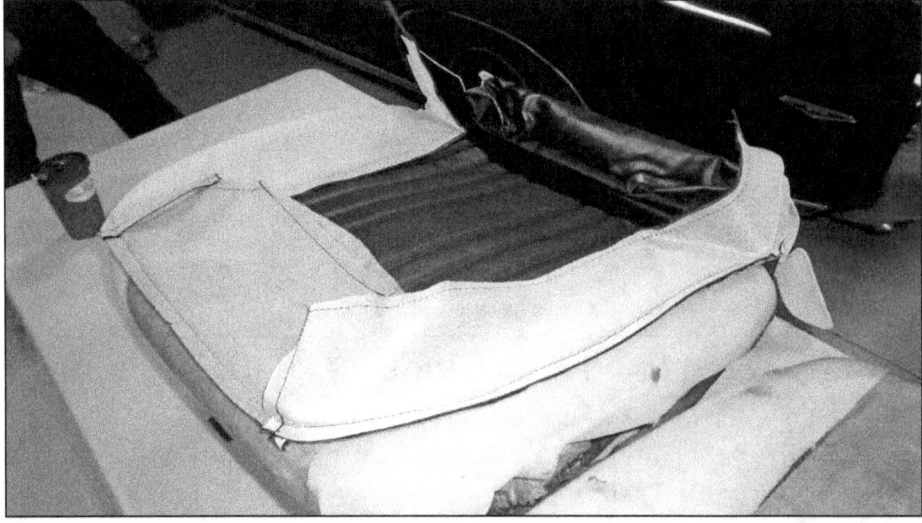

4 Lay the new seat cover over the seat cushion and check for the general fit. Some brands of reproduction covers may fit a little better than others, but with a bit of coaxing, you can attain a satisfactory and attractive outcome.

Insert Rod into Seat Cover

5 Carefully guide the reinforcement rod through the sheaths built into the seat cover. There are sheaths located around the bottom perimeter and also in the area between the main seating area and the side bolsters. Use a wire cutter to trim off excess coat hanger.

Attach Hog Rings

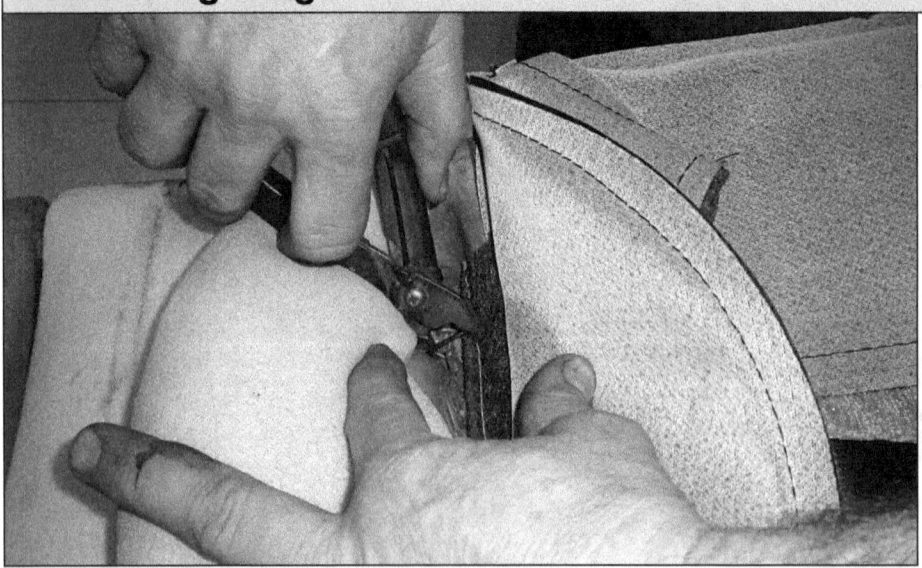

6 Attach the hog rings at approximately the same spacing as they were originally applied at the factory. If you are using the original cushions, you can see the holes for the originals. If you are using reproductions, use the originals as a guide for proper placement. There is no benefit to using too many and you could actually cause the sheath to separate from the cover.

INTERIOR

Attach Hog Rings (Continued)

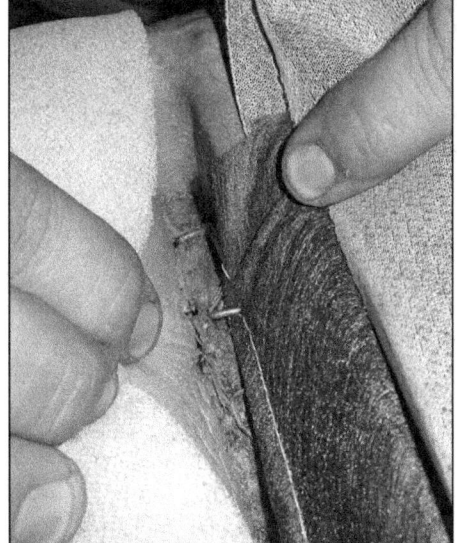

7 The installed hog rings should look like this. They have properly secured the reinforcement rod and sheath on the seat cover to the cushion and seat frame. Continue the process on both sides of the seat cushion bun.

8 With the seat base upside down, carefully pull the cover over the bottom of the frame. The arrows reveal the mounting points for the hog rings. They are the tabs cut into the metal seat frame. Pull the seat cover's reinforcement rod and sheath over the lip of the seat frame and attach the hog rings to the tabs.

9 Continue fastening the lower cover to the seat base until all tabs have been hog ringed.

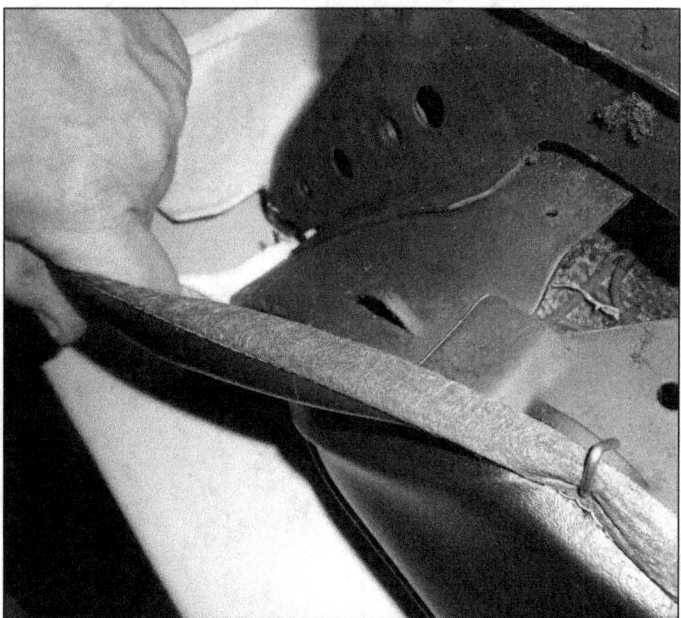

10 The hog rings follow the perimeter of the seat cover and connect to the frame to anchor the fabric. The seat cover is stretched tight for a finished look. The reinforcement rod is in the sheath. The vinyl in the seat cover has been properly pierced and the hog rings connect it to the seat frame.

Attach Hog Rings (Continued)

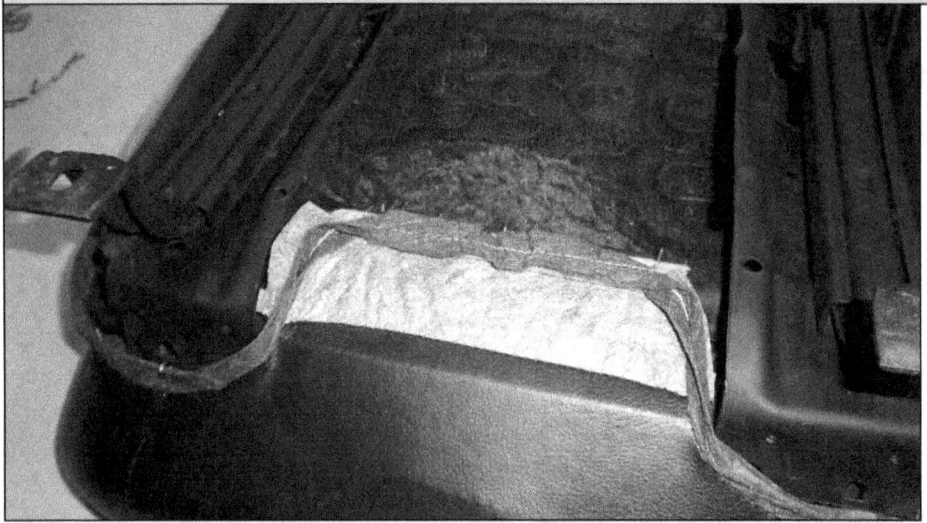

11 Three hog rings secure the vinyl in the center section of the seat. Evenly stretch the seat cover over the seat frame.

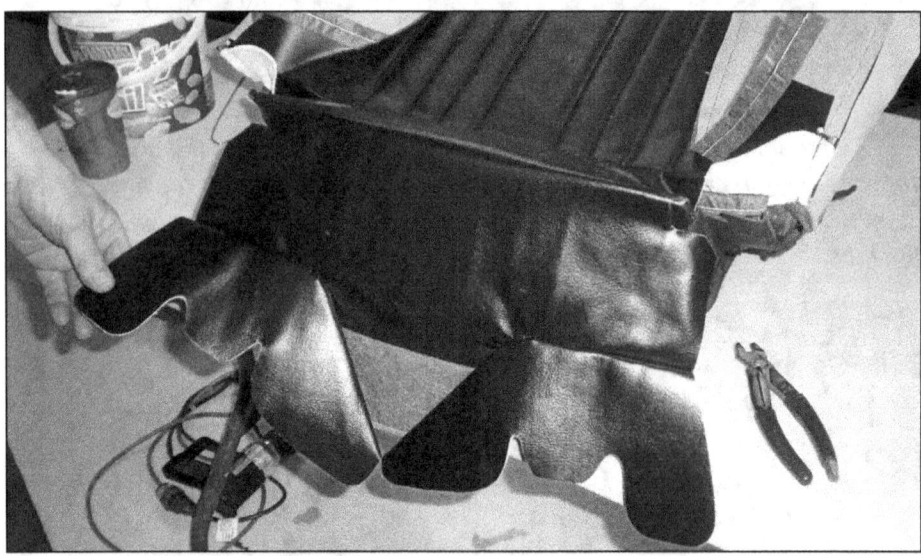

12 After you attach the hog rings on the front and sides of the seat base, move to the back side. Fold out the flaps of upholstery and test fold them around the seat frame. Identify the tabs or holes made for the hog rings.

Install Cardboard Kick Guard

13 If your cardboard kick guard is in good condition, it can be reused. If it is damaged or missing, a new one can be purchased. If available, the original can be used as a pattern to make a new one out of fresh cardboard. Likewise, a length of coat hanger can be used in the bottom sheath.

Position the Seat Cover Flaps

14 With the cardboard positioned, stretch the flaps of the seat cover over the edge of the seat frame and use pliers to crimp the hog rings over the seat cover so it's secured in position.

Install Seat Back Stops

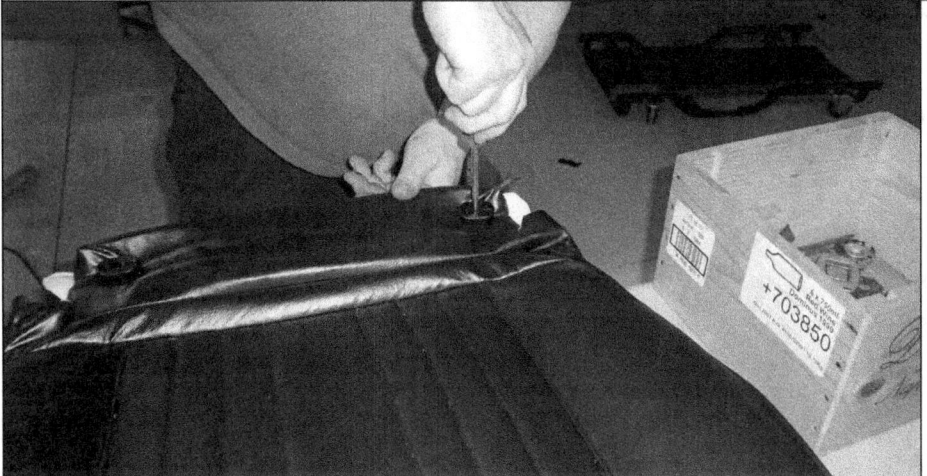

15 Screw the seat back stops back into place. Use a screwdriver to pierce the upholstery and drive the screws into the screw holes.

Use Heat Gun to Remove Wrinkles

16 Wrinkles will undoubtedly appear and they won't go away unless they are dealt with. Use a heat gun to remove them. A hair dryer isn't strong enough to perform this operation and a heat gun quickly damages the vinyl if left in one place too long. The best results come from keeping the heat gun moving at all times and gently smoothing the vinyl with your fingers. Don't get too rough or the heated vinyl can distort.

Inspect Complete Seat Bottom

17 The completed seat bottom looks as good as new. Set it aside for re-uniting with the seat back later.

Reupholster Seat Back

18 Begin the procedure for reupholstering the seat back by removing the trim medallion from the original seat cover and installing it on the new cover. Carefully measure the location and recheck it before you punch two small holes through the upholstery. Fasten the trim medallion to the seat cover by bending the retaining tabs against the upholstery panel. After you confirm the proper measurements, this should only take a minute or two.

Install and Anchor Upholstery on Seat Back

19 Installing the seat back upholstery is pretty much the same as for the base. Position the seat cover on the frame and carefully pull it over the edges.

Install Retaining Rods and Hog Rings

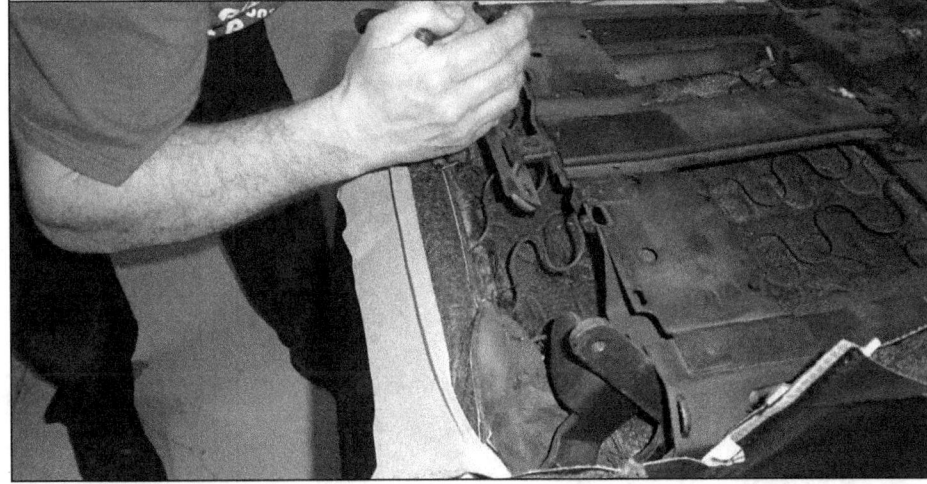

20 Fabricate retaining rods from coat hangers, and slide them into the sheaths. Once in place, hook the hog rings around the sheaths and anchor the hog rings on the frame. Be sure to look for the mounting tabs or holes on the perimeter of the seat frame.

Install Hog Rings

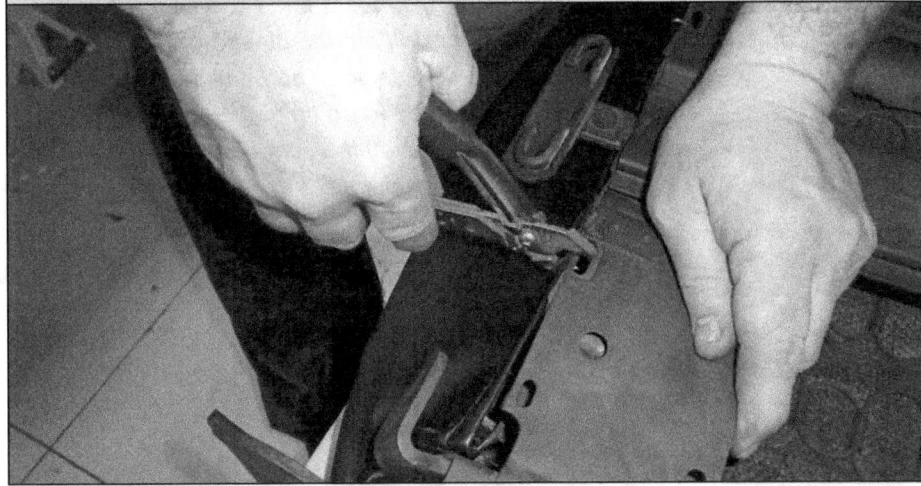

21 Hook the hog rings through the seat cover and around the seat frame. These slots on the bottom of the seat back are the factory mounting points for the hog rings to secure the seat cover. Complete the hog-ring installation for the rest of the seat back.

Attach Top of Seat Cover

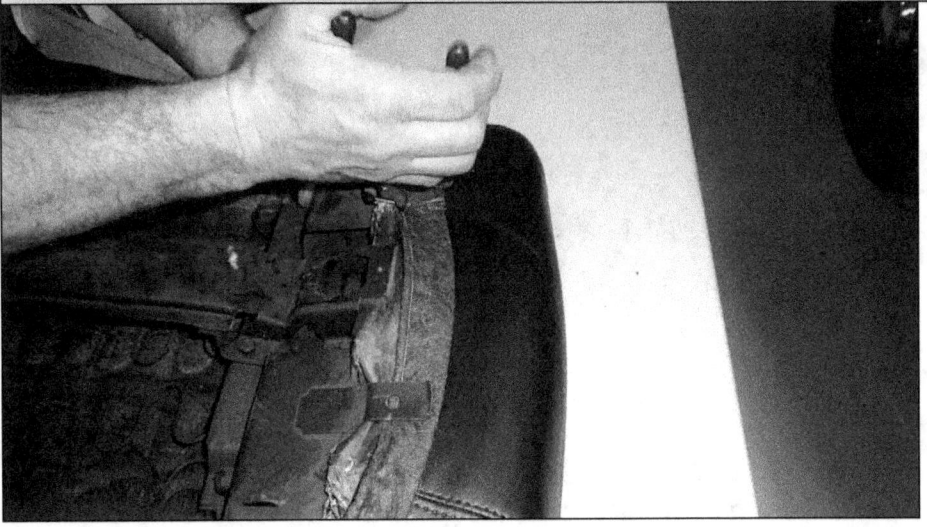

22 Hook the top of the seat cover around the wire frame with hog rings and use the pliers to crimp the hog rings to the frame. Attach the top of the seat cover along the area just below where the plastic back attaches.

Bolt Seat Bottom to Seat Back

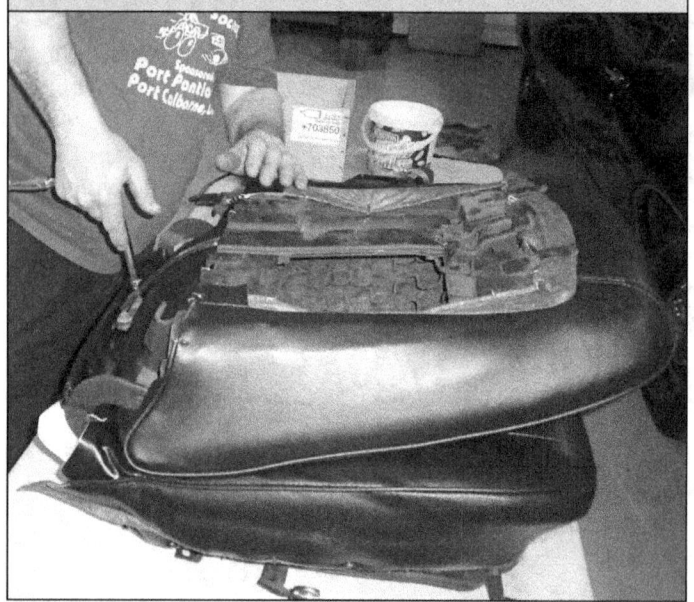

23 Drive two bolts through the mounting bracket on the seat back to secure it to the seat bottom. Do not apply a lot of torque to the bolts. They do not need to be any tighter than what you can do with a small ratchet. A little Lock-Tite to secure these bolts is a good idea.

Locate Attachment Point

24 These reproduction seat trim panels do not have the holes drilled in them for their attachment to the seat frames. Locate the attachment points and carefully drive the screws through or drill out the plastic. If the holes are too large, the stock screws don't hold the panel in place. The seat back also needs to go on at this time. If you are using a reproduction, install the seat back release button on the original attaching points.

This completed seat looks as good as new and is ready for installation.

CHAPTER 10

BODY ASSEMBLY AND ALIGNMENT

This portion of the restoration is where the fruits of all of your hard work start to come together—that pile of parts begins to take shape and start to look like a car.

This is also the time that the quality of your work needs to be top-shelf. Just as the fit and finish of the interior reflects on the rest of the car to its occupants, the quality of the exterior is the first impression that either has people nodding their heads in approval or curling their lips and saying, "Yeah, right."

I always loved the term "bolt-on sheet metal," because it is the embodiment of the over-simplification of what it really takes to assemble a car. Sure, you are fastening those pieces using bolts and wrenches, but it is so much more than that. There is a long process of properly aligning body panels, and like the construction of a building, each part builds upon the previous one. If the foundation isn't right, the rest will not be either.

That being said, most mass-produced cars have a point short of perfection for panel alignment. The trick is to watch for areas of improvement while understanding there is likely a point just short of perfection that is actually the limit of production tolerances.

To help illustrate this and to give you an idea of what is considered acceptable, I asked noted Pontiac GTO restorer Imran Chaudary to demonstrate the ins and outs of assembly and alignment of body panels. He has built a solid reputation in the Pontiac community for his

The proper alignment of the bolt-on sheetmetal is one of those things that you might not notice right away, but is one of the first things you pick up on when things are amiss. Imran Chaudary restored this 1973 GTO, and all the panels were expertly aligned. The seams were measured, trial fitted, aligned, and then bolted down for good. He always builds a foundation of proper alignment by starting at the doors and working forward.

ability to bring GTOs back from the dead. Being in Canada and having a much smaller pool of suitable restoration candidates, Chaudary is used to restoring GTOs most Americans would consider parts cars.

The car being assembled for the following how-to sequence is an original Carousel Red Ram Air III 1969 GTO Judge owned by Sam Ranalli, of Mississauga, Ontario. He had Imran perform the majority of the restoration, sending the paint work to AGG First Canadian. Fortunately, the Judge was a very solid car to begin with, needing nothing in the way of panel replacement for rust. The restoration was fairly straightforward, needing the usual mechanical and interior replacements.

When it came time to re-assemble the body, Imran had two helpers assist with the panel alignment. The process for proper panel alignment is most definitely not a one-person job. Actually, the more the merrier—to a point, of course. Body panel alignment is a big job needing a lot of hands to do correctly. It is nearly impossible to push on a panel from two or more different directions if there is only one of you. Having three or four friends helping during this portion of the procedure saves time and frustration. Trust me, it will still be frustrating but at least it will be possible to do with a group. Having a pizza delivery service and frosty beverages also helps attract cheap labor.

The Process

The idea of proper body alignment is a lot like building a house. It starts with having a proper foundation and building upon it, one piece at a time. With that notion, start at the farthest point back for the bolt-on front sheet metal. Two-door body styles, like those used on a GTO, require starting at the doors. If the doors aren't right, nothing else is going to line up. From there, each of the front fenders is installed and aligned. After those are done, the hood is added and then the front bumper. If any of them is not properly aligned, nothing installed after them will be in alignment and won't be until the initial problem is corrected.

Aside from the manpower and the usual assortment of wrenches and sockets, it is very helpful to begin by determining the amount of gap that is appropriate for the GTO's body panels. For quick measurement purposes, a piece of wood lath or a strip of soft plastic of the proper thickness can be used as a gauge to determine how far off a particular body panel is.

Once the door has been hung, the bolts are tightened to a "snug" position and checked for fit. Fortunately, doors are usually the easiest panels to properly align, relatively speaking. They are connected at the main body on just one end and by adjusting those bolts and the striker on the opposite end, it's usually not a major ordeal. If the main body has been tweaked by a collision or excessive use (drag racing, wheelies, etc.), it is tougher to do.

Surprises

As with the restoration of any car more than 40 years old, the idea that things will go completely without trouble is a fairy tale. As that great philosopher Murphy once said, "Anything that can go wrong, will go wrong, and at the worst possible moment." For Sam Ranalli's 1969 GTO Judge, that something ended up being the Endura bumper. At some point in the Judge's life, it came into contact with something solid enough to push the nose back about 3/8 inch, yet did not blemish the urethane Endura material.

This is a situation where the body shop should have noticed the problem and dealt with it beforehand. After painting the main body and the bolt-on panels separately, the terms of the job dictated that all the panels be test fitted on the car for any obvious problems. As it turned out, the worker assigned to the project bolted everything up except the bumper (he wasn't one of the two who were sent to Imran's shop). He incorrectly assumed that since all the other panels were fine, the bumper was as well, and unfortunately for him, his lack of initiative cost him his job.

The body shop did make the situation right. After considering the possibility of prepping and painting a backup bumper Sam had, they took the slightly bent bumper, brought it back their shop, bent it back into its original shape, and it lined up fine. I'm told the process isn't anything an owner wants to see in person, but the results were perfect, and the gorgeous paint they laid down on it wasn't damaged in the process—a win-win.

The bottom line is that this hiccup slowed the process enough where it almost prevented Sam from debuting the Judge at the show he wanted. Obviously, no one died over it, but it was an inconvenience for the owner that could have been avoided if that particular bodyman spent the extra 30 minutes or whatever to do the entire test-fitting job as he was supposed to.

Door Alignment

Measure Door Gap

1 This driver-side door is freshly bolted onto the GTO Judge body, but as you can see, the alignment is not even close. Ideally the door gaps between the front fender, rocker panel and rear quarter should be equal or as close to the same as possible.

2 Production tolerances sometimes come short of perfection, but successful outcomes are indeed possible. Here, the door gap is too wide and the door slumps down in a rather unattractive fashion. Body fit is a critical detail that either makes or breaks a restoration, so you need to ensure the door properly lines up. Begin the process with the door striker, as this is the rearmost section of the alignment process. Be sure to have a star screwdriver fitting with your ratchet, as well as 5/8- and 9/16-inch sockets and some wooden laths of various thicknesses. Once you've determined the proper door gap clearance, find the lath that matches that gap measurement; it may take some sanding to get the proper thickness. It works like a feeler gauge on a spark plug and provides you with a quick and simple gauge to check for proper panel gaps.

Adjust Striker Plate

3 The striker needs to be properly positioned to ensure proper latch operation. The striker must line up with the quarter panel. The striker is the component that sets the alignment of the rear of the door. The striker must also align with the latch on the door and in such a way that the trailing edge of the door also lines up with the leading edge of the rear quarter panel. Using the rear of the door as a guide for height alignment, position the striker so that when closed, the trailing edge of the door is at the same height as the quarter. Visually inspect the window channel moldings for the door and quarter glass to help determine the proper height. You are now able to align the rear of the door and quarter panel and use a star screwdriver-type socket to tighten it when you have achieved the proper position.

Adjust Door to Attain Correct Spacing

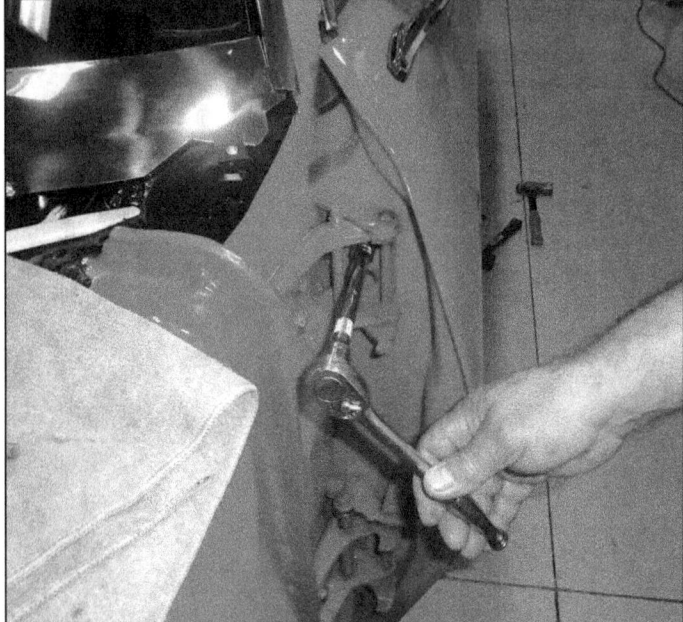

4 The GTO door has two hinges, an upper and lower, that join the front of the door to the firewall/cowl section of the main body and also allow for normal opening and closing. One is a body-side hinge and the other is a door-side hinge. Adjust both hinges for proper door alignment.

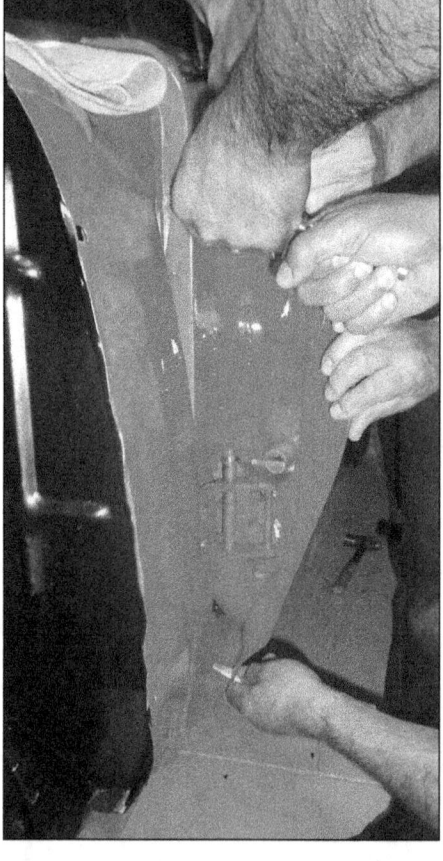

5 Use a ratchet and 9/16-inch socket to loosen the bolts on the hinge. There are a total of eight mounting points for each door. You can loosen the bolts on the door side first to see if you can get the proper position without having to loosen all eight. Have your assistants help reposition the door, using a lath as a measuring tool to determine the proper gap.

Align Driver-Side Door

6 This door came into alignment quite easily. Just by chance, the preliminary bolting on of the door hinges was fairly close. The driver-side door came into alignment quite easily because of our early luck getting the striker into alignment with only two tries. Now it is time to move to the other side. The passenger's side came as a bit more of a challenge.

Align Passenger-Side Door

7 Once the striker is properly positioned, loosen the hinges to achieve proper alignment. Having people holding the door and taking direction really makes a positive difference.

Install Splash Guard

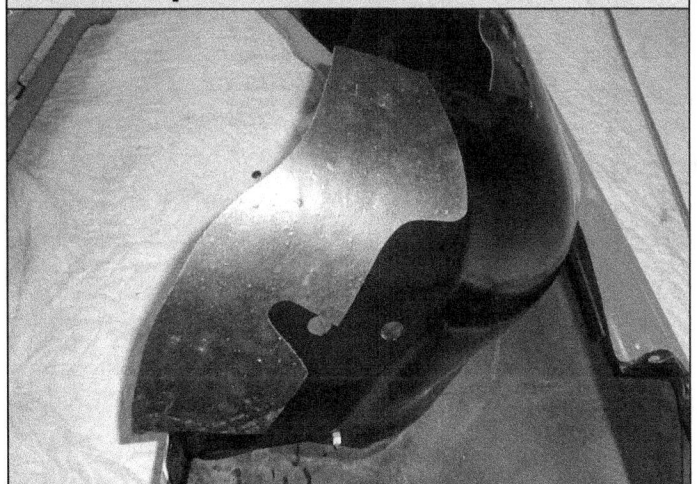

8 Bolt the inner fender with splash guard to the outer fender and ready it for installation. The procedure is fairly simple and can be accomplished by a single person without any assistance. There are five 5/16-inch standard bolts with retaining clips that attach the two panels together using a socket. Since the bolt holes are only large enough for the bolts themselves, there shouldn't be any alignment problems here; it only goes on one way. Tighten the bolts to 35- to 40 ft-lbs, a little more than "snug."

Mask Bodywork to Protect Paint

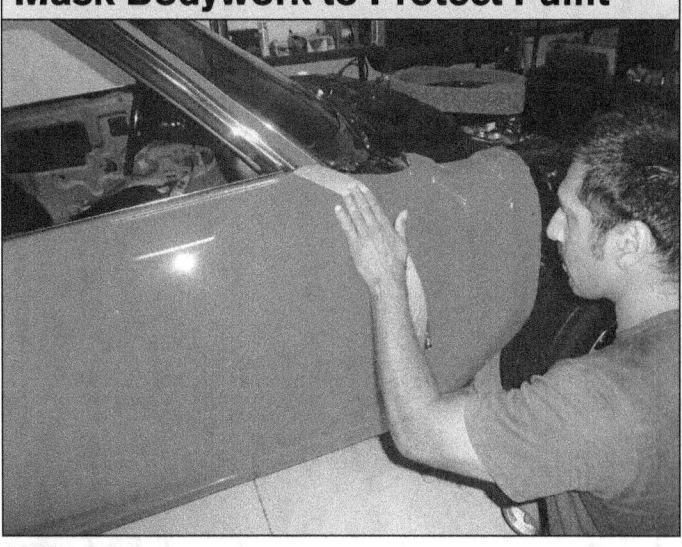

9 Regular blue interior wall masking tape works great, and 3M makes a great interior painting masking tape that works well in this application. The tape protects paint from chips and scrapes. Best of all, it comes off very easily and doesn't harm the new paint. Don't hesitate to tape up the back side of the door or fender or any other areas you may be concerned about protecting, for that matter.

Check Door Gaps

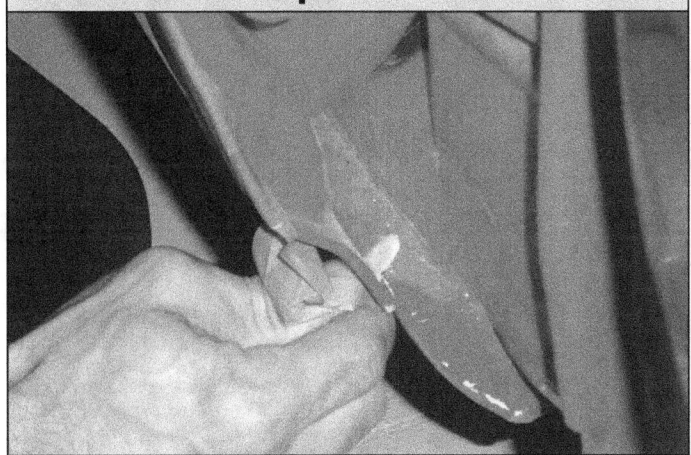

10 To begin the alignment procedure, do some preliminary measuring of the entire area to see how far off the door is after the initial bolt-up. Check the gap between the door and the rocker using the lath as a "feeler gauge." If you see that there are variations, say for example, the gap is narrower at the front of the door, you have to either raise the hinges, lower the striker, or both, using the star screwdriver bit. In this case the striker was fine as is but the hinges had to come up.

Adjust Door Hinge

11 In order to get the door where you want it, the side of the hinge that connects to the body may need to be moved up. After loosening the bolts with a 9/16-inch socket wrench, place a wooden block under the hinge and carefully lift up with a floor jack. Slowly pump up the jack until the feeler gauge shows that there is an even gap between the door and the rocker panel, as well as the trailing edge of the door and the leading edge of the rear quarter panel. Verify this with the lining up of the window trim moldings. Again, it is nothing more than trial and error with several helping hands and a lot of patience.

Tighten Door Hinge Bolts

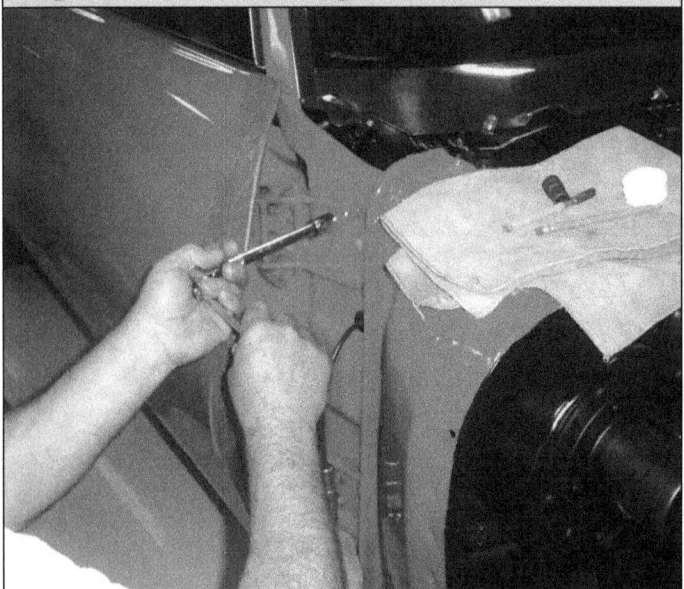

12 Once properly positioned, tighten the door hinge bolts with a 9/16-inch socket wrench. Since the doors are going to get more use and movement than the fenders, a little more torque might be in order, but don't go above 40 ft-lbs or you may have some distortion problems. Additionally, 40-plus-year-old metal in a stress area is probably a little work hardened, so don't push the issue.

Adjust for Final Fit

13 After a little bit more test fitting and moving the door hinges around slightly, you will achieve the proper alignment. If the alignment procedure is successful, the door exhibits an even gap with the rear quarter from the top to bottom. Though it is not as visible, the gap between the door and the rocker is also right on the money. With both doors installed and properly aligned, you can now move to the front fenders, as the "foundation" of the alignment procedure is now complete. Again, it is nothing more than trial and error with several helping hands and a lot of patience.

Front Fender Fitting and Alignment

Install Fender Badge

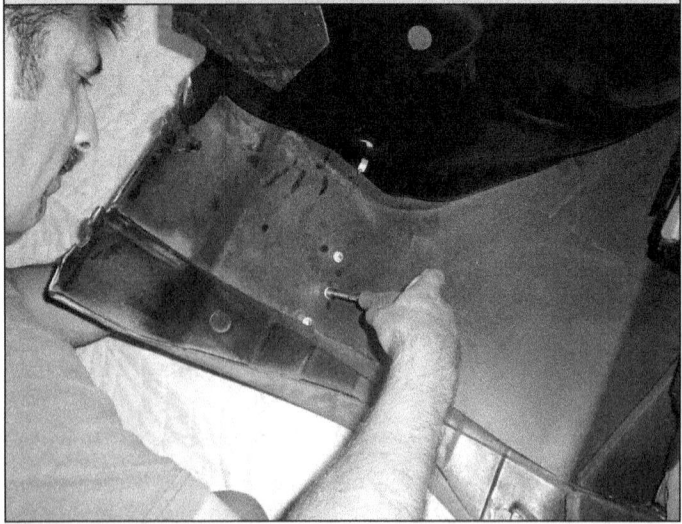

1 Use the supplied sheet-metal nuts and a nut driver to install the GTO fender badge. Don't use a lot of force, as the bolts strip under excessive torque, so remember that "snug" is more than enough.

Position Fender on Body

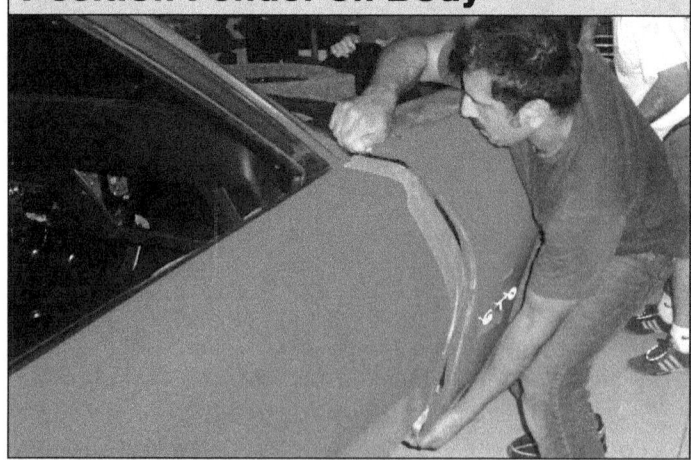

2 Make sure that the inner and outer fenders are securely fastened and there are no other issues. Then carefully position the passenger-side front fender on the body, taking care not to hit the door. The tape is there just in case. This is another one of those times when having a few friends helping is a real bonus.

Position Fender on Body (Continued)

3 Attach the inner/outer fender unit to the cowl and to the core support. There is no connection between the inner fender and the frame. There are two core thread screws that go into the cowl that use a 3/8-inch socket and large 2-inch washers. Another 3/8-inch screw goes in at the base of the A-pillar. There are also two 3/8-inch bolts at the bottom of the fender just ahead of the door, two in the lower front valance and two more that go into the core support just behind the bumper. At bottom is a contoured rectangular bracket with one 5/16-inch bolt that connects to the radiator core support and one 5/16-inch bolt to the lower portion of inner fender. Start with the lower bolts and, once they are properly positioned, work your way up.

Check Gap of Fender

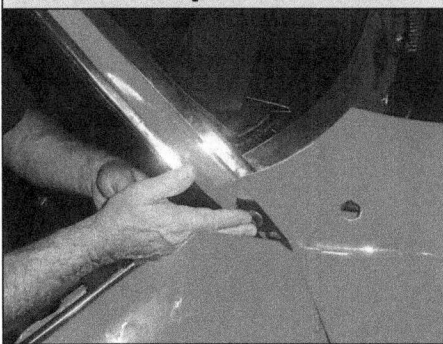

4 With the bottom bolts located and tightened, establish the gap between the door and the fender with the wooden lath feeler gauge. By just fastening the lower bolts, you are able to make the necessary changes systematically, without having to go back and re-do everything. By taking the tightening of bolts in steps, you can keep a handle on the alignment as the bolts go in and make adjustments as necessary.

Tighten Fender Bolt at Firewall

5 When you get to the top bolts (those at the A-pillar, the cowl, and the upper section of the core support), tighten them only 1/3 of the way, as they need to be movable for the next step, which is aligning to the gaps between the hood and the front fenders. Keeping them somewhat loose facilitates the hood alignment process.

Align Inner Fenders

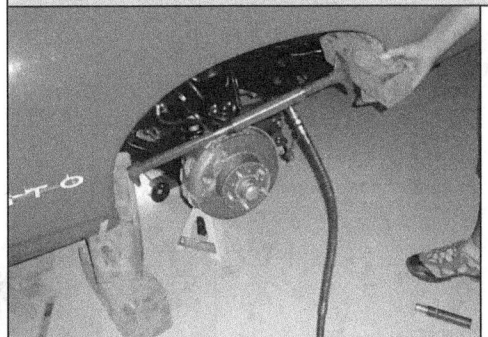

6 Getting the fender unit to line up correctly to the three factory-drilled holes in the cowl may take some "encouragement" in the form of a small hydraulic ram. The ram adjusts with a small foot pump mechanism that makes it easy to gently move the panels without causing undue stress on them. These items can be a huge help, but they can easily damage the rather fragile sheet metal, so you need to carefully adjust them and not exert excessive force on the sheet metal. After all, it can bend and buckle if care is not taken. Put wood blocks between the ram and the sheet metal, and gently add pressure. Only a fraction of an inch is needed to get them properly lined up to the holes. Once again, check your fit. You may need to make some adjustments (moving the fender edge closer or farther away from the hood) to get proper alignment with the hood but for this portion of the procedure, you are done. Replicate the procedure for the other front fender. Go slowly and be very careful. Another way to achieve similar results is to carefully modify the bolt holes in the fenders to make them more oval-shaped to allow for some additional adjustment. This may be an attractive option if the fenders are very close and need only a fraction of an inch or if you don't have access to a hydraulic ram.

Hood Installation

Prepare to Install Hood Hinges

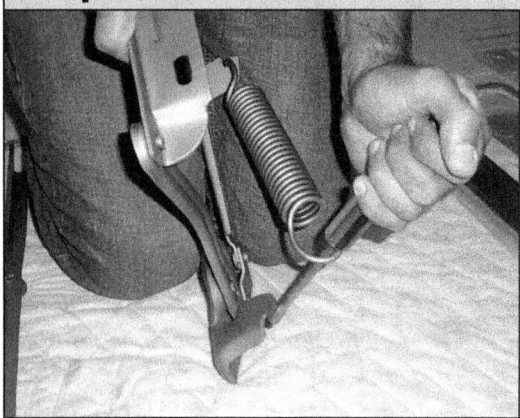

1 Getting the hood hinge assemblies ready for installation is easy but you need to be careful with this operation. Use a screwdriver to install the spring on the hinge. Place the rear of the spring in its perch and hook the other end around the shaft of the screwdriver. Place the end of the screwdriver over the other spring perch. By holding the base of the hood hinge very firmly in one hand, and the screwdriver in the other, stretch the spring by extending the screwdriver forward. As it expands, the spring slides down the screwdriver shaft and pops right into the other perch. Depending on your strength level, you may want to use a longer screwdriver to get more of a mechanical advantage, as the spring is pretty stiff.

Install Hood Hinges

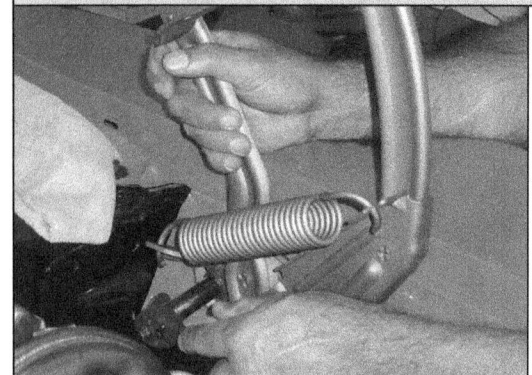

2 Install the hood hinge assemblies using a socket wrench. There are two bolts that attach each hinge assembly to the fender and two more that locate the hood. All are 7/16 inch and should be tightened to 35 to 40 ft-lbs.

Install Hood

3 Installing the hood is, at the least, a three-person operation, one for each side and one to tighten the bolts. Take extra care to make sure that you don't jam the hood into the top of the fenders, as it is so easy to do and then it is repair time. Again, take your time and avoid any sudden moves.

4 Tighten the bolts part way and get a preliminary assessment of the alignment of the hood to the fenders.

Install Hood (Continued)

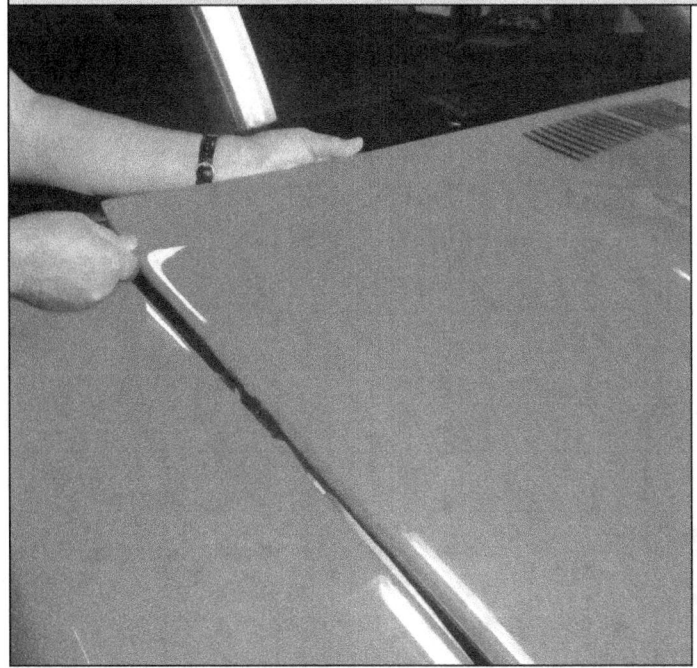

5 Even when the hood isn't tightened down completely, it may be obvious that the fender is too far away from the hood, so a proper adjustment is needed. In that case, loosen the top fender bolts, move the fender in, and test the gap for uniformity.

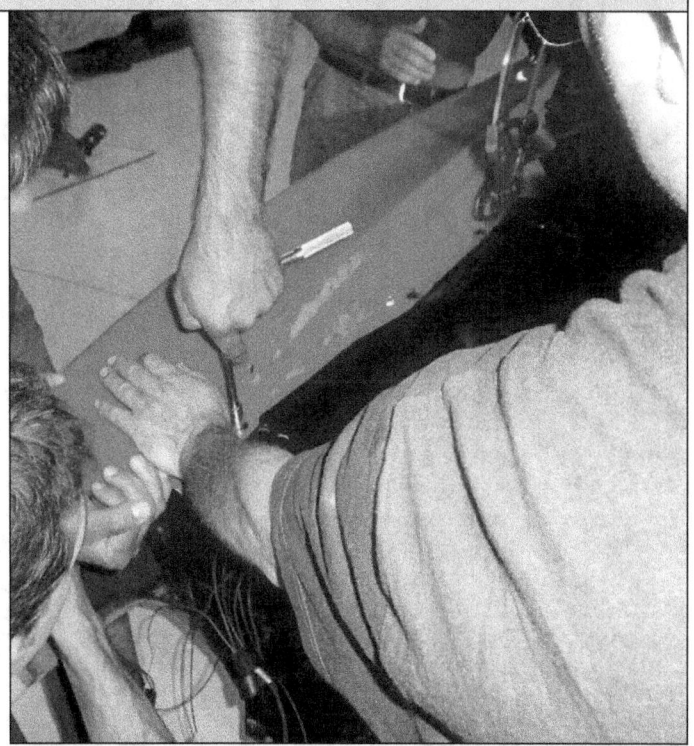

6 Once you have verified the correct gaps between the hood and the fenders, retighten the bolts to the fender and the hood.

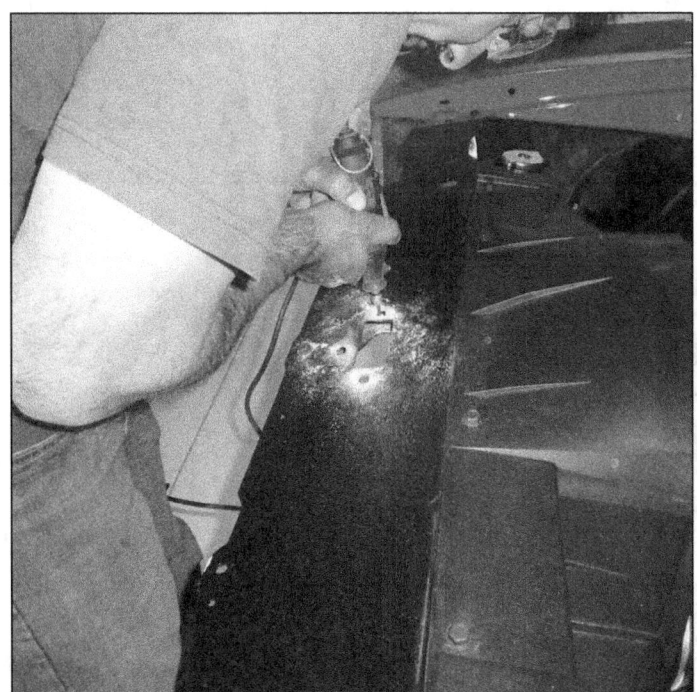

7 Use a die grinder to enlarge the holes for the hood latch in order to move it slightly to line up with the catch on the underside of the hood panel.

8 This allows for the typical operation of the hood release and prevents it from causing any alignment issues, as it is easy to have the hood sit too high up relative to the bumper.

CHAPTER 10

Bumper Installation

Install Bumper Bracket

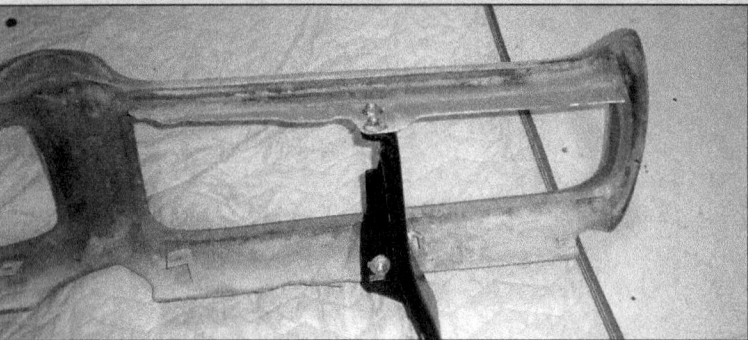

1 *This Endura bumper bracket is in its proper location on the bumper. The brackets are 3/4 inch and are tightened to 35 to 40 ft-lbs of torque.*

Install Frame Extensions

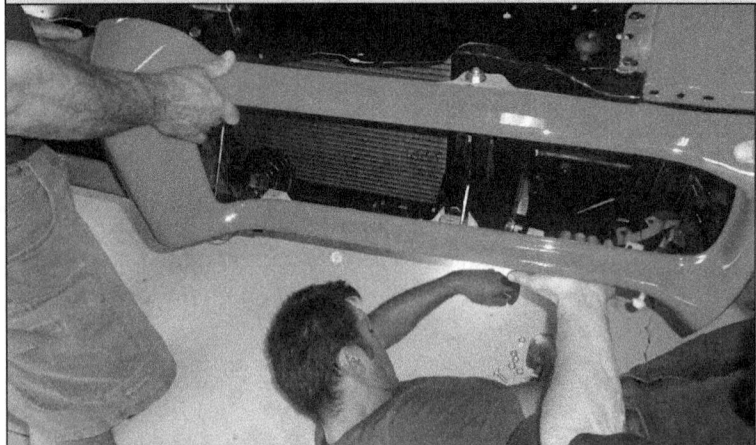

2 *With an assistant holding the bumper in place, tighten the bumper brackets to the frame extensions and to 35 to 40 ft-lbs.*

Check Bumper Fitment

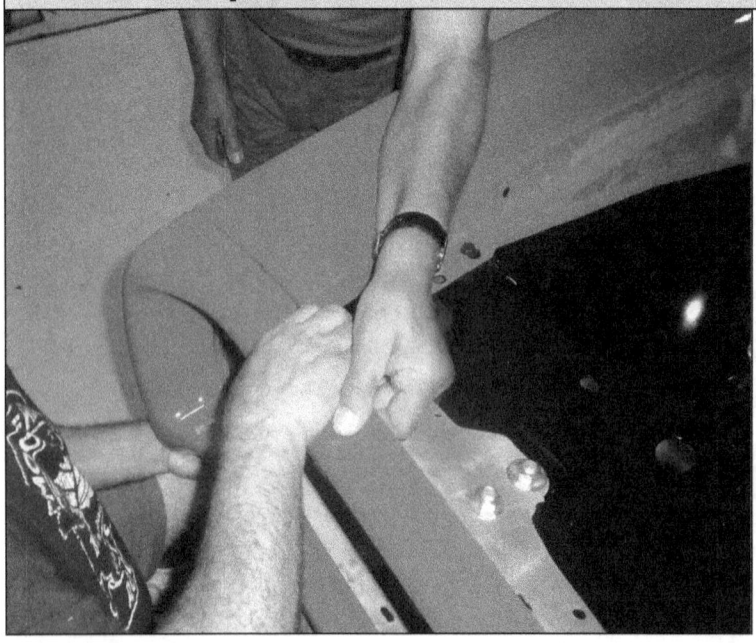

3 *Tighten the remaining bolts and check the bumper for fit. The gap should be even at the fender. And it should evenly align with the hood.*

Check Bumper Fitment (Continued)

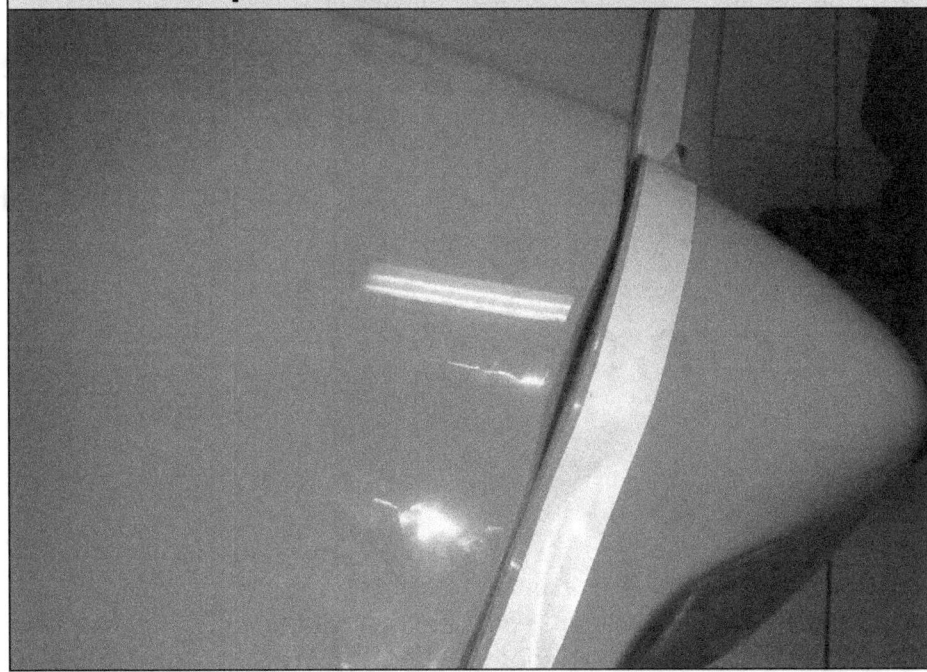

4 You may find the alignment is uneven and the leading edge of the hood is almost making contact with the bumper. Even though the bumper appears to be in good condition and even preps well for paint, the inescapable fact may be that the bumper frame is bent slightly, causing the uneven gap.

5 The masking tape shows where the trailing edge of the bumper should be. There are three options at this point, all of which involve removing the bumper again. The first option is to get another bumper, test fit it to make sure it is not bent, prep and paint it to match, and then install it.

The second option is to mill off that mount on the trailing edge of the bumper. That can work in some cases, but it is only advisable if the amount to be removed can be measured in thousandths of an inch. If yours is off way too much, the bumper will not look right and will likely be shred in the process. This re-contoured Endura bumper fits as it should with a uniform gap and no interference issues with the hood. Additionally, the hood opens and closes as it should and the bumper is completely integrated to the rest of the car.

The third option is to true up the bumper. The center section was apparently struck with enough force to bend it back about 3/8 inch without leaving a mark on the Endura material. This is what the owner opted for. After a few hours of carefully bending, twisting, and tweaking, the center of the bumper was put back where it was originally and that 3/8-inch depression was eliminated. Unfortunately, the procedure ended up cracking the paint on the bumper, so it was stripped to the bare elastomer surface, reprimed, and repainted. Luckily, using some paint left over from the car, there weren't any blending or color-matching problems. While we could have used another bumper, this one was the original, so there is some originality retained, even though in the end, there was a lot of extra work.

CHAPTER 11

ELECTRICAL

The wiring systems of the 1964–1974 Pontiac GTOs are probably closer in complexity to a Model T Ford than anything currently in showrooms. While that may be true, wiring systems are still a point of fear and loathing among many restorers of Pontiac GTOs and other muscle car era machines. The truth is, it really isn't that bad if you plan ahead. Armed with a decent set of tools, a little patience, and a shop manual with complete wiring diagrams, you are able to restore function to those areas of the electrical system that are no longer operational.

Over the course of 40 or more years, it is likely that your GTO, like any vehicle that age, has developed some wiring problems. Perhaps the backup lamps no longer work or a power window is no longer operational, and maybe the engine won't fire. In that amount of time, wiring may deteriorate, grounds may fail, or perhaps some past owner tried to install aftermarket gauges and needlessly started hacking away at wires, causing shorts and other problems. Whatever the case, the goal is to get everything working reliably and as originally intended.

The wiring condition is probably a pretty good indicator of the condition of the rest of the car. If your car was well taken care of, chances are you will have less trouble than a GTO that had been abused the majority of its life. Since I have not advocated the restoration of GTOs that are clearly good for nothing other than parts, I assume that the electrical system is generally in decent shape but in need of some help.

In this chapter I show you how to repair the consequences of an electrical fire or other catastrophic failure, several trouble spots, and what you need to do for a successful outcome. I also show you some upgrading options that can be easily added for more convenience and enjoyment.

Vintage radios can be restored at home if you have the skills or by a number of companies such as Antique Radio Doctor. If the radio still works, you can restore the push-buttons, face, and knobs, so it appears factory new. Remove the face plate, clean out the dust, and put a fresh dab of red paint on the station indicator. Replacement knobs and face-plate decals are available from most restoration parts suppliers and fishing line can be used to repair the loss of movement on the station indicator. (Photo Courtesy Scott Tiemann)

ELECTRICAL

Of all the electrical connections on your GTO, chances are that the battery cables and terminals have seen more use and abuse than any other part that carries current. Often, the terminals have been overtightened and distorted. Also, jumper cables have gouged them and battery acid has corroded them. If the cables on your battery are still in decent shape, they can be cleaned up along with the battery terminals. If they need to be replaced, make sure that you get cables of sufficient gauge thickness; it is more important than how they look, as cables that are too thin can cause too much resistance and can heat up. Unless you are competing in concours judging, pass on 6-gauge battery cables and reproduction tar-top batteries. Get a modern replacement battery and at least 4-gauge cables. These batteries cost less and work better than the originals ever did. (Photo Courtesy Imran Chaudary)

Inspection of the Wiring

Before you begin the inspection, take stock of your car's electrical system. Make notes about which electrical parts work and which are non-functional. Are all of the lights working, including the license plate lamp, the reverse lamps, and the interior lighting? What about the cigar lighter? Is the element burned out or is the socket not working? (Yes, they are cigar lighters, not cigarette lighters; check your owner's manual.)

Once you have a complete list of electrical components that are not working, take the time to familiarize yourself with the wiring diagrams in the shop manual before taking any direct action. This gives you the opportunity to isolate each trouble spot and figure out where the most logical failure point is. Problems can usually be traced to a switch failure, break in the wiring connection, faulty ground, or defective device, be it a bulb, motor, or radio. Use your multi-tester to see if power is actually getting to the device. If it is, the

While it certainly is not the cause of all electrical problems, more often than not, a faulty ground is the main source of trouble, especially in a car of this age. Over the years, ground wires and straps become corroded, break, or fall off, and fray to the point that they no long conduct electricity. Ground straps are particularly important on a full-frame car, as they provide a path between the body and frame where electricity can flow. With the body isolated from the frame with rubber body mounts, interior electrics really have no way to complete a circuit without them. Unibody cars do not have this level of reliance on ground straps like a conventional body-on-frame design, but even the stub-framed 1974 GTOs need them more than a modern car.

A wiring diagram from your shop manual lists the number of grounding points and their locations. If they are missing or no longer functional, correct replacements are available.

Once the grounds have been attended to, it is time to move on to the other connections in the car. A multi-tester is a very handy and useful item for tracking down shorts and bad connections.

After 40 years or more, ground straps are often frayed, corroded, or even broken. Those in good condition and with a solid chassis connection are especially important on full-frame cars, such as 1964-1973 GTOs. These provide a path for the electricity to flow between the body and the frame and therefore allow the circuit to be completed. Rubber body mounts isolate these units, and for the stereo and lighting system to properly function, you need the ground straps in good working order. The number of ground straps varies from year to year and generation to generation, so check with your shop manual for their location on your particular car. Replacing them is a snap; just unbolt them from the firewall and the frame and bolt in their replacements. Use new washers, remove corrosion, and clean the area to the bare metal for the best contact. (Photo Courtesy Scott Tiemann)

CHAPTER 11

The wiring passes from the front of the car to the rear. Most notably, the wiring for the taillights and reverse lamps, as well as side-marker lamps, are routed and protected by plastic or rubber tubes. These tubes keep the wiring dry and safe from the constant rubbing caused by passenger footwear on the carpeting. Most often these tubes are in good shape and can be reused, as long as the carpeting is intact on your car and the floorboards aren't rusted out. Use a multi-tester to make sure that all the wiring is still functional and replace the wiring that does not complete a circuit. Simply connect the multi-tester's probes to the connections to see if current passes though the wiring. If it does, the gauge on the face of the multi-tester moves to show the current flow. If if doesn't, it stays at zero. (Photo Courtesy Scott Tiemann)

A wiring diagram causes nightmares for many car enthusiasts, and that includes me. The thing to keep in mind is that while the wiring diagrams in your shop manual are not going to look exactly like this, they nonetheless illustrate where everything is and what everything does. Testing individual pieces, figuring out if there is a wiring issue, a ground issue, or a blown bulb goes a lot faster with a multi-tester, such as one from Radio Shack. (Photo Courtesy Scott Tiemann)

device is malfunctioning. If not, look for the connection failure.

Internal breaks in the wiring are often found with a multi-tester, and they can be tough to get at, often showing up in plug-in connectors in plastic or rubber housings; they are in turn part of a larger harness. Sometimes, it is a simple fix, as when a wire was pulled and stretched enough that it came out of the back side of a plug-in connector. Perhaps a plastic wire insulator cracked with age and exposed a bare wire to some bare metal and a short was caused. Keep an eye out for obvious problems like that.

Before you start cutting into wire insulation or taking plug-in connectors apart, make sure that replacement pieces are available. The good news is that many of these pieces are still available or are being reproduced. Lectric Limited has become a great source not only of harnesses, but also of correct switches, ground straps, connectors, bulbs, and other items that help get your electrical system back to its original operational condition.

The repairs themselves do not end up looking exactly like the original wiring, but that is not a problem, most of it is not visible anyway. It is important that the repairs are performed correctly and are as durable as the circuit was when new, if not more durable. That means splicing the wires together and then soldering them with resin-core solder and covering the bare wire connection using shrink wrap. From there, it needs to be heated with a hair dryer or heat gun for a permanent, weatherproof connection. This is no place for a quick wrap of electrical tape or other solutions that won't last. You don't want to be pulling up carpeting

ELECTRICAL

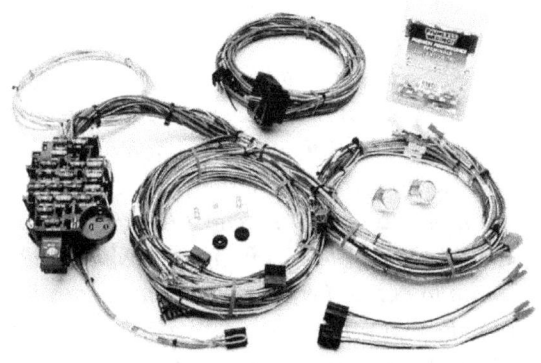

A wiring harness is a wearable item, and after more than 40 years, it may be simply worn out. If you're performing a complete restoration, it's a good opportunity to install a new harness. Routing and securing the harness is much easier if the engine and interior have been removed because you have full access to do the work. If your wiring harness has been substantially damaged, burned, or deteriorated beyond repair, you need to install a new one.

Painless offers exceptional reproduction wiring harnesses. Its universal GM muscle car kit fits all GM A-, F-, and X-Body cars from 1964 to 1974 and an optional engine compartment harness can also be included. It is a more generic version of what was offered in the cars originally and uses standard GM plugs, fittings, and color coding. Installation can be accomplished using the same procedures as for a factory-original harness. This kit even includes labels for connections, which makes the installation, well, painless. The system includes comprehensive instructions, which can be downloaded from the website. (Photo Courtesy Painless Performance Products)

The starter relay is exposed to the elements, and as a result, it tends to fail. Fortunately, it is a fairly simple item to get at and to repair or replace. Use a multi-tester to measure the voltage and resistance and then compare them to the actual specs. Also, inspect the wiring to the relay and determine if there's any damage such as cut, chafed, or frayed wires. When the relay fails, often it's just a matter of cleaning off all the terminals, and the starter is operational again. However, starter relay replacements are inexpensive and plentiful through most restoration parts houses. (Photo Courtesy Scott Tiemann)

or taking apart your dash again. Do it right and do it once.

Harness Replacement

If the wiring harness is just too brittle, broken down, and deteriorated to provide any more useful service, you need a replacement. Again, the aftermarket has OE-quality replacements that bring function and reliability to your electrical system. Replacement harnesses are available from Painless Products and Lectric Limited; they are very nice, very robust units. There are some differences, though, not based on quality but by application.

Lectric Limited has two series of harnesses—the Original Design Series and the Custom Update Series. The first is an exact-reproduction wiring harness, manufactured using the original GM blueprints, with the correct color coding, connectors, and wrappings. You can order exact-replacement dash, engine, and front and rear lamp harnesses. This is a great choice for concours and stock driver restorations, as it is a harness designed with production-style components and has a very authentic appearance.

The Original Design Series also allows for some minor modifications. Lectric Limited has already designed modified versions that accommodate some commonly-requested alterations from stock, such as adding HEI or a newer alternator, as well as alternator relocation. These changes can be added to the basic wiring layout.

The Custom Update Series is a great solution to updating the wiring for modified vehicles, so if you're looking to do a full pro-touring style of build, you have that option. This harness is a little more of a do-it-yourself approach to wiring and you

CHAPTER 11

Depending on the year and the option level, a GTO could be equipped with a 37-amp alternator. That was barely enough to charge the battery and keep the car running at the same time. Low-amp alternators were great for race cars because they didn't use as much power to turn them. But if you are adding any power options, it makes sense to upgrade to a higher-amperage version.

Installing an alternator is one of the easiest things to do on a GTO. First, remove the battery cables from the terminals, making sure they don't come in contact with the terminals. Loosen the bolts that hold the alternator to the mounting bracket. This creates slack in the belt so it can be removed. Disconnect the terminal and the ground wire attached to the back of the alternator. Remove the bolts securing the alternator. Place the new alternator in the designated position and torque the new bolts. Plug the terminal back in and attach the ground wire at the back of the alternator. Slip the belt over the pulley and push the alternator up with your hand. Use a flat-head screwdriver to push against the belt. You should be able to push it out 1/4 inch to obtain the correct tension. Torque the bolts to hold the alternator in this desired position. Reconnect battery terminals.

Compatible units with up to 200 amps are available from Year One and others if you are adding EFI and an in-car entertainment system. Lower-amperage versions are also available for restorations with more modest power requirements.

Although the alternator is usually blamed for charging problems, you need to check on the voltage regulator as well. Look for breaks in the circuit and use a multi-tester to confirm the resistance ratings in the shop manual. If cleaning the contacts still does not bring the readings to spec, replace it. If it is not operating properly, the alternator cannot properly charge the battery, preventing long-term operation. Replacements are readily available and installation is a plug-and-play procedure.

need to cut the wiring to the desired length and add the connectors yourself. The upside is that you can design a custom system for your exact needs and save some money by finishing it yourself.

The Painless wiring kit is a universal GM kit designed for 1964–1974 intermediates, as well as F- and X-Body cars. Knowing that most of the GM mid-size offerings were more the same than they were different, especially from an electrical standpoint, Painless engineered a wiring harness that works with any of these vehicles. Although the kit uses standard GM plugs and other hardware common to these vehicles, it is more of a Swiss Army knife approach—it is not a perfect reproduction product but it is designed to be a functionally identical replacement for GM's offerings from that period. Like the Lectric Limited approach, you can mix and match different harnesses, such as interior, engine compartment, and front and rear lighting; and there are options within those items as well. Once the harness is

ELECTRICAL

A high-performance modern electronic distributor can be a visually subtle change, but it also pays big dividends in performance and convenience. This unit, manufactured by Pertronix, replaces the breaker points, so the spark consistency is stronger and more precise. As you know, points are wearable items, and over time the gap needs to be maintained for maximum performance. Even under perfect adjustment, an electronic ignition provides a more powerful and precise spark than a points ignition. The spark is also much more intense, which increases power and mileage. While converting the standard points-type distributor to a later GM HEI unit has been a popular upgrade in the past, it is visually incorrect for a 1960s-era car. If your GTO is equipped with a Tri-Power system, an HEI interferes with the rear carburetor and as a result, does not fit. This conversion does a great job of bringing your ignition system performance up to date without sacrificing your authentic-looking engine compartment. It is a simple modification well worth the cost. (Photo Courtesy of Pertronix Corporation)

If you are upgrading your ignition system with an electronic distributor module, a coil upgrade is also necessary. This Pertronix coil is designed for compatibility with its module and provides lower resistance. Make sure your ignition components are all compatible, as damage or lack of ignition can result. (Photo Courtesy Pertronix Corporation)

installed, its deviations from the original design would take some serious sleuthing to detect.

Trouble Spots

Every Pontiac GTO model year has idiosyncrasies and problems; the service bulletins help solve those problems. However, there are common areas that affect all Pontiacs and likely all GM cars from that era. Most are associated with age.

Starting System

Starters and starter solenoids can wear out over time; ballast resistors can also be the culprit. Since there are still a lot of Pontiacs from this era on the road, finding replacement starters, solenoids, and accessories is pretty easy. Even high-torque versions are available if you have a hard-starting, big-inch engine with a lot of compression. Of course, if this is a concours-style restoration, you have to rebuild your original pieces, which is much more expensive. It is likely that a rebuilder in your area can handle the job.

Ignition switches can also be problematic, and dash-mounted switches can become especially loose. It is not unusual to find mid 1960s era Pontiacs that can be started with a screwdriver. If they can get that sloppy, they can also fail to complete the circuit and leave you without a means to get your car started and running.

Charging System

With an older car, the charging system, like other areas of the electrical system, is prone to grounding issues, which can put additional strain on the alternator and voltage regulator. When repairing or replacing these components, be sure to replace all of the ground straps to ensure the proper function and longevity of these refurbished components.

The alternator wears out over time, and if your original, correctly date-coded unit is in need of rebuilding, it is something that can be done at home, or it can be commercially performed. Most kits include detailed directions and the job can be handled with normal hand tools.

Upgrades

Upgrading the charging system in the quest to make your driver-quality GTO a better-performing machine is important. An upgraded stereo, high-performance ignition system, electric fans, and add-on air-conditioning system all contribute to the electrical demands made on your charging system. A stock alternator is hard-pressed to keep up.

In the mid 1970s, GM replaced the old-style alternator having the

CHAPTER 11

Although concours judges like to see a set of original T-3 headlamps with the molded-in triangle, the truth is, they were not that great, performance-wise. A modern set of replacement sealed-beam headlamps is a wise addition to a driver-type restoration. As an example, Hella H-4 lamps are a huge improvement over the originals and are available just about anywhere, including Amazon.com. Just be sure to save the original T-3s, if they are still with the car, as they are quite valuable. (Photo Courtesy Scott Tiemann)

If your car has an aftermarket tach or other accessory gauges installed, the decision to retain them is based on your restoration type and their condition. If you are performing a concours-style resto and none of the gauges work, remove them. If they are period-correct and you are performing a weekend driver restoration effort, it is worthwhile to retain them. In the case of this car, a 1964 Royal Bobcat GTO, they were retained, as the car was restored not to 100-percent stock, but to the configuration that it was in when it was featured in the March 1964 issue of Car and Driver *magazine. Since the gauges were in very good original condition, they were simply disassmbled, cleaned, and re-assembled. (Photo Courtesy Scott Tiemann)*

external voltage regulator with a more modern, SI (systems integrated) series, single-wire alternator with the internal voltage regulator. It offered more charging power and reliability, as the regulator was more protected from the elements. Converting your GTO to take advantage of these newer alternators is a simple procedure. Conversion kits are available from several sources to upgrade your system to maintain those elevated requirements.

Higher-amperage SI alternators are a sensible upgrade that helps your car handle the additional strain. Units up to 200 amps are available from Year One and other sources that can be adapted to your GTO. A power level like that more than covers any upgrade in your plan.

Ignition

The ignition system actually gives you a lot of warning that things are amiss. With hundreds of millions of revolutions over the course of its life, the ignition has no doubt deteriorated somewhat over time and is likely in need of some attention.

Other than when it gets wet, the ignition system rarely leaves you hanging. As it wears, however, the performance of your engine gradually reduces until it starts misfiring, running rough, and dropping a cylinder or two. The main causes for this sort of trouble are the distributor cap, breaker points, plug wires, and plugs themselves.

Replacing the distributor cap, wires, and plugs is simple. As the wires get older, their resistance increases, and less electricity makes its way to the plugs, reducing performance. Recent advancements in plug wire technology bring new levels of performance with a new generation

ELECTRICAL

Like the radios, original speakers can be reconditioned and restored to like-new appearance and operation. Most radio restoration companies also service speakers. Reproduction speakers are also available. If appearance is not a concern, much higher quality speakers can be substituted and fit into the stock locations. (Photo Courtesy Scott Tiemann)

The stereo in Les Iden's 1966 GTO is an interesting blend of old and new. The car features a reproduction of the 1966 Pontiac A-Body AM/FM radio from Antique Auto Radio. It looks authentic on the outside but uses all modern internals. With a shallower chassis, it allows for easier installation and features mini-plug inputs so you can hardwire an iPod or satellite radio receiver directly into it. It also features 45 watts of power in each of its four channels and is an excellent alternative for those wishing for modern sound with an authentic look.

of low-resistance wires that still look like factory items.

Spark plugs wear over time as well and should be replaced, taking the time to read the old ones for signs of engine condition and possible problems. Engine builders have preferences for various brands and it never hurts to hear what their recommendations are for your particular engine combination.

Replace the breaker points on any street-driven restoration with an electronic control module and compatible coil, like those from Pertronix. They add to the efficiency and intensity of the spark, making the most of your new, low-resistance plug wires and fresh spark plugs. More spark translates to a little more power, a little better fuel economy, and reduced exhaust emissions. It's a very worthwhile addition to your street-driven GTO.

Lighting

Even though the wiring system for your GTO's lighting is fairly simple, it can still cause problems and more often than not, those problems are related to the condition of the sockets for the bulbs and the grounds. Check the shop manual to determine where the lighting grounds are and how many there should be; and make the necessary repairs to bring them back to factory specs.

Next, inspect the lamp sockets for corrosion and damage. Clean the terminals of all corrosion and make sure they are making proper contact with the bulbs at their particular connection points. Headlamps have prongs that fit into their sockets, while most of the rest of the bulbs use barrel-type sockets. Order and install new sockets and bulbs as needed.

The original T-3 headlamps were good for their day, but newer replacements are readily available that provide superior illumination for night driving. This is another safety-oriented upgrade that can be easily integrated into your driver restoration. If your car still has any operational T-3 headlamps, remove and safely store them, as even used ones command a hefty price from concours restorers.

Audio

Providing a great-sounding but authentic-looking sound system has been a problem for muscle car fans—either you had one that looked authentic or you had one that sounded great. For some reason, the two really didn't mix, even though promises to that effect were commonplace right up to a few years ago. Unfortunately, most of them were underpowered and overpriced junk. I hate to see a late-model aftermarket stereo in the dash of a classic muscle car because it just looks so incorrect. I am not a purist by any stretch, but the clash of design eras just comes off as clunky, unintegrated, and anachronistic. I like old and new, just not in some grotesque Frankendash mismatch.

I recently photographed a car feature on my friend Les Iden's modified 1966 GTO for POCI's *Smoke Signals* magazine and must admit, I was completely fooled by the head unit he had in his dash. I thought it was a stock 1966 A-Body radio. When he told me he had a custom sound system, I asked if he hid it in the glovebox. He said that it was right in the stock location. I had to do a double-take.

Upon closer inspection, I was amazed to find an extremely stealthy and really fantastic-sounding AM/FM stereo. Manufactured by Antique Auto Radio, this head unit fits in the stock location but is only about 3 inches deep, taking up less space than a stock radio. This unit also accepts auxiliary inputs from an iPod, mp3 player, or a satellite receiver. It's a great-looking and great-sounding system. If you like to bring your music with you, this is a very viable option. In the case of Les' 1966, the shallow chassis dimensions were especially helpful since he had added an aftermarket air-conditioning system and needed the room behind the radio for ducting.

In addition to the 1966 A-Body Pontiac, Antique Auto Radio also offers a similar reciever for 1969–1972 A-Bodies, and more will undoubtedly be released in the future. Custom builds are also available that can fit in stock radio chassis for vehicles not listed.

SOURCE GUIDE

5speeds.com

Ames Performance Engineering
10 Pontiac Drive
P.O. Box 572
Spofford, NH 03462
(800) 421-2637
www.amesperf.com

Antique Auto Club of America
501 W. Governor Road
P.O. Box 417, Hershey, PA 17033
(717) 534-1910
www.aaca.org

Antique Automobile Radio, Inc.
700 Tampa Road
Palm Harbor FL 34683
(800) 933-4926
(727) 785-8733
www.antiqueautomobileradio.com

Baer Racing
2222 West Peoria Avenue
Phoenix, Arizona 85029
(602) 233-1411
www.baer.com

Bill Hirsch Auto
396 Littleton Avenue
Newark, NJ 07103
(973) 642-2404
(800) 828-2061
www.hirschauto.com

California Pontiac Restoration
820 Poinsettia Street
Santa Ana, CA 92701
(877) 504-8124
Tech Line (714) 245-9800

Classic Industries
18460 Gothard Street
Huntington Beach, CA 92648-1229
(714) 847-6887
www.classicindustries.com

Cruisin' Tigers GTO Club
(630) 541-6029
www.cruisintigersgto.com

D&D Automobilia
211 Rawley Avenue
Mount Airy, NC 27030
(336) 429-2188
www.danddautomobilia.com

Dashboard Restorations USA
P.O. Box 1401
Brush Prairie, WA 98606 USA
(360) 892-4075
www.dashboardrestorations.com

Detroit Iron Information Systems
1311 Quail Creek Trail
Cedar Park, TX 78613
(877) 893-8123
(512) 528-9725
www.detroitironis.com

Classic Restorations
150 Route 17
Sloatsburg, NY 10974
(845) 712-5500
www.classicresto.com

Dynamat
Inc. 3042 Symmes Road
Hamilton, OH 45015
(513) 860-5094
www.dynamat.com

The Eastwood Company
263 Shoemaker Road
Pottstown, PA 19464
(610) 323-9099
www.eastwood.com

FatMat Sound Control Inc.
20 Park Road
Painesville OH 44077
www.fatmat.com

The Finishing Touch
5580 Northwest Highway
Chicago, IL 60630
(800) 403-4545
www.thefinishingtouchinc.com

Gary's Steering Wheel Restoration
2677 Ritner Highway
Carlisle, PA 17015
(717) 243-5646
www.garyssteeringwheel.com

Global West Suspension
655 S. Lincoln Avenue
San Bernardino, CA 92408
(909) 890-0759
www.globalwest.net

GTO Association of America
P.O. Box 213
Timnath, CO 80547
www.gtoaa.org

High Performance Pontiac Magazine
9036 Brittany Way
Tampa, FL 33619
(813) 675-3477
www.higperformancepontiac.com

Hotchkis Performance
8633 Sorensen Avenue
Santa Fe Springs, CA 90670
(888) 735-6425
International (562) 907-7757
www.hotchkis.net

Inline Tube
15066 Technology Drive
Shelby Township, MI 48315
(800) 385-9452
www.inlinetube.com

Just Dashes
5941 Lemona Avenue
Van Nuys CA 91411
(818) 780-9005
www.justdashes.com

SOURCE GUIDE

KBS Coatings
1101 Cumberland Crossing, #180
Valparaiso, IN 46383-2356
(877) 548-9323
www.kbs-coatings.com

Lectric Limited
6750 W. 74th Street, Suite A
Bedford Park, IL 60638 USA
(866) 624-1850

Legendary Auto Interiors, Ltd.
121 West Shore Boulevard
Newark, NY 14513
(800) 363-8804
www.legendaryautointeriors.com

Master Power Brakes
Phone (888) 351-8785
www.mpbrakes.com

Midwest Transmission Supply
8625 I Street
Omaha, NE 68127
(402) 731-4500

Morris Custom Classics, LLC
(864) 987-0032

National Parts Depot
www.npdlink.com

Original Parts Group, Inc.
1770 Saturn Way
Seal Beach, CA 90740
(800) 243-8355
www.originalpartsgroup.com

Painless Performance
2501 Ludelle Street
Fort Worth, Texas 76105
(817) 244-6212
www.painlesswiring.com

Performance Years
2705 Clemens Road Building 105A
Hatfield, PA 19440
Phone (267) 638-3500
www.performanceyears.com

Phoenix Graphix
400 S. 79th Street
Chandler, AZ 85226
(800) 941-4550
www.phoenixgraphix.com

PHS
P.O. Box 183251
Shelby Twp., MI 48218
(586) 781-5164
www.phs-online.com

Pontiac Heaven
(480) 899-7873
www.pontiacheaven.org

Pontiac-Oakland Club International
P.O. Box 68, Dept. CT
Maple Plain, MN 55359
(877) 368-3454
www.poci.org

POR-15, Inc.
P.O. Box 1235
Morristoen, NJ 07962
(800) 726-0459
www.por15.com

Power Steering Services
2347 East Kearney Street
Springfield, MO 65803
(417) 864-6676
www.powersteering.com

Quality Restorations
Poway, CA 92064
(858) 271-7374
www.qualityrestorations.com

Brew City Engineering, Inc.
P.O. Box 180095
Delafield, WI 53018
(877) BCE-0203
www.rediscoverradio.com

SD Performance
446 Harrison St., Unit #81A
Sumas, WA 98295
(604) 392-2211
www.sdperformance.com

Society of Automotive Historians
c/o Cornerstone Registration, Ltd.
P.O. Box 1715
Maple Grove, MN 55311-6715
www.autohistory.org

Ssnake-Oyl Product Inc.
114 N. Glenwood
Tyler, TX 75702
(800) 284-7777
Tech Line (903) 526-4500
www.ssnake-oyl.com

SSBC Performance Brake Systems
11470 Main Road
Clarence, NY 14031
(800) 448-7722
www.ssbrakes.com

Stencils & Stripes Unlimited
1108 South Crescent
Park Ridge, IL 60068
(847) 692-6893
www.stencilsandstripes.com

Supercar Specialties, Scott Tiemann
11817 E Grand River Avenue
Portland, MI 48875-8443

T&B Transmission & Gear
3402 West Oregon Road
Deer Park, WA 99006
(509) 276-2998
www.tbtrans.com

The Parts Place
630 Enterprise Avenue
Dekalb, IL 60115
(630) 365-1800
www.thepartsplaceinc.com

Trim Tags, Inc.
900 Port Clinton Ct. W
Buffalo Grove, IL 60089-6637
(847) 478-TAGS
www.trimtags.com

Wallaceracing.com
(Pontiac information source)

Wilwood Engineering
4700 Calle Bolero
Camarillo, CA 93012
(805) 388-1188
www.wilwood.com

Year One
P.O. Box 521
Braselton, GA 30517
(800) 932-7663
www.yearone.com

www.ingramcontent.com/pod-product-compliance
Lightning Source LLC
Chambersburg PA
CBHW051407070526
44584CB00023B/3326